The KIM
HARGREAVES
COLLECTION

The KIM HARGREAVES COLLECTION

A Rowan Original

FOREWORD BY KAFFE FASSETT

MACMILLAN PUBLISHING COMPANY
NEW YORK

MAXWELL MACMILLAN INTERNATIONAL
NEW YORK   OXFORD   SINGAPORE   SYDNEY

Macmillan Publishing Company
866 Third Avenue
New York, NY 10022

Macmillan Publishing Company is part of the Maxwell Communication Group of Companies.

Library of Congress Cataloging-in-Publication Data

The Kim Hargreaves collection/foreword by Kaffe Fassett.
p.   cm.
"A Rowan original."
ISBN 0-02-548171-1
1. Knitting—Patterns.   2. Sweaters.   I. Hargreaves, Kim.
TT825.K449 1991   91-14043
746.9'2—dc20   CIP

First published in Great Britain in 1991
by Anaya Publishers Ltd.

Editor   Margaret Maino
Designer   David Fordham
Photographer   Tim Bret-Day
Pattern Checkers   Wyn Greggains, Hilary Swaby
Chartist   Sarah Heron
Illustrator   Conny Jude
Detail Photographs   Ray Moller

Macmillan books are available at special discounts for bulk purchases for sales promotions, premiums, fund-raising, or educational use. For details, contact:

Special Sales Director
Macmillan Publishing Company
866 Third Avenue
New York, NY 10022

10 9 8 7 6 5 4 3 2 1

Typeset in Great Britain by SX Composing Ltd, Rayleigh, Essex
Color reproduction by Columbia Offset, Singapore
Printed in China

CONTENTS

FOREWORD
BY
KAFFE FASSETT

Some years ago a rather shy young girl came with her mother to a workshop where the public, under my guidance, were given the chance to experiment with yarns and ideas. The small knitted sample she produced at the end of the class had a startlingly original use of colour and alerted me to Kim's potential. I remember making a mental note to keep an eye on her. . . .

With this collection she emerges as an exciting designer with a rare boldness of design and a flair for rich colour combinations. I wish her the best of luck.

INTRODUCTION

I COME FROM a family of knitters and was taught the skill at an early age. At my village school in Holmfirth, Yorkshire, even the boys were encouraged to knit by our enthusiastic teacher, Miss Bland. I have vivid memories of my first efforts – a brightly-coloured striped tea cosy that was my mother's pride and joy.

Growing up in a small textile community surrounded by creative people was a great background for me. I could spend hours making things for myself or searching for clothes in a jumble sale. Even today I am a fan of jumble sales and second-hand shops; many of my 'discoveries' end up in my wardrobe, often after I have adapted them.

When it comes to my own designs I create knitwear for real people in everyday situations such as going to work, walking the dog, going out to dinner or to a party. This book has given me the opportunity to design garments for all these occasions – from casual comfortable sweaters for outdoor wear to glittering eye-catching evening wear.

The majority of my designs are for women because I love body-conscious feminine shapes and interesting details such as collars, pockets and unusual buttons – these features are my hallmarks. However many of the heavier outdoor garments in this collection can be worn by either men or women, and some designs are specifically for men. Of course I have not forgotten the children: my children's designs are scaled-down versions of the adult garments, often re-coloured to show the versatility of the pattern.

Part of my work as the in-house designer for Rowan Yarns (who

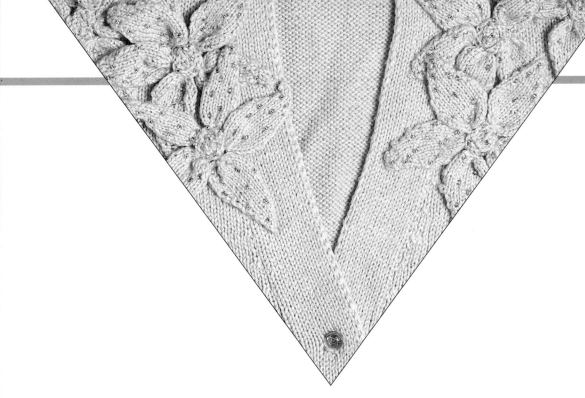

produce all the beautiful yarns that I've used) involves planning and
developing new yarns. Over the years I have become very aware of the
different types of yarn that are available and how to make the most of
their individual qualities in various styles and patterns. Thick, tweedy
yarns for warmth and rugged cable patterns, a perfect blend of wool
and cotton for definition in stitchwork designs or a luxurious silk or
plush chenille to resemble velvet – I have used all these yarns and
many others, including basic wools and cottons, for a collection that
reflects the versatility of knitted fabrics.

My own initiation into the world of textiles and hand-knitting was
very low-key. At seventeen I began working at the Rowan mill (where
the yarns are developed) at weekends and during my school holidays.
After leaving school I joined the Rowan team full-time and my rôle
with the company has developed as Rowan has grown – from packing
orders, filling shelves and printing tapestries to my present position.

Originally Rowan's wonderful yarns in a vast range of colours gave
me the incentive to take up knitting again. Stephen Sheard, the co-
owner and creative driving force of Rowan Yarns, was aware of my interest in design so he encouraged me to pursue my own ideas. Later a
workshop given by Kaffe Fassett at Styal Mill in Cheshire gave me a
fresh insight into colour and design; this was an incredible boost to
my confidence and my career really took off from there. Soon after-
wards Stephen approached me to come up with suggestions for
simple classic garments which Rowan published as a collection in
1987. These first designs are still amongst my favourites.

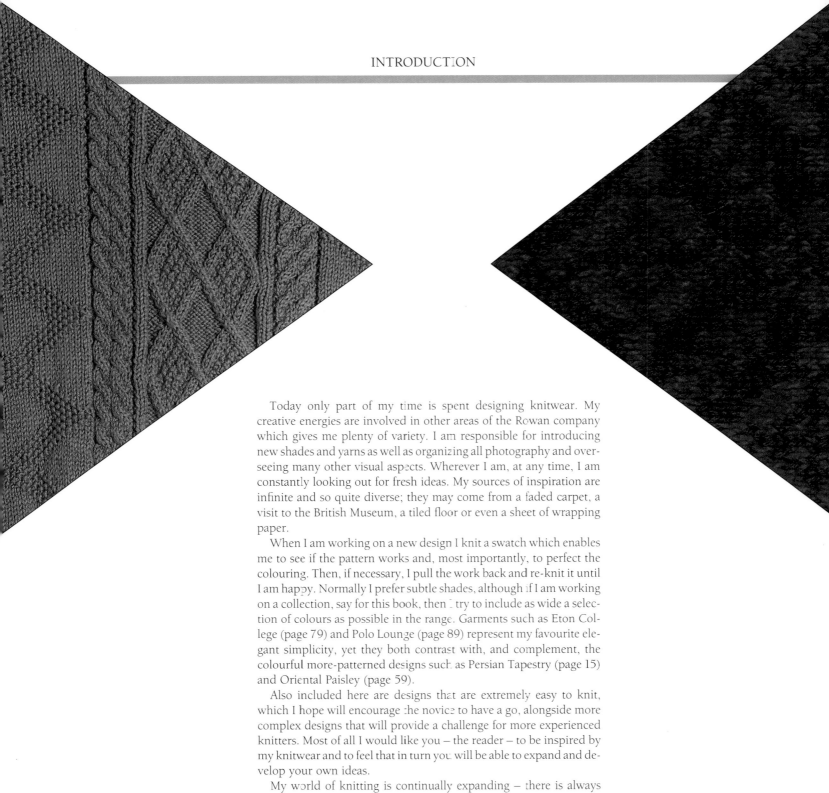

Today only part of my time is spent designing knitwear. My creative energies are involved in other areas of the Rowan company which gives me plenty of variety. I am responsible for introducing new shades and yarns as well as organizing all photography and overseeing many other visual aspects. Wherever I am, at any time, I am constantly looking out for fresh ideas. My sources of inspiration are infinite and so quite diverse; they may come from a faded carpet, a visit to the British Museum, a tiled floor or even a sheet of wrapping paper.

When I am working on a new design I knit a swatch which enables me to see if the pattern works and, most importantly, to perfect the colouring. Then, if necessary, I pull the work back and re-knit it until I am happy. Normally I prefer subtle shades, although if I am working on a collection, say for this book, then I try to include as wide a selection of colours as possible in the range. Garments such as Eton College (page 79) and Polo Lounge (page 89) represent my favourite elegant simplicity, yet they both contrast with, and complement, the colourful more-patterned designs such as Persian Tapestry (page 15) and Oriental Paisley (page 59).

Also included here are designs that are extremely easy to knit, which I hope will encourage the novice to have a go, alongside more complex designs that will provide a challenge for more experienced knitters. Most of all I would like you – the reader – to be inspired by my knitwear and to feel that in turn you will be able to expand and develop your own ideas.

My world of knitting is continually expanding – there is always something new for me to learn or to try and I hope that I can inspire you to keep experimenting. Ultimately, whether you knit one of my designs, adapt one of my patterns or create your own entirely, I hope you have great pleasure in both knitting and wearing it.

Kim Hargreaves

SPRIGS & GARLANDS

Browsing through a book on early nineteenth century wall hangings, I was impressed by an elegant pattern of sprigged flowers with deep scalloped and garlanded borders. Although the original version was made in rich silks and gold threads, it still looked fresh and pretty. For a more affordable version I have used Aran yarn for the background with gold chenille replacing the golden threads.

SIZES

To fit 87/92[92/96:96/102]cm (34/36[36/38:38/40]in) bust
Actual size 129.5[134.5:138.5]cm (51[53:54¾]in)
Sleeve seam 40.5cm (16in)
Length to shoulder 66[68.5:71]cm (26[27:28]in)
Figures in square brackets [ ] refer to larger sizes; where there is only one set of figures, it applies to all sizes

MATERIALS

7[8:9])×100g hanks of Rowan Magpie in main shade A (Natural 002)
1×50g ball of Rowan Designer DK in shade B (665) – used double throughout
1×50g ball of Rowan Fine Cotton Chenille in shade C (383) – used double throughout
1×100g hank of Rowan Chunky Cotton Chenille in each of 3 shades D, E and F (370, 373, 372)
1 ball of Designer DK in shade G (650) – used double throughout
1 hank of Chunky Cotton Chenille in shade H (364)
1 ball of Designer DK in shade J (65) – used double throughout
Pair each of 4mm (US6) and 5mm (US8) knitting needles
11 buttons

TENSION

18 sts and 23 rows to 10cm (4in) over patt using 5mm (US8) needles

NOTE

Magpie Aran and Chunky Cotton Chenille are used single throughout; Fine Cotton Chenille and Designer DK are used double throughout

BACK

Using 4mm (US6) needles and A, cast on 112(116:120) sts. Work 2.5cm (1in) in K2, P2 rib, ending with a WS row and inc 3 sts evenly across last row. 115[119:123] sts.
Change to 5mm (US8) needles.
Beg with a K row, cont in st st and work 88[94:100] rows in patt from Chart 1. Strand colours loosely across back of work where appropriate or use small, separate balls of yarn for individual motifs. Link one shade to the next by twisting them around each other where they meet on the WS to avoid making gaps.

Shape armholes

Cast off 5 sts at beg of next 2 rows. 105[109:113] sts. Cont in patt without shaping until row 146[152:158] has been completed, so ending with a P row.

Elisabeth, wearing 'Sprigs and Garlands' and Jennifer, in the child's version of 'Laurel Crown', enjoy the sunshine out in the garden. The loose casual shape of Elisabeth's cardigan is formalized with a deep border at the lower edge featuring swags and garlands that are reminiscent of early French tapestries.

Shape shoulders and back neck

Cast off 12[12:13] sts at beg of next 2 rows.
Next row Cast off 12[13:13] sts, patt until there are 17 sts on right-hand needle, turn and complete right side of neck first.
Next row Cast off 4 sts, patt to end.
Cast off rem 13 sts.
With RS of work facing, rejoin yarn to rem sts, cast off centre 23[25:27] sts, patt to end.
Next row Cast off 12[13:13] sts, patt to end.
Complete as given for other side of neck.

POCKET LININGS
(make 2)

Using 5mm (US8) needles and A, cast on 22 sts. Beg with a K row, work 40 rows in st st, ending with a P row. Cut off yarn and leave sts on a holder.

LEFT FRONT

Using 4mm (US6) needles and A, cast on 56[56:60] sts. Work 2.5cm (1in) in K2, P2 rib, ending with a WS row and inc 1[3:1] sts evenly across last row. 57[59:61] sts.
Change to 5mm (US8) needles.
Beg with a K row, cont in st st and work 42 rows in patt from Chart 1, so ending with a P row. *

Place pocket lining

Next row Patt 15[17:19] sts, sl next 22 sts onto a holder, patt across 22 sts of pocket lining, then patt to end.
** Cont in patt from Chart until row 88[94:100] (row 89[95:101] for right front) has been completed, so ending at side edge.

Shape armhole

Cast off 5 sts at beg of next row. 52[54:56] sts. Cont in patt without shaping until row 131[135:139] (row 132[136:140] for right front) has been completed, so ending at front edge.

Shape neck

Cast off 4 sts at beg of next row and 3 sts at beg of foll 2 alt rows. 42[44:46] sts. Dec one st at neck edge on next 3 rows, then on 2[3:4] foll alt rows. 37[38:39] sts. Work 3 rows without shaping, so ending at armhole edge.

Shape shoulder

Cast off 12[12:13] sts at beg of next row and 12[13:13] sts at beg of foll alt row. Work one row. Cast off rem 13 sts.

RIGHT FRONT

Work as given for left front to *
Place pocket lining
Next row Patt 20 sts, sl next 22 sts on to a holder, patt across 22 sts of pocket lining, then patt to end.

Complete as given for Left Front from ** to end, noting the bracketed exceptions.

SLEEVES

Using 4mm (US6) needles and A, cast on 44 sts. Work 2.5cm (1in) in K2, P2 rib, ending with a WS row and inc one st at end of last row. 45 sts.
Change to 5mm (US8) needles.
Beg with a K row, cont in st st and patt from Chart 2, inc one st at each end of 3rd and

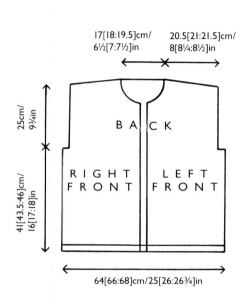

17[18:19.5]cm/ 6½[7:7½]in   20.5[21:21.5]cm/ 8[8¼:8½]in

BACK

25cm/ 9¾in

41[43.5:46]cm/ 16[17:18]in

RIGHT FRONT   LEFT FRONT

64[66:68]cm/25[26:26¾]in

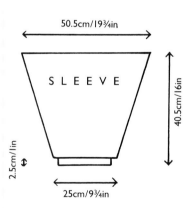

50.5cm/19¾in

SLEEVE

40.5cm/16in

2.5cm/1in

25cm/9¾in

With its comfortable shape and elegant pattern of sprigged flowers against an Aran-weight wool background, 'Sprigs and Garlands' is a jacket that will look special on any occasion. The pockets, inset neatly behind the lower garlanded border, are a practical feature.

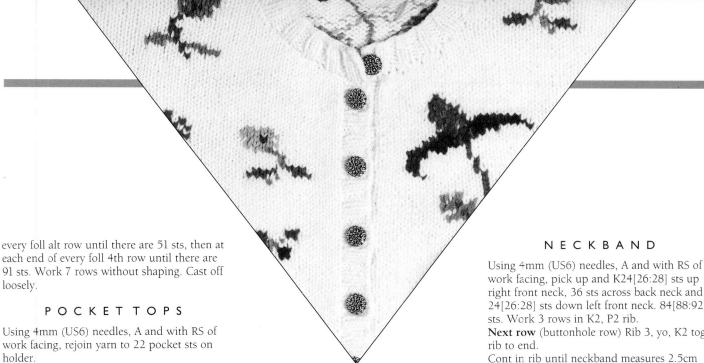

every foll alt row until there are 51 sts, then at each end of every foll 4th row until there are 91 sts. Work 7 rows without shaping. Cast off loosely.

POCKET TOPS

Using 4mm (US6) needles, A and with RS of work facing, rejoin yarn to 22 pocket sts on holder.
1st row (RS) K to end.
2nd row K2, (P2, K2) to end.
3rd row P2, (K2, P2) to end.
Rep 2nd and 3rd rows twice more.
Cast off in rib.

BUTTON BAND

Using 4mm (US6) needles, A and with RS of work facing, pick up and K112[116:120] sts evenly down left front. Work 2.5cm (1in) in K2, P2 rib. Cast off in rib.

BUTTONHOLE BAND

Using 4mm (US6) needles, A and with RS of work facing, pick up and K112[116:120] sts evenly down right front. Work 2 rows in K2, P2 rib.
Next row (buttonhole row) Rib 9[11:8], (yo, K2 tog, rib 9[9:10]) 9 times, yo, K2 tog, rib 2[4:2].
Cont in rib until buttonhole band measures 2.5cm (1in) from beg. Cast off in rib.

NECKBAND

Using 4mm (US6) needles, A and with RS of work facing, pick up and K24[26:28] sts up right front neck, 36 sts across back neck and 24[26:28] sts down left front neck. 84[88:92] sts. Work 3 rows in K2, P2 rib.
Next row (buttonhole row) Rib 3, yo, K2 tog, rib to end.
Cont in rib until neckband measures 2.5cm (1in) from beg. Cast off in rib.

TO MAKE UP

Press on WS using a warm iron over a damp cloth. Sew sleeve tops in position, matching centre of sleeve to shoulder seam and sewing final rows to cast-off sts at underarm. Join side and sleeve seams. Sew down pocket linings on WS of work and pocket tops on RS of work. Press seams. Sew on buttons.

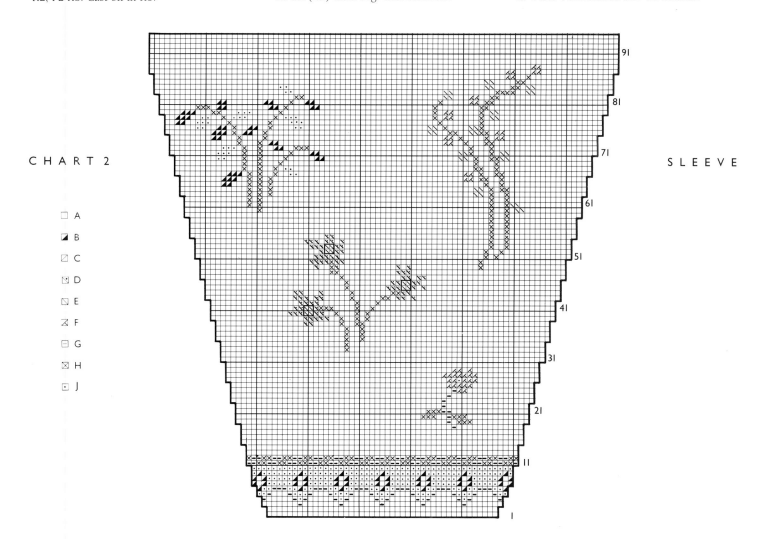

CHART 2

SLEEVE

□ A
◩ B
▨ C
◨ D
◩ E
▨ F
⊟ G
⊠ H
⊡ J

PERSIAN TAPESTRY

I have used a traditional Fair Isle design in just two colours for the main body of this sweater and off-set it at the hem and cuffs with a strong geometric border in contrasting colours. The adult's version – which I feel would also look very good on a man – is knitted in rich autumnal shades of DK and chenille; the child's sweater has a border in soft pastel tones.

SIZES

To fit 66[71:86:91:97]cm (26[28:34:36:38]in) chest/bust
Actual size 83[91:115:119:123]cm (32½[36:45¼:47:48½]in)
Length to shoulder 46[51:62.5:64:66]cm (18[20:24¾:25:26]in)
Sleeve seam 34[34:45:45:45]cm (13½[13½:17¾:17¾:17¾]in)
Figures in square brackets [ ] refer to larger sizes; where there is only one set of figures, it applies to all sizes.

MATERIALS

Colourway 1 – child's sweater
20[21]×25g hanks of Rowan Lightweight DK in main shade A (charcoal 625)
2×100g hanks of Rowan Chunky Cotton Chenille in shade B (Fern 364)
1×50g ball of Rowan Designer DK in shade C (Salmon 668)
2×25g hanks of Lightweight DK in shade D (rust 27)
2×50g balls of Designer DK in shade E (pink 667)
2×25g hanks of Lightweight DK in shade F (gold 8)
2×50g balls of Designer DK in shade G (mauve 666)
2[3]×25g hanks of Lightweight DK in shade H (mustard 664)
4[5]×25g hanks of Lightweight DK in shade J (sage green 421)
2[3]×25g hanks of Lightweight DK in shade K (duck egg 665)

Colourway 2 – adult's sweater
28[28:29]×25g hanks of Rowan Lightweight DK in main shade A (charcoal 625)
5[6:6]×50g balls of Rowan Fine Cotton Chenille in shade B (Oak 397)
2[2:3]×25g hanks of Lightweight DK in shade C (chestnut 663)
2×25g hanks of Lightweight DK in shade D (airforce 65)

2×25g hanks of Lightweight DK in shade E (shrimp 24)
1×25g hank of Rowan Botany in shade F (gold 521)
1×100g hank of Rowan Chunky Cotton Chenille in shade G (Fern 364)
2×25g hanks of Botany in shade H (duck egg 528)
4[4:5]×25g hanks of Lightweight DK in shade J (khaki 407)
1×25g hank of Lightweight DK in shade K (bronze 77)
Pair each of 4mm (US6) and 5mm (US8) knitting needles

NOTE

All yarns are used double throughout the design with the exception of Chunky Cotton Chenille, which is used as a single strand and Botany which is used as 3 strands together

TENSION

20 sts and 21 rows to 10cm (4in) over patt using 5mm (US8) needles

BACK

Using 4mm (US6) needles and A, cast on 80[88:112:116:120] sts.
Work 7 rows in K2, P2 rib.
Inc row Rib 20[22:28:29:30], * M1, rib

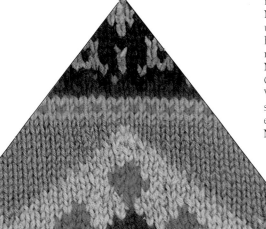

20[22:28:29:30], rep from * to end. 83[91:115:119:123] sts.
Change to 5mm (US8) needles.
Beg with a K row, cont in st st and work 92[102:126:130:134] rows in patt from Chart. Strand yarns loosely across back of work where appropriate or use small, separate balls of yarn for individual motifs. Link one shade to the next by twisting them around each other where they meet on the WS to avoid making gaps.

Shape shoulders and back neck
Cast off 9[10:13:13:13] sts at beg of next 2 rows.
Next row Cast off 10[10:13:13:13] sts, patt until there are 14[16:18:18:18] sts on right-hand needle, turn and complete this side of neck first.
Next row Cast off 4 sts, patt to end. Cast off rem 10[12:14:14:14] sts.
With RS of work facing, rejoin yarn to rem sts, cast off centre 17[19:27:31:35] sts, patt to end. 24[26:31:31:31] sts.
Next row Cast off 10[10:13:13:13] sts, patt to end.
Next row Cast off 4 sts, patt to end. Cast off rem 10[12:14:14:14] sts.

CHART 1

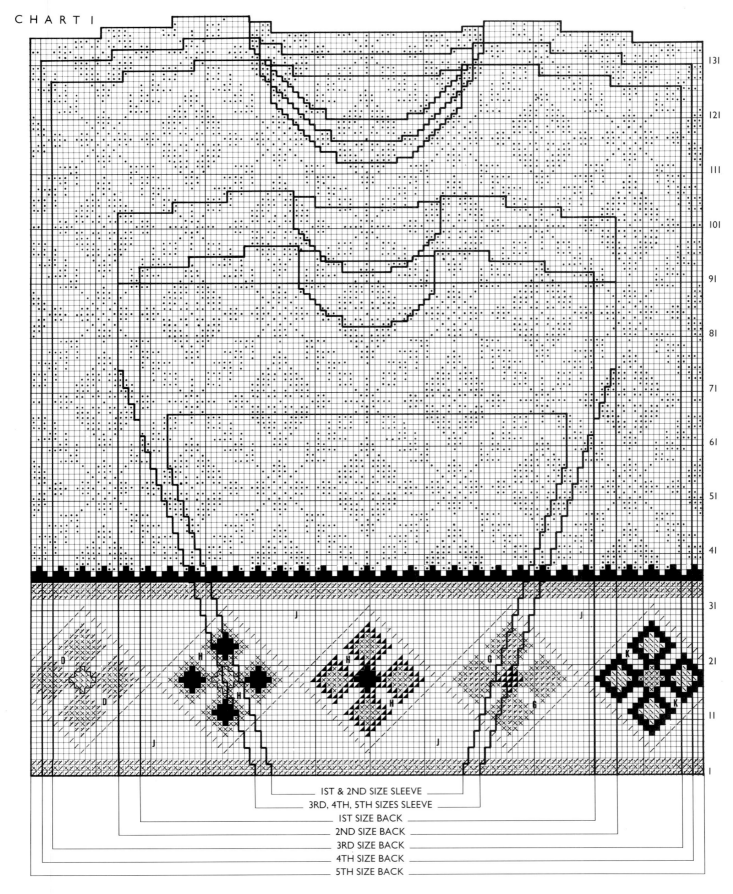

131
121
111
101
91
81
71
61
51
41
31
21
11
1

1ST & 2ND SIZE SLEEVE
3RD, 4TH, 5TH SIZES SLEEVE
1ST SIZE BACK
2ND SIZE BACK
3RD SIZE BACK
4TH SIZE BACK
5TH SIZE BACK

KEY

☐	☐	☐	☐ or ■	⊠	⊘	☐ or ◩	☐ or ◩	☐	☐ or ◪
A	B	C	D	E	F	G	H	J	K

Anna, on a visit to a museum, wears her 'Persian Tapestry' sweater. The close tones of the stylish main fabric are balanced by the colourful patterns at the lower edge.

FRONT

Work as given for back until row
82[92:112:116:120] has been completed.

Shape neck
Next row Patt 37[41:52:53:54], turn and
leave rem sts on a spare needle.
Cont on these sts for first side of neck.
Cast off 3 sts at beg of next row, then dec one
st at neck edge on next 5[6:9:10:11] rows.
29[32:40:40:40] sts.
Work 3[2:3:2:1] rows straight.

Shape shoulder
Cast off 9[10:13:13:13] sts at beg of next row
and 10[10:13:13:13] sts at beg of foll alt row.
Work 1 row. Cast off rem 10[12:14:14:14] sts.
With RS of work facing, rejoin yarn and cast
off centre 9[9:11:13:15] sts, patt to end.
37[41:52:53:54] sts.
Work 1 row, then complete to match first
side.

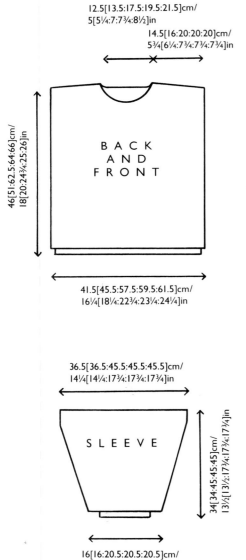

12.5[13.5:17.5:19.5:21.5]cm/
5[5¼:7:7¾:8½]in

14.5[16:20:20:20]cm/
5¾[6¼:7¾:7¾:7¾]in

46[51:62.5:64:66]cm/
18[20:24¾:25:26]in

**BACK
AND
FRONT**

41.5[45.5:57.5:59.5:61.5]cm/
16¼[18¼:22¾:23¼:24¼]in

36.5[36.5:45.5:45.5:45.5]cm/
14¼[14¼:17¾:17¾:17¾]in

34[34:45:45:45]cm/
13½[13½:17¾:17¾:17¾]in

SLEEVE

16[16:20.5:20.5:20.5]cm/
6¼[6¼:8:8:8]in

SLEEVES

Using 4mm (US6) needles and A, cast on
32[32:40:40:40] sts.
Work 7 rows in K2, P2 rib.
Inc row 1st and 2nd sizes only Rib 8, * M1,
rib 8, rep from * to end.
3rd, 4th and 5th sizes only Inc one st at
centre of row.
All sizes 35[35:41:41:41] sts.
Change to 5mm (US8) needles.
Beg with a K row, cont in st st and patt from
Chart, inc one st at each end of every 3rd row
until there are 73[73:91:91:91] sts. Cont
without shaping until row 68[68:90:90:90:]
has been completed, ending with a P row.
Cast off loosely.

NECKBAND

Join right shoulder seam. Using 4mm (US6)
needles, A and with RS of work facing, pick
up and K16[16:20:20:20] sts down left front
neck, 9[9:11:13:15] sts from front neck,

*In the child's version of 'Persian Tapestry'
the gold-coloured chenille yarn used against
a plain wool background creates a plush
textured fabric.*

16[16:20:20:20] sts up right front neck and
27[27:37:39:45] sts from back neck.
68[68:88:92:100] sts.
Work 7 rows in K2, P2 rib.
Cast off in rib.

TO MAKE UP

Press on WS using a warm iron over a damp
cloth. Join left shoulder and neckband seam.
Mark position of underarms
18[18:23:23:23]cm (7[7:9:9:9]in) down from
shoulders on back and front. Sew in sleeves
between markers, matching centre of sleeve
top to shoulder seam. Join side and sleeve
seams. Press seams.

LAUREL CROWN

A coronation robe in red and gold provided the original inspiration for this sweater. To reproduce the soft effect of velvet I used a black chenille background for the woman's version scattered with laurel sprigs in yellow chenille to replace the gold threads. Other jewel colours, including rich green or deep purple, would be equally suitable as background colours. The deep border at the hem and cuffs is easy to knit in a two-colour Fair Isle pattern. I love over-size sweaters like this for outdoor wear. Its shape looks especially good teamed with leggings.

SIZES

To fit 61[71:86:91:97]cm (24[28:34:36:38]in) chest/bust
Actual size 76.5[87.5:127.5:132:139]cm (30¼[34½:50¼:52:54¾]in)
Length to shoulder 41[45.5:67:70:73]cm (16[17¾:26½:27½:28¾]in)
Sleeve seam 34.5[34.5:48:48:48]cm (13¾[13¾:19:19:19]in)
Figures in square brackets [ ] refer to larger sizes; where there is only one set of figures, it applies to all sizes

MATERIALS

Colourway 1 – child's sweater
7[8]×50g balls of Rowan Fine Cotton Chenille in main shade A (Ecru 376)
2×100g hanks of Rowan Chunky Cotton Chenille in shade B (Fern 364)
2×50g balls of Rowan Designer DK in shade C (bronze 650)
Colourway 2 – adult's sweater
15[15:16]×50g balls of Rowan Fine Cotton Chenille in main shade A (Black 377)
2×100g hanks of Rowan Chunky Cotton Chenille in shade B (Fern 364)
2[3:3]×50g balls of Rowan Designer DK in shade C (bronze 650)
Pair of 4mm (US6) knitting needles
Pair of 5mm (US8) knitting needles

TENSION

18 sts and 25 rows to 10cm (4in) over patt using 5mm (US8) needles

NOTE

All yarns are used double throughout the design with the exception of Chunky Cotton Chenille, which is used as a single strand

BACK

Using 4mm (US6) needles and A, cast on 60[68:92:96:100] sts.
Work 3[3:7:7:7] rows in K2, P2 rib.
Inc row Rib 6[4:2:4:2], * M1, rib 6[6:4:4:4], rep from * to last 6[4:2:4:2] sts, M1, rib to end. 69[79:115:119:125] sts.
Change to 5mm (US8) needles.
Beg with a K row, cont in st st and patt from Chart, work 96[108:158:166:172] rows. Strand yarns loosely across back of work where appropriate or use small, separate balls of yarn for individual motifs. Link one shade to the next by twising them around each other where they meet on the WS to avoid making gaps.

Shape shoulders
Child's sweater
Cast off 21[26] sts at beg of next 2 rows.
Cast off rem 27 sts.
Adult's sweater
Cast off 13[14:15] sts at beg of next 4 rows and 14[14:15] sts at beg of next 2 rows.
Cast off rem 35 sts.

FRONT

Work as given for back until row 84[94:140:148:154] has been completed.

Shape neck
Next row Patt 30[35:53:55:58] sts, turn and leave rem sts on a spare needle.
Cont on these sts for first side of neck.
* Cast off 3 sts at beg of next row. Dec one st at neck edge on next 3[3:5:5:5] rows, then on every foll alt row until 21[26:40:42:45] sts rem.
Work 1[3:1:1:1] rows straight, so ending row 96[108:158:166:172] (row 97[109:159:167:173] for right front).
Child's sweater
Cast off these 21[26] sts.
Adult's sweater
Cast off 13[14:15] sts at beg of next and foll alt row. Work 1 row. Cast off rem 14[14:15] sts.
With RS of work facing, rejoin yarn to next st and cast off centre 9 sts, patt to end. 30[35:53:55:58] sts.
Patt 1 row.
Now complete to match first side of neck from * to end noting the bracketed exception.

Overleaf *A London park is the setting for a winning pose struck by Anna wearing a 'Laurel Crown' sweater in the adult's colourway.*

CHART I

☐ A
⊡ B
⊠ C

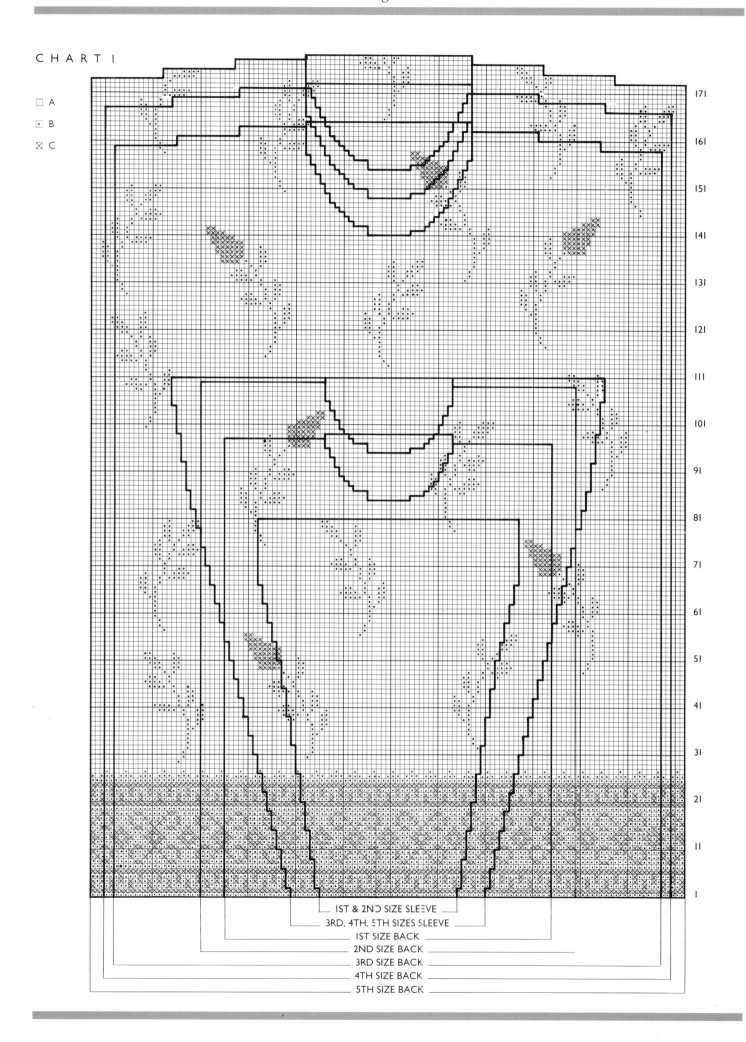

171
161
151
141
131
121
111
101
91
81
71
61
51
41
31
21
11
1

1ST & 2ND SIZE SLEEVE
3RD, 4TH, 5TH SIZES SLEEVE
1ST SIZE BACK
2ND SIZE BACK
3RD SIZE BACK
4TH SIZE BACK
5TH SIZE BACK

SLEEVES

Using 4mm (US6) needles and A, cast on 28[28:40:40:40] sts.
Work 2.5[2.5:4:4:4]cm (1[1:1½:1½:1½]in) in K2, P2 rib but inc one st at centre of last row. 29[29:41:41:41] sts.
Change to 5mm (US8) needles.
Beg with a K row, cont in st st and patt from Chart, inc one st at each end of 3rd and every foll 6th[6th:4th:4th:4th] row until there are 47[47:85:85:85] sts, then at each end of every

foll 4th[4th:6th:6th:6th] row until there are 55[55:91:91:91] sts.
Work straight until row 80[80:110:110:110] has been completed. Cast off.

NECKBAND

Join right shoulder seam. With RS of work facing, A and using 4mm (US6) needles, pick up and K16[18:22:24:26] sts down left front neck, 9 sts from front neck, 16[18:22:24:26] sts up right front neck and 27[27:35:35:35]

sts across back neck. 68[72:88:92:96] sts.
Work 5[5:7:7:7] rows in K2, P2 rib.
Cast off in rib.

TO MAKE UP

Press lightly on WS using a warm iron over a damp cloth. Mark position of underarms 15[15:25:25:25]cm (6[6:10:10:10]in) down from shoulders on back and front. Sew in sleeves between markers. Join side and sleeve seams. Press seams.

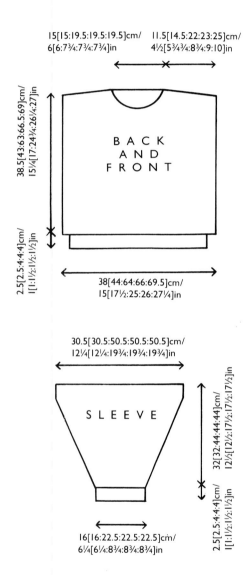

Knitted in a chunky-weight yarn, this sweater with its comfortable loose shape is perfect for wearing on cooler days around town or in the country. The plush effect of the dark chenille makes a sumptuously rich background fabric for the sprigged buds and border patterns. A softer colourway, featuring ecru as the main colour, is shown on a child (see page 10).

SLOANE SQUARE

A lot of inspiration for my designs comes from studying Persian textiles. The idea for this cardigan originated from a carpet. Although I liked the pattern, I wanted a change from the traditional rich, dark colours. Instead I chose the muted shades of a pure wool yarn, with a touch of chenille, to look as though the colours have faded with time.

SIZES

To fit 86/91[91/97:97/102]cm (34/36[36/38:38/40]in) bust
Actual size 123[129.5:136]cm (48½[51:53½]in)
Length to shoulder 66[68.5:71]cm (26[27:28]in)
Sleeve seam 44cm (17½in)
Figures in square brackets [ ] refer to larger sizes; where there is only one set of figures, it applies to all sizes

MATERIALS

26[26:27] × 25g hanks of Rowan Lightweight DK in main shade A (fawn 82)
1 × 100g hank of Rowan Magpie in shade B (Peppercorn 610) – used single throughout
2 × 50g balls of Rowan Fine Cotton Chenille in shade C (Maple 396)
3 hanks of Lightweight DK in shade D (rust 663)
3 hanks of Lightweight DK in shade E (green 421)
4 hanks of Lightweight DK in shade F (petrel blue 65)
2 hanks of Lightweight DK in shade G (mauve 423)
2 hanks of Lightweight DK in shade H (pale turquoise 665)
3 × 50g balls of Rowan Designer DK in shade J (pale mauve 118)
Pair each of 4mm (US6) and 5mm (US8) knitting needles
8 buttons

NOTE

All yarns are used double throughout the design with the exception of Magpie, which is used as a single strand

TENSION

18 sts and 23 rows to 10cm (4in) over patt using 5mm (US8) needles

BACK

Using 4mm (US6) needles and A, cast on 108[116:120] sts.
Work 2.5cm (1in) in K2, P2 rib, ending with a WS row and inc 3[1:3] sts evenly across last row. 111[117:123] sts.
Change to 5mm (US8) needles.

Beg with a K row, cont in st st and work 88[94:100] rows in patt from Chart 1. Strand shades loosely across back of work where appropriate or use small, separate balls of yarn for individual motifs.

Shape armholes
Cast off 6 sts at beg of next 2 rows. 99[105:111] sts. Work straight until row 146[152:158] has been completed, ending with a P row.

This flower patterned cardigan is a perfect companion for spending a casual day in town. Knitted mainly with two strands of a lightweight double knitting wool to give an Aran-weight thickness the cardigan is a stylish answer to the problem of what to wear on spring or autumn days when the weather is too warm for a coat.

CHART I

□ A
⊡ B
◩ C
⊠ D
◪ E
◣ F
■ G
⧅ H
◢ J

160

140

130

120

110

100

90

80

70

60

50

40

30

20

10

0

CHART 2

- ☐ A
- ⊡ B
- ◩ C
- ☒ D
- ◨ E
- ◩ F
- ■ G
- ◩ H
- ◪ J

SLEEVE

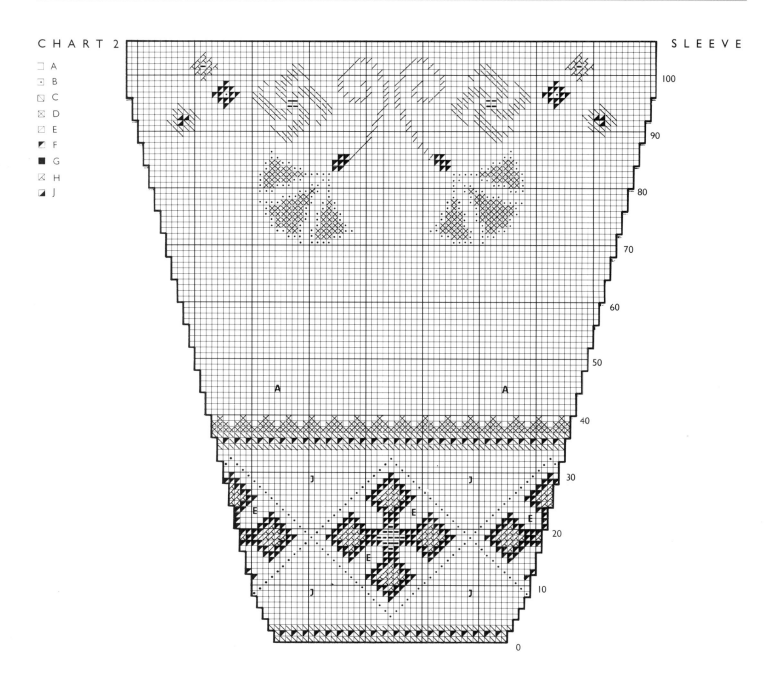

Shape shoulders

Cast off 10[11:12] sts at beg of next 2 rows and 11[12:13] sts at beg of following 4 rows. Cast off rem 35 sts.

LEFT FRONT

Using 4mm (US6) needles and A, cast on 52[56:60] sts.
Work 2.5cm (1in) in K2, P2 rib, ending with a WS row and inc 3[2:1] sts evenly across last row. 55[58:61] sts.
Change to 5mm (US8) needles.
Beg with a K row, cont in st st and work 88[94:100] rows from Chart 1 (work 89[95:101] rows for right front), so ending at side edge.

Shape armhole

Cast off 6 sts at beg of next row. 49[52:55] sts.

Work straight until row 127[133:139] (row 128[134:140] for right front) has been completed, so ending at front edge.

Shape neck

Cast off 6 sts at beg of next row and 3 sts at beg of foll alt row. 40[43:46] sts.
Dec one st at neck edge on next 5 rows, then on foll 3 alt rows. 32[35:38] sts.
Work 5 rows straight, so ending at armhole edge.

Shape shoulder

Cast off 10[11:12] sts at beg of next row and 11[12:13] sts at beg of foll alt row. Work one row. Cast off rem 11[12:13] sts.

RIGHT FRONT

Work as given for Left Front, noting the bracketed exceptions.

SLEEVES

Using 4mm (US6) needles and A, cast on 40 sts. Work 2.5cm (1in) K2, P2 rib, ending with a WS row and inc one st at end of last row. 41 sts.
Change to 5mm (US8) needles.
Beg with a K row, cont in st st and patt from Chart 2, inc one st at each end of 3rd and 3 foll alt rows. 49 sts.
Inc one st at each end of every foll 4th row until there are 93 sts. Work straight until 106 rows have been completed, ending with a P row. Cast off loosely.

BUTTON BAND

Using 4mm (US6) needles, A and with RS of work facing, pick up and K104[108:112] sts evenly down left front. Work 3.5cm (1¼in) in P2, K2 rib. Cast off in rib.

BUTTONHOLE BAND

Using 4mm (US6) needles, A and with RS of work facing, pick up and K104[108:112] sts evenly down right front. Work 3 rows in K2, P2 rib.

Next row (buttonhole row) Rib 2[4:4], (cast off 2, rib until there are 14 sts on right-hand needle after cast-off group) 6 times, cast off 2, rib to end.

Next row Rib to end casting on 2 sts over each buttonhole on previous row.

Work straight until buttonhole band measures 3.5cm (1¼in) from beg. Cast off in rib.

NECKBAND

Join shoulder seams. Using 4mm (US6) needles, A and with RS of work facing, pick up and K38 sts up right front neck, 36 sts across back neck and 38 sts down left front neck. 112 sts. Work 3 rows in P2, K2 rib.

Next row (buttonhole row) Rib 4, cast off 2, rib to end.

Next row Rib to end casting on 2 sts over buttonhole on previous row.

Work straight until neckband measures 3.5cm (1¼in) from beg. Cast off in rib.

TO MAKE UP

Press on WS using a warm iron over a damp cloth. Sew sleeve tops in position, matching centre of sleeve to shoulder seam and sewing final rows to cast-off sts at underarm. Join side and sleeve seams. Press seams. Sew on buttons.

19.5cm/7¾in

17.5[19.5:21]cm/6¾[7¾:8¼]in

51.5cm/20¼in

66[68.5:71]cm/26[27:28]in

BACK

RIGHT FRONT

LEFT FRONT

25cm/9¾in

2.5cm/1in

SLEEVE

48.5cm/19¼in

61.5[65:68]cm/24¼[25½:26¾]in

30.5[32:34]cm/12[12½:13½]in

25.5cm/10in

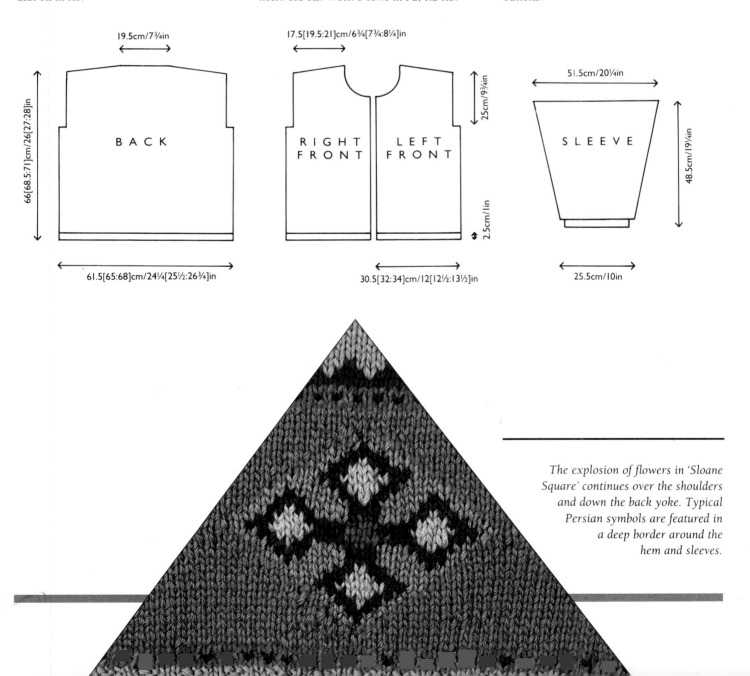

The explosion of flowers in 'Sloane Square' continues over the shoulders and down the back yoke. Typical Persian symbols are featured in a deep border around the hem and sleeves.

DRAGON FANTASY

This generously sized cardigan is a perfect spring or autumn coat for either town or country. I first saw the dragon pattern, with its enchanting border of entwined leaves, on a nineteenth century carpet. I have used subtle changes of colour for my bold dragon motifs and leaf borders, then placed them against a charcoal grey fabric for an understated, expensive look. To make the pattern appear more prominent use a stone or mushroom coloured background.

SIZES

To fit 86/91[91/97:97/102]cm (34/36[36/38:38/40]in) bust
Actual size 127[132:136]cm (50[52:53½]in)
Length to shoulder 64.5[67:70]cm (25¼[26½:27½]in)
Sleeve seam 47cm (18½in)
Figures in square brackets [ ] refer to larger sizes; where there is only one set of figures, it applies to all sizes.

MATERIALS

35[35:36]×25g hanks of Rowan Lightweight DK in main shade A (moss green 61)
6×25g hanks of Lightweight DK in shade B (charcoal 625)
3×25g hanks of Lightweight DK in shade C (shrimp 78)
3×25g hanks of Lightweight DK in shade D (sage green 421)
2×25g hanks of Lightweight DK in shade E (rust 663)
1×25g hank of Lightweight DK in shade F (duck egg 665)
1×25g hank of Lightweight DK in shade G (gold 86)
1×25g hank of Lightweight DK in shade H (airforce 88)
1×25g hank of Lightweight DK in shade J (navy 97)
1×25g hank of Lightweight DK in shade K (beige 58)
Pair each of 4mm (US6) and 5mm (US8) knitting needles
10 buttons

NOTE

All yarns are used double throughout the design

TENSION

18 sts and 23 rows to 10cm (4in) over patt using 5mm (US8) needles

BACK

Using 4mm (US6) needles and A, cast on 96[100:104] sts.
Work 8cm (3in) in K2, P2 rib, ending with a RS row.
Inc row Rib 2[4:6], inc in next st, * rib 4, inc in next st, rep from * to last 3[5:7] sts, rib to end. 115[119:123] sts.
Change to 5mm (US8) needles
Beg with a K row, cont in st st and work 72[78:84] rows in patt from Chart 1. Strand yarns loosely across back of work where appropriate or use small, separate balls of yarn for individual motifs. Link one shade to the next by twisting them around each other where they meet on the WS to avoid making gaps.

Shape armholes

Cast off 6 sts at beg of next 2 rows. 103[107:111] sts.
Cont in patt without shaping until row 130[136:142] has been completed, ending with a P row.

Shape shoulders

Cast off 12[11:12] sts at beg of next 2 rows and 11[12:12] sts at beg of foll 4 rows. Cast off rem 35[37:39] sts.

POCKET LININGS
(make 2)

Using 5mm (US8) needles and A, cast on 22[24:24] sts. Beg with a K row, work 22 rows st st, ending with a P row. Cut off yarn and leave sts on a holder.

LEFT FRONT

Using 4mm (US6) needles and A, cast on 48[48:52] sts. Work 8cm (3in) in K2, P2 rib, ending with a RS row.
Inc row Rib 3[3:5], inc in next st, * rib 4[3:4], inc in next st, rep from * to last 4[4:6] sts, rib to end. 57[59:61] sts
Change to 5mm (US8) needles.
Beg with a K row, cont in st st and work 38[42:46] rows in patt from Chart 1. **

Place pocket lining

Next row Patt 16, sl next 22[24:24] sts onto a holder, patt across 22[24:24] sts of pocket lining, then patt to end.
*** Cont in patt from Chart 1 until row 72[78:84] (row 73[79:85] for right front) has been completed, so ending at side edge.

Shape armhole

Cast off 6 sts at beg of next row. 51[53:55] sts.
Cont in patt without shaping until row 117[121:125] (row 118[122:126] for right front) has been completed, so ending at front edge.

Shape neck

Cast off 6 sts at beg of next row and 3 sts at beg of foll alt row. 42[44:46] sts. Dec one st at neck edge on next 6 rows, then on foll 2[3:4] alt rows, so ending at armhole edge.

Shape shoulder

Cast off 12[11:12] sts at beg of next row and 11[12:12] sts at beg of foll alt row. Work one row. Cast off rem 11[12:12] sts.

CHART I

- □ A
- ⊡ B
- ⊠ C
- ☑ D
- ⊠ E
- ⊟ F
- ◪ G
- ⊠ H
- ⊠ J
- ⊡ K

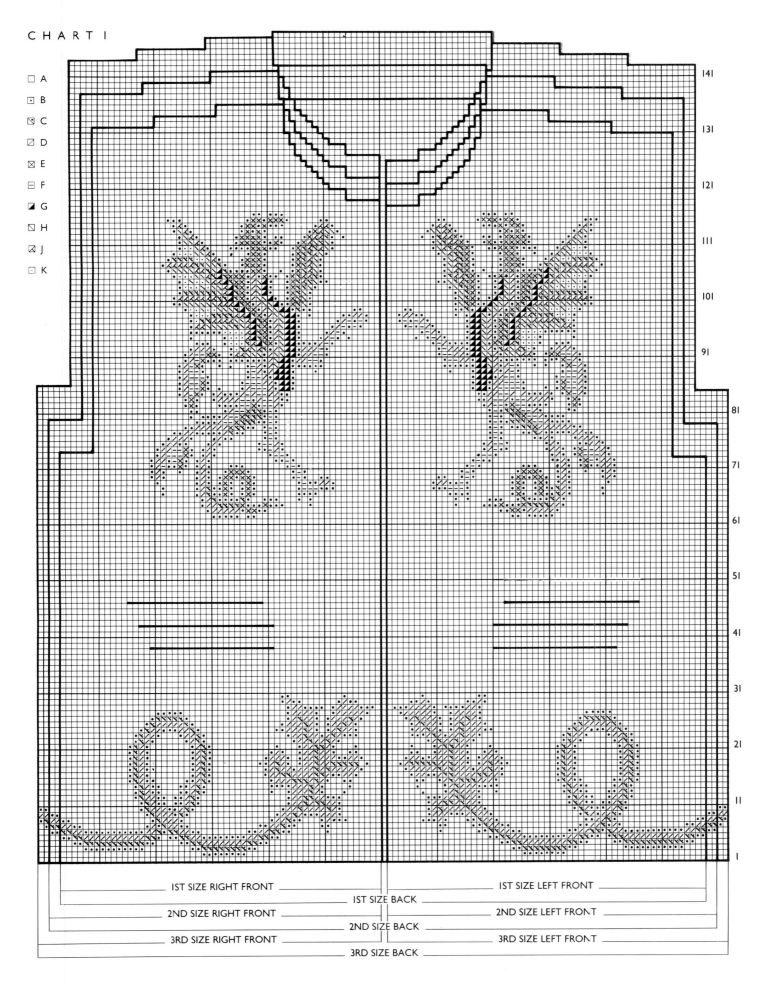

141
131
121
111
101
91
81
71
61
51
41
31
21
11
1

1ST SIZE RIGHT FRONT _____ 1ST SIZE LEFT FRONT _____
1ST SIZE BACK _____
2ND SIZE RIGHT FRONT _____ 2ND SIZE LEFT FRONT _____
2ND SIZE BACK _____
3RD SIZE RIGHT FRONT _____ 3RD SIZE LEFT FRONT _____
3RD SIZE BACK _____

CHART 2   SLEEVE

□ A
⊡ B
☒ C
☑ D
⊠ E
⊟ F
◢ G
⊠ H
☒ J
⊡ K

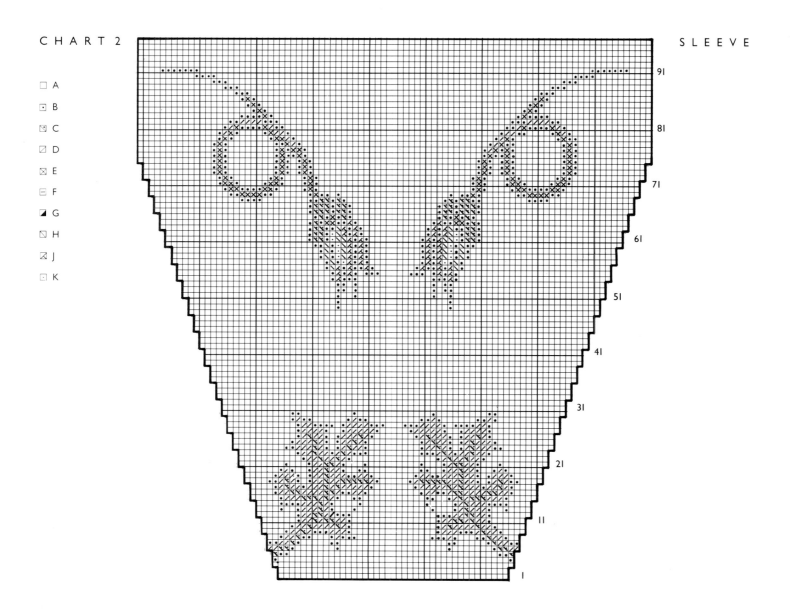

91
81
71
61
51
41
31
21
11
1

RIGHT FRONT

Work as given for left front to **.

Place pocket lining
Next row Patt 19[19:21], sl next 22[24:24] sts
on to a holder, patt across 22[24:24] sts of
pocket lining, then patt to end.
Complete as given for left front from *** to
end, noting the bracketed exceptions.

SLEEVES

Using 4mm (US6) needles and A, cast on 36
sts. Work 9cm (3½in) in K2, P2 rib, ending
with a RS row.
Inc row Rib 1, inc in next st, * rib 7, inc in
next st, rep from * to last 2 sts, rib 2. 41 sts.
Change to 5mm (US8) needles.
Beg with a K row, cont in st st and patt from
Chart 2, inc one st at each end of every 3rd
row until there are 91 sts.
Cont in patt without shaping until row 96 has
been completed, ending with a P row. Cast
off loosely.

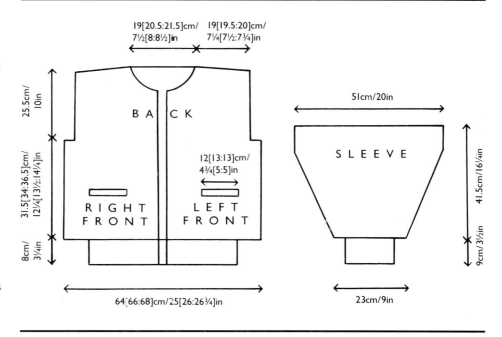

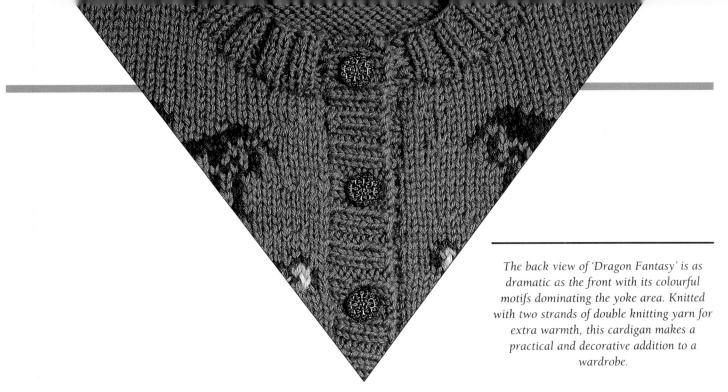

The back view of 'Dragon Fantasy' is as dramatic as the front with its colourful motifs dominating the yoke area. Knitted with two strands of double knitting yarn for extra warmth, this cardigan makes a practical and decorative addition to a wardrobe.

POCKET TOPS

Using 4mm (US6) needles, A and with RS of work facing, rejoin yarn to 22[24:24] pocket sts on holder.
1st row K2[3:3], P2, (K2, P2) to last 2[3:3] sts, K to end.
2nd row P2[3:3], K2, (P2, K2) to last 2[3:3] sts, P to end.
Rep 1st and 2nd rows twice more.
Cast off in rib.

NECKBAND

Join shoulder seams. Using 4mm (US6) needles, A and with RS of work facing, pick up and K25[26:27] sts up right front neck, 32[34:36] sts across back neck and 25[26:27] sts down left front neck. 82[86:90] sts.
Work 7 rows in K2, P2 rib as given for 1st size of pocket tops. Cast off in rib.

BUTTON BAND

Using 4mm (US6) needles, A and with RS of work facing, pick up and K120[124:124] sts evenly down left front. Work 8 rows in P2, K2 rib. Cast off in rib.´

BUTTONHOLE BAND

Using 4mm (US6) needles, A and with RS of work facing, pick up and K120[124:124] sts evenly up right front. Work 3 rows in P2, K2 rib.
Next row (buttonhole row) Rib 5[3:3], (cast off 2, rib until there are 10[11:11] sts on right-hand needle after cast-off group) 9 times, cast off 2, rib to end.
Next row Rib to end, casting on 2 sts over each buttonhole on previous row.
Rib 3 more rows. Cast off in rib.

TO MAKE UP

Press on WS using a warm iron over a damp cloth. Sew sleeve tops in position, matching centre of sleeve to shoulder seam and sewing final rows to cast-off sts at underarm. Join side and sleeve seams. Sew down pocket linings on WS of work and pocket tops on RS of work. Press seams. Sew on buttons.

BALMORAL TWEED

Living, as I do, close to the Yorkshire Pennines I know how invaluable a thick woollen sweater can be on a cold day. Balmoral Tweed is a chunky sweater full of decorative Aran patterns and textures that will appeal to both men and women. This sweater can be knitted very quickly in chunky Fox Tweed – a beautiful pure wool yarn in moorland tones with subtle flecks of colour.

SIZES

To fit 97/102[102/107:107/112]cm (38/40[40/42:42/44]in) bust/chest
Actual size 130[135:140]cm (51[53:55]in)
Length to shoulder 69[71:74]cm (27[28:29]in)
Sleeve seam (with cuff turned back) 50cm (19½in)
Figures in square brackets [ ] refer to larger sizes; where there is only one set of figures, it applies to all sizes.

MATERIALS

25[26:27]×50g hanks of Rowan Fox Tweed DK (Seal 852)
Pair each 5½mm (US9) and 6½mm (US10½) knitting needles
Cable needle

NOTE

Yarn is used double throughout the design

TENSION

16 sts and 20 rows to 10cm (4in) over patt using 6½mm (US10½) needles

SPECIAL ABBREVIATIONS

CR5R Cross 5 Right thus: sl next 3 sts onto cable needle and leave at back of work, K2, then P1 and K2 from cable needle
CR3R Cross 3 Right thus: sl next st onto cable needle and leave at back of work, K2, then P1 from cable needle
CR3L Cross 3 Left thus: sl next 2 sts onto cable needle and leave at front of work, P1, then K2 from cable needle
C4L Cable 4 Left thus: sl next 2 sts onto cable needle and leave at front of work, K2, then K2 from cable needle
C4R Cable 4 Right thus: sl next 2 sts onto cable needle and leave at back of work, K2, then K2 from cable needle

PATTERN PANEL
(worked over 15 sts)

Row 1 (RS) P5, CR5R, P5.
Row 2 K5, P2, K1, P2, K5.
Row 3 P4, CR3R, K1, CR3L, P4.

Row 4 K4, P2, K1, P1, K1, P2, K4.
Row 5 P3, CR3R, K1, P1, K1, CR3L, P3.
Row 6 K3, P2, K1, [P1, K1] twice, P2, K3.
Row 7 P2, CR3R, K1, (P1, K1) twice, CR3L, P2.
Row 8 K2, P2, K1, (P1, K1) 3 times, P2, K2.
Row 9 P1, CR3R, K1, (P1, K1) 3 times, CR3L, P1.
Row 10 K1, P2, K1, (P1, K1) 4 times, P2, K1.
Row 11 P1, K3, P1, (K1, P1) 3 times, K3, P1.
Row 12 K1, P3, K1, (P1, K1) 3 times, P3, K1.
Row 13 P1, CR3L, K1, (P1, K1) 3 times, CR3R, P1.
Row 14 K2, P3, K1, (P1, K1) twice, P3, K2.
Row 15 P2, CR3L, K1, (P1, K1) twice, CR3R, P2.
Row 16 K3, P3, K1, P1, K1, P3, K3.
Row 17 P3, CR3L, K1, P1, K1, CR3R, P3.
Row 18 K4, P3, K1, P3, K4.
Row 19 P4, CR3L, K1, CR3R, P4.
Row 20 K5, P5, K5.
Row 21 P5, CR5R, P5.
Row 22 K5, P2, K1, P2, K5.
Row 23 P4, CR3R, P1, CR3L, P4.
Row 24 K4, P2, K3, P2, K4.
Row 25 P4, K2, P3, K2, P4.
Row 26 As row 24.
Row 27 P4, CR3L, P1, CR3R, P4.
Row 28 K5, P2, K1, P2, K5.
These 28 rows form Pattern Panel 1.

PATTERN PANEL 2
(worked over 22 sts)

Row 1 (RS) P2, K2, P3, K2, P4, K2, P3, K2, P2.
Row 2 K2, P2, K3, P2, K4, P2, K3, P2, K2.
Row 3 P2, (CR3L, P2) twice, (CR3R, P2) twice.
Row 4 (K3, P2) twice, K2, (P2, K3) twice.
Row 5 P3, CR3L, P2, CR3L, CR3R, P2, CR3R, P3.
Row 6 K4, P2, K3, P4, K3, P2, K4.
Row 7 P4, CR3L, P2, C4R, P2, CR3R, P4.
Row 8 K5, P2, K2, P4, K2, P2, K5.
Row 9 P5 (CR3L, CR3R) twice, P5.
Row 10 K6, P4, K2, P4, K6.
Row 11 P6, C4L, P2, C4L, P6.
Row 12 As row 10.
Row 13 P5, (CR3R, CR3L) twice, P5.
Row 14 As row 8.
Row 15 P4, CR3R, P2, C4R, P2, CR3L, P4.
Row 16 As row 6.

Row 17 P3, CR3R, P2, CR3R, CR3L, P2, CR3L, P3.
Row 18 As row 4.
Row 19 (P2, CR3R) twice, P2, (CR3L, P2) twice.
Row 20 As row 2.
Rows 21 to 28 Rep rows 1 and 2 four times.
These 28 rows form Pattern Panel 2.

BACK

Using 5½mm (US9) needles cast on 88 sts.
Rib row 1 P1, K2, * P2, K2, rep from * to last st, P1.
Rib row 2 K1, P2, * K2, P2, rep from * to last st, K1.
Rep these 2 rows for 7cm (2¾in), ending with row 1.
Inc row Rib 5[1:1], for **2nd and 3rd sizes only** (M1, rib 2[1] sts) 2[4] times, for **all sizes** M1, rib 10, M1, rib 2, M1, rib 4, (M1, rib 2)

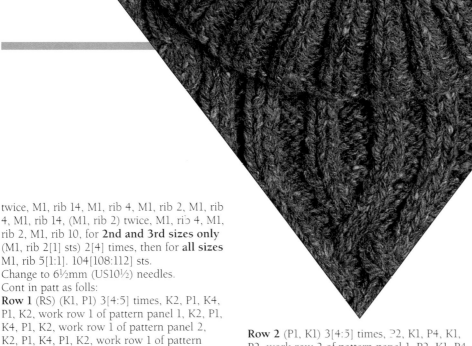

twice, M1, rib 14, M1, rib 4, M1, rib 2, M1, rib 4, M1, rib 14, (M1, rib 2) twice, M1, rib 4, M1, rib 2, M1, rib 10, for **2nd and 3rd sizes only** (M1, rib 2[1] sts) 2[4] times, then for **all sizes** M1, rib 5[1:1]. 104[108:112] sts.
Change to 6½mm (US10½) needles.
Cont in patt as folls:
Row 1 (RS) (K1, P1) 3[4:5] times, K2, P1, K4, P1, K2, work row 1 of pattern panel 1, K2, P1, K4, P1, K2, work row 1 of pattern panel 2, K2, P1, K4, P1, K2, work row 1 of pattern panel 1, K2, P1, K4, P1, K2, (P1, K1) 3[4:5] times.

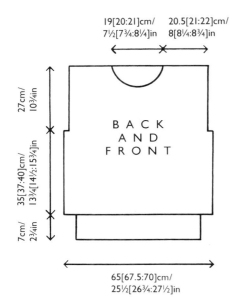

19[20:21]cm/ 7½[7¾:8¼]in   20.5[21:22]cm/ 8[8¼:8¾]in

27cm/ 10¾in

35[37:40]cm/ 13¾[14½:15¾]in

7cm/ 2¾in

BACK AND FRONT

65[67.5:70]cm/ 25½[26¾:27½]in

55.5cm/21¾in

SLEEVE

42cm/16½in

10cm/4in (folded back) cuff

29.5cm/11¾in

Warren appreciates the rugged appeal and warmth of the Aran patterned sweater knitted in an unusual chunky tweed yarn.

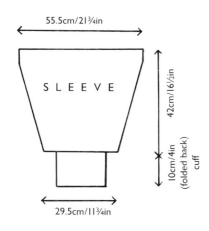

Row 2 (P1, K1) 3[4:5] times, P2, K1, P4, K1, P2, work row 2 of pattern panel 1, P2, K1, P4, K1, P2, work row 2 of pattern panel 2, P2, K1, P4, K1, P2, work row 2 of pattern panel 1, P2, K1, P4, K1, P2, (K1, P1) 3[4:5] times.
Row 3 (P1, K1) 3[4:5] times, K2, P1, C4L, P1, K2, work row 3 of pattern panel 1, K2, P1, C4R, P1, K2, work row 3 of pattern panel 2, K2, P1, C4L, P1, K2, work row 3 of pattern panel 1, K2, P1, C4R, P1, K2, (K1, P1) 3[4:5] times.
Row 4 (K1, P1) 3[4:5] times, P2, K1, P4, K1, P2, work row 4 of pattern panel 1, P2, K1, P4, K1, P2, work row 4 of pattern panel 2, P2, K1, P4, K1, P2, work row 4 of pattern panel 1, P2, K1, P4, K1, P2, (P1, K1) 3[4:5] times.
The first and last 6[8:10] sts form Irish Moss st.
Cont in Irish Moss st over these 6[8:10] sts, working corresponding pattern rows of pattern panels 1 and 2 as now set and working cables on 5th and every foll 6th row until back measures 42[44:47]cm (16½[17½:18½]in) from cast-on edge, ending with a WS row.

Shape armholes
Cast off 4 sts at beg of next 2 rows. 96[100:104] sts.
Work straight until armholes measure 27cm (10¾in) from beg of shaping, ending with a WS row.

Shape shoulders
Cast off 33[34:35] sts at beg of next 2 rows.
Cast off rem 30[32:34] sts.

FRONT
Work as given for back until armholes measure 21cm (8¼in) from beg of shaping, ending with a WS row.

Shape neck
Next row Patt 43[44:45], turn and leave rem sts on a spare needle.
Cont on these sts for first side of neck.
Cast off 3 sts at beg of next row, then dec one st at neck edge on every row until 33[34:35] sts rem.
Work straight until front measures same as back up to shoulders, ending at armhole edge.

Shape shoulder
Cast off rem 33[34:35] sts.
With RS of work facing, rejoin yarn to next st and cast off centre 10[12:14] sts, patt to end. 43[44:45] sts.
Patt 1 row.
Now complete to match first side of neck.

SLEEVES
Using 5½mm (US9) needles cast on 44 sts.
Beg with rib row 1, work in rib as given for back for 20.5cm (8in), ending with row 1.
Inc row Rib 3, M1, rib 18, M1, rib 20, M1, rib 3. 47 sts.
Change to 6½mm (US10½) needles.
Cont in patt as folls:
Row 1 (RS) (K1, P1) 3 times, K2, P1, K4, P1, K2, work row 1 of pattern panel 1, K2, P1, K4, P1, K2, (P1, K1) 3 times.
Row 2 (P1, K1) 3 times, P2, K1, P4, K1, P2, work row 2 of pattern panel 1, P2, K1, P4, K1, P2, (K1, P1) 3 times.
Row 3 (P1, K1) 3 times, K2, P1, C4L, P1, K2, work row 3 of pattern panel 1, K2, P1, C4R, P1, K2, (K1, P1) 3 times.
Row 4 (K1, P1) 3 times, P2, K1, P4, K1, P2, work row 4 of pattern panel 1, P2, K1, P4, K1, P2, (P1, K1) 3 times.
The first and last 6 sts form Irish Moss st.
Cont to work cables on 5th and every foll 6th row and working each corresponding row of pattern panel 1 as now set, inc and work into Irish Moss st one st at each end of next and foll 4 alt rows. 57 sts.
Now inc one st at each end of every foll 4th row until there are 89 sts.
Work straight until sleeve measures 62.5cm (24¾in) from cast-on edge, ending with a WS row. Cast off loosely.

COLLAR
Join right shoulder seam. With RS of work facing, join on yarn and using 5½mm (US9) needles, pick up and K20 sts down left front neck, 10[12:14] sts from front neck, 20 sts up right front neck and 30[32:34] sts across back neck. 80[84:88] sts.
Beg with rib row 2, work in rib as given for back for 12cm (4¾in).
Cast off in rib.

TO MAKE UP
Do not press. Join left shoulder and collar seam, reversing seam on collar for last 6cm (2¼in).
Sew sleeve tops in position, matching centre of sleeve to shoulder seam and sewing final rows to cast-off sts at underarm. Join side and sleeve seams, reversing seam on cuffs for last 10cm (4in). Turn back collar and cuffs.

CHELSEA STYLE

I love the vest style of this man's sweater – and it is so simple to knit as it features basic horizontal stripes with deep borders of geometric motifs. I chose the yarn and colours to echo the faded tones of an Indian rug. The yarn, Silkstones, is a luxurious blend of silk and wool; here it is combined with Grainy Silk which is the same yarn with a flecked tweed effect.

SIZES

To fit 86/91[91/97:97/102]cm (34/36[36/38:38/40]in) chest
Actual size 126[132:138]cm (49½[52:54½]in)
Length to shoulder 67[69:71]cm (26½[27:28]in)
Sleeve seam 46cm (18in)
Figures in square brackets [ ] refer to larger sizes; where there is only one set of figures, it applies to all sizes.

MATERIALS

8[8:9]×50g hanks of Rowan Grainy Silk in main shade A (Twig 809)
2×50g hanks of Rowan Silkstones in shade B (Teal 828)
3×50g hanks of Silkstones in shade C (Chilli 826)
2×50g hanks of Silkstones in shade D (Mulled Wine 830)
2[3:3]×50g hanks of Silkstones in shade E (Dried Rose 825)
2[2:3]×50g hanks of Silkstones in shade F (Olive Grey 827)
2×50g balls of Rowan Fine Cotton Chenille in shade G (Lacquer 388)
2×50g balls of Fine Cotton Chenille in shade H (Privet 394).
Pair each of 3¼mm (US3) and 4½mm (US7) knitting needles
4 buttons

NOTE

All yarns are used double throughout the design

TENSION

20 sts and 27 rows to 10cm (4in) over patt using 4½mm (US7) needles

The colours in the patterning on 'Chelsea Style' are repeated as stripes in the ribbing at the lower edge, cuffs and around the neckband.

BACK

Using 3¼mm (US3) needles and A, cast on 100[104:108] sts.
** Work in K2, P2 rib thus: 2 rows A, 1 row B, 1 row E, 1 row B.
Cont with A only, work until rib measures 8cm (3in) from cast-on edge, ending with a RS row **.
Inc row Rib 12[11:10], inc in next st, * rib 2, inc in next st, rep from * to last 12[11:10] sts, rib to end. 126[132:138] sts.
Change to 4½mm (US7) needles.
Beg with a K row, cont in st st and work 90[96:102] rows from Chart. Strand yarns loosely across back of work where appropriate or use small, separate balls of yarn for individual motifs. Link one shade to the next by twisting them around each other where they meet on the WS to avoid making gaps.

Shape armholes
Cast off 6 sts at beg of next 2 rows. 114[120:126] sts.
Cont in patt without shaping until row 156[162:168] has been completed.

Shape neck
Next row Patt 43[46:49], turn and complete this side first.
Cast off 4 sts at beg of next row.
Do not cast off but cut off yarn and sl rem 39[42:45] sts on a spare needle.
With RS of work facing, rejoin yarn and cast off centre 28 sts, patt to end. Work 1 row, then complete as given for other side of neck.

POCKET LININGS
(make 2)

Using 4½mm (US7) needles and A, cast on 26 sts. Beg with a K row, work in st st for 10cm (4in), ending with a P row. Cut off yarn and leave sts on a holder.

FRONT

Work as given for back until row 102[106:110] has been completed.

Place pocket lining
Next row Patt 14[16:18], * sl next 26 sts onto a holder, patt across 26 sts of pocket lining *, patt 34[36:38], rep from * to *, then patt to end.
Cont in patt from Chart until row 126[132:138] has been completed.

Divide for front opening
Next row Patt 54[57:60], turn and leave rem sts on a spare needle.
Cont on these sts for first side of neck.
Patt until row 141[147:153] (row 142[148:154] for second side of neck) has been completed, so ending at inner edge.

Shape neck
Cast off 3 sts at beg of next and foll 2 alt rows. Dec one st at neck edge on next 4 rows,

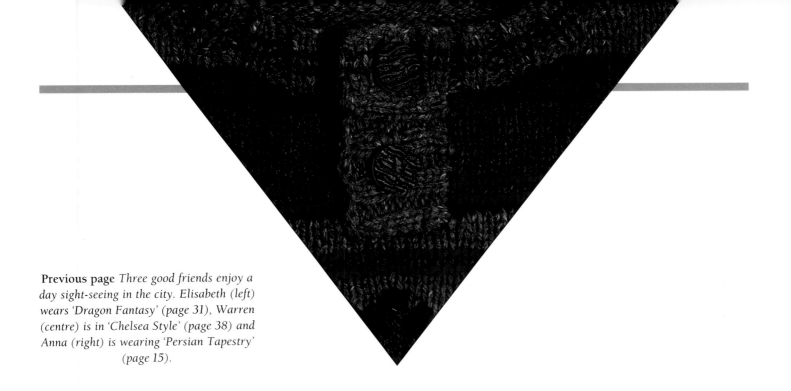

then on foll 2 alt rows. 39[42:45] sts. Work 4 rows without shaping, so ending row 158[164:170] (row 159[165:171] for second side of neck).

Do not cut off yarn but leave these 39[42:45] sts on a spare needle.

With RS facing, rejoin yarn and cast off centre 6 sts, patt to end.

Now complete to match first side, noting the bracketed exceptions.

SLEEVES

Using 3¼mm (US3) needles and A, cast on 40 sts.

Work as given for back from ** to **

Inc row Rib 2, inc in next st, * rib 6, inc in next st, rep from * to last 2 sts, rib 2. 46 sts.

Change to 4½mm (US7) needles.

Beg with a K row, cont in st st and patt from Chart foll sleeve detail, inc one st at each end of every 3rd row until there are 96 sts, then on every foll 5th row until there are 102 sts. Work straight until row 105 has been completed. Using A only, work 7 more rows. Cast off loosely.

POCKET TOPS

Using 3¼mm (US3) needles, A and with RS of work facing, rejoin yarn to 26 pocket sts on holder.

1st row (RS) P1, K1, P2, (K2, P2) to last 2 sts, K1, P1.

2nd row K1, P1, K2, (P2, K2) to last 2 sts, P1, K1.

Next row (buttonhole row) Using B, rib 12, cast off 2, rib to end.

Next row Using E, rib to end casting on 2 sts at cast-off group.

Rib 1 row B and 1 row A.

Using A, cast off in rib.

BUTTON BAND

Using 3¼mm (US3) needles, A and with RS of work facing, pick up and K16 sts along front opening.

1st row K1, (P2, K2) to last 3 sts, P2, K1.

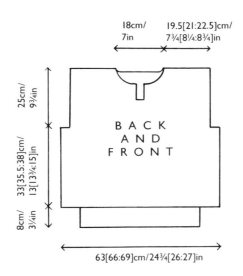

18cm/ 7in   19.5[21:22.5]cm/ 7¾[8¼:8¾]in

25cm/ 9¾in

BACK AND FRONT

33[35.5:38]cm/ 13[13¾:15]in

8cm/ 3¼in

63[66:69]cm/24¾[26:27]in

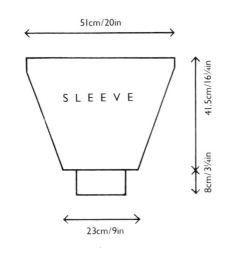

51cm/20in

SLEEVE

41.5cm/16¼in

8cm/3¼in

23cm/9in

2nd row K3, (P2, K2) to last 5 sts, P2, K3.

Rib 10 more rows. Cast off in rib.

BUTTONHOLE BAND

Using 3¼mm (US3) needles, A and with RS of work facing, pick up and K16 sts along front opening. Work 5 rows rib as given for button band.

Next row (buttonhole row) Rib 7, cast off 2, rib to end.

Next row Rib to end, casting on 2 sts at cast-off group.

Rib 5 more rows. Cast off in rib.

SHOULDER SEAMS

Graft back and front shoulders together on RS of work as folls

With wrong sides together take a st from front and back and K them tog, take next 2 sts tog in the same way, then pass first st over second st, cont to cast off in this way until all sts are worked, so forming a seam on the right side of work.

NECKBAND

Using 3¼mm (US3) needles, A and with RS of work facing, pick up and K 36 sts up right front neck, 40 sts across back neck and 36 sts down left front neck. 112 sts.

Work 2 rows rib as given for button band.

Next row (buttonhole row) Using B, rib 5, cast off 2, rib to end.

Next row Using E, rib to end, casting on 2 sts at cast-off group.

Rib 1 row B and 3 rows A.

Using A, cast off in rib.

TO MAKE UP

Press on WS using a warm iron over a damp cloth. Sew sleeve tops in position, matching centre of sleeve to shoulder seam and sewing final rows to cast-off sts at underarm. Join side and sleeve seams. Sew down pocket linings on WS of work and pocket tops on RS of work. Sew base of buttonhole and button bands to front opening. Press seams. Sew on buttons.

CHART 1

A ☐
B ◣
C ▨ or ☐
D ⊠
E ◿
F ⊡ or ☐
G ◺
H ⊟

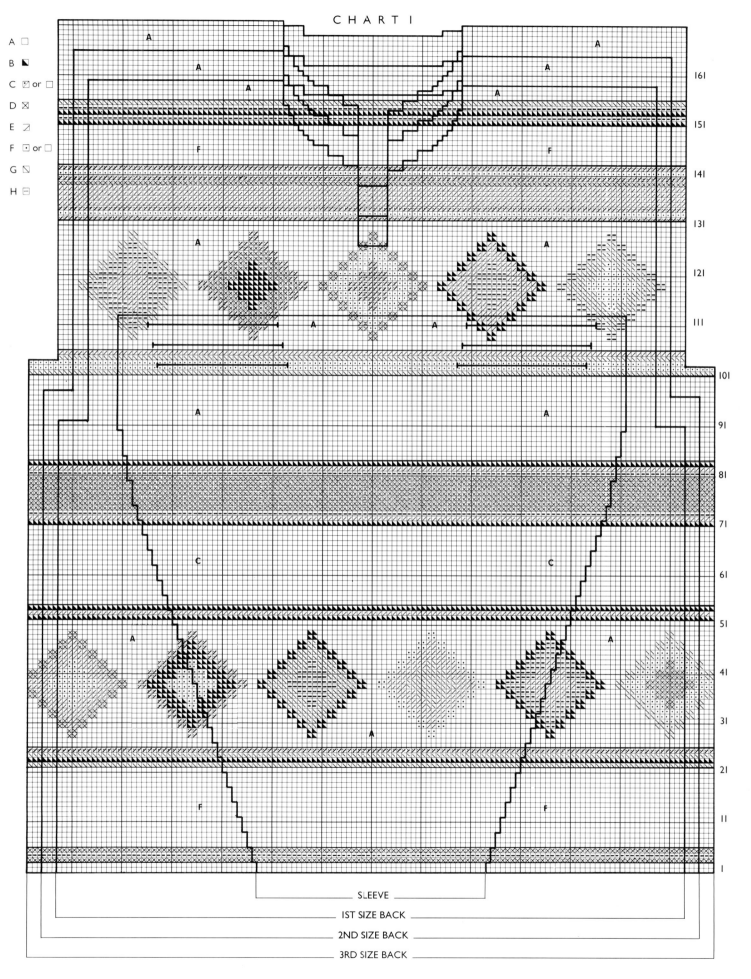

161
151
141
131
121
111
101
91
81
71
61
51
41
31
21
11
1

SLEEVE

1ST SIZE BACK

2ND SIZE BACK

3RD SIZE BACK

SISSINGHURST CASTLE

My own wardrobe contains many plain understated clothes; their timeless quality really is my style. Here I have taken a classic, long-line cardigan and made it more feminine and fitted by shaping the side seams. Worked in stocking stitch and knitted in Lightweight DK, this very wearable cardigan features pockets and a neat shawl collar.

SIZES

To fit 86[91:97]cm (34[36:38]in) bust
Actual size 102[105.5:109]cm (40[41½:43]in)
Length to shoulder 62.5[65:67]cm (24¾[25½:26½]in)
Sleeve seam 47cm (18½in)
Figures in square brackets [ ] refer to larger sizes; where there is only one set of figures, it applies to all sizes.

MATERIALS

28[29:30]×25g hanks of Rowan Lightweight DK (chestnut 663)
Pair each of 2¾mm (US2) and 3¼mm (US3) knitting needles
6 buttons

TENSION

28 sts and 34 rows to 10cm (4in) over st st using 3¼mm (US3) needles

POCKET LININGS
(make 2)

Using 3¼mm (US3) needles cast on 33[35:35] sts. Beg with a K row, work 24[26:28] rows st st, so ending with a P row. Cut off yarn and leave these sts on a holder.

LEFT FRONT

** Using 2¾mm (US2) needles cast on 75[77:81] sts.
Rib row 1 K1tbl, * P1, K1tbl, rep from * to end.
Rib row 2 P1tbl, * K1, P1tbl, rep from * to end.
Rep these 2 rows for 9cm (3½in), ending row 2 but for **2nd size only** inc one st at centre of last row . 75[78:81] sts.

Change to 3¼mm (US3) needles.
Beg with a K row, cont in st st, work 6[8:12] rows, so ending with a P row. **
Dec row K3, K2tog, K to end.
Work 3 rows.
Rep last 4 rows 3 times more, then work the dec row again. 70[73:76] sts.
P 1 row.

Place pocket lining
Next row K13[12:11] sts, sl next 33[35:35] sts on a holder, K the 33[35:35] sts of pocket lining, K to end.
P 1 row.
Cont to shape side edge as before on next and every foll 4th row until 64[67:70] sts rem.
Work 9[9:7] rows straight, so ending at side edge.
3rd size only
Next row K to last 2 sts, K2tog.
Next row P. 69 sts.
All sizes
Inc row K3, M1, K to end.
*** Cont to inc as now set on 10[10:7] foll 4th rows and **at the same time** dec one st at front edge on 4th[2nd:5th] row and 5[5:3] foll 7th rows. 69[72:73] sts.
3rd size only
Cont to shape front edge, inc one st at side edge on 3 foll 6th rows. 74 sts.

All sizes
69[72:74] sts.
Keeping side edge straight, cont to shape front edge as before until 68[70:72] sts rem.
***
Work 1[2:3] rows straight, so ending at side edge.

Shape armhole
Next row Cast off 2 sts, K to end.
P 1 row.
Next row K3, K3togtbl, K to end.
**** Cont to shape front edge as before, dec 2 sts at armhole edge as now set on foll 2 alt rows. 59[61:63] sts.
Keeping armhole edge straight, cont to shape front edge as before until 53[54:55] sts rem.
Work straight until front measures 62.5[65:67]cm (24¾[25½:26½]in) from cast-on edge, ending at armhole edge.

Shape shoulder
Cast off 17[18:18] sts at beg of next row and 18 sts at beg of foll alt row. Work 1 row. Cast off rem 18[18:19] sts.

RIGHT FRONT

Work as given for left front from ** to **.
Dec row K to last 5 sts, K2togtbl, K3.
Work 3 rows.
Rep last 4 rows 3 times more, then work the dec row again. 70[73:76] sts.
P 1 row.

Place pocket lining
Next row K24[26:30], sl next 33[35:35] sts on a holder, K the 33[35:35] sts of pocket lining, K to end.
P 1 row.
Cont to shape side edge as before on next and

Elegantly displayed in a formal setting, 'Sissinghurst Castle' is a classically shaped design that flatters the figure. The pockets are inset above a deep ribbed lower edge and a shawl collar trims the V neckline.

every foll 4th row until 64[67:70] sts rem.
Work 9[9:7] rows straight, ending front edge.
3rd size only
Next row K2tog, K to end.
Next row P. 69 sts.
All sizes
Inc row K to last 3 sts, M1, K3.
Now work as given for left front from *** to
***
Work 2[3:4] rows straight, so ending at side
edge.

Shape armhole
Next row Cast off 2 sts, P to end.
Next row K to last 6 sts, K3tog, K3.
Now complete as given for left front from
**** to end.

BACK

Using 2¾mm (US2) needles cast on
149[155:161] sts.
Work in rib as given for left front for 9cm
(3½in), ending row 2 but inc one st at centre
of last row. 150[156:162] sts.
Change to 3¼mm (US3) needles.
Beg with a K row, cont in st st, work 6[8:12]
rows, so ending with a P row.
Dec row K3, K2tog, K to last 5 sts, K2togtbl,
K3.
Work 3 rows.
Cont to dec as now set on next and every foll
4th row until 128[134:140] sts rem.
Beg with a P row, work 9[9:7] rows straight,
so ending with a P row.
Inc row K3, M1, K to last 3 sts, M1, K3.
Work 3 rows.
Cont to inc as now set on next and every foll
4th row until there are 150[156:156] sts, then
for **3rd size only** on every foll 6th row until
there are 162 sts.
Beg with a P row, work until back measures
the same as fronts up to beg of armhole
shaping, ending with a P row.

Shape armholes
Cast off 2 sts at beg of next 2 rows.
Next row K3, K3togtbl, K to last 6 sts, K3tog,
K3.
P 1 row.
Rep last 2 rows twice more. 134[140:146] sts.
Work straight until back measures same as
fronts up to beg of shoulder shaping, ending
with a P row.

Shape shoulders and back neck
Cast off 17[18:18] sts at beg of next 2 rows.
Next row Cast off 18 sts, then K until there
are 18[18:19] sts on right-hand needle, turn
and complete this side first.
P 1 row. Cast off rem 18[18:19] sts.
With RS of work facing, rejoin yarn to next st
and cast off centre 28[32:36] sts, K to end.
36[36:37] sts.
Next row Cast off 18 sts, P to end.
K 1 row. Cast off rem 18[18:19] sts.

SLEEVES

Using 2¾mm (US2) needles cast on 63 sts.
Work in rib as given for left front for 9cm

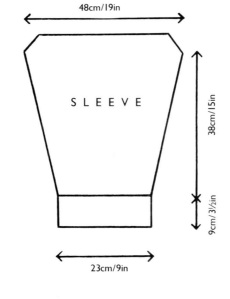

10[11.5:13]cm/
4[4½:5¼]in

19[19:19.5]cm/
7½[7½:7¾]in

BACK

23cm/
9in

30.5[33:35]cm/
12¼[13:13¾]in

RIGHT FRONT

LEFT FRONT

9cm/
3½in

53.5[55.5:58]cm/
21¼[21¾:23]in

48cm/19in

SLEEVE

38cm/15in

9cm/3½in

23cm/9in

(3½in), ending row 2 but inc one st at centre
of last row. 64 sts.
Change to 3¼mm (US3) needles.
K 1 row and P 1 row.
Inc row K3, M1, K to last 3 sts, M1, K3.
P 1 row.
Rep last 2 rows 5 times more, then work the
inc row again. 78 sts.
Inc one st as now set at each end of every foll

4th row until there are 134 sts.
Work 3 rows straight.

Shape top
Cast off 2 sts at beg of next 2 rows.
Next row K3, K3togtbl, K to last 6 sts, K3tog,
K3.
Next row P.
Rep last 2 rows twice more.
Cast off rem 118 sts.

SHAWL COLLAR AND FRONT BANDS

Join shoulder seams. Using 2¾mm (US2)
needles cast on 9 sts.
Rib row 1 K2tbl, * P1, K1tbl, rep from * to
last st, K1tbl.
Rib row 2 K1, * P1tbl, K1, rep from * to end.
Rep these 2 rows until band, slightly
stretched, fits up left front to beg of shaping,
ending with row 2.
Inc one st at beg of next and every foll alt row
until there are 65 sts.
Place a marker at shaped edge on last row.
Work straight until collar fits up left front to
shoulder seam. Place a second marker at
shaped edge on last row.
Work straight until collar fits across back
neck from second marker to right shoulder
seam. Place a third marker at shaped edge on
last row.
Work straight until collar from 3rd marker, is
the same depth as between 2nd and 1st
markers.
Dec one st at shaped edge on next and every
foll alt row until 9 sts rem, so finishing at end
of right front shaping.
Sew on the collar and bands so far. Mark the
position of 6 buttons on left front band, the
first 3 rows above cast-on edge, the second 4
rows below top of rib, the 3rd one 6 rows
above second, the last one level with beg of
front shaping and the rem two equally spaced
between third and last.
Make buttonholes to correspond with
markers thus:
Buttonhole row 1 (RS) Rib 4, cast off 2, rib
to end.
Buttonhole row 2 Rib to end casting on 2 sts
over those cast off in previous row.
Work 3 rows after last buttonhole.
Cast off in rib.

POCKET TOPS
(Alike)

With RS of work facing and using 2¾mm
(US2) needles, rejoin yarn to 33[35:35]
pocket sts on holder.
Work 6 rows in rib as given for left front.
Cast off in rib.

TO MAKE UP

Press lightly on WS using a warm iron over a
damp cloth. Sew remainder of band to right
front. Sew in sleeves, matching centre of
sleeve top to shoulder seam. Join side and
sleeve seams. Sew down pocket linings to WS
of work and pocket tops to RS of work. Sew
on buttons. Press seams.

KENSINGTON GARDENS

*Much of the research that I do for my design material involves studying
antique textiles; rugs and carpets are an endless source of inspiration.
Although most of my designs are knitted in heavier weight yarns such as
Aran or double knitting, it made a pleasant change for me to work in 4 ply
yarns; I was able to get a lot more detail into the pattern.
This long-line sweater, with its colourful intricate flower motifs encased in a
golden trellis against a black background, is quite a challenge even for an
experienced knitter, but the finished result justifies the effort.*

SIZES

To fit 86[91:97]cm (34[36:38]in) bust
Actual size 110[115:119]cm (43½[45¼:47]in)
Length to shoulder 70[72.5:75]cm
(27½[28½:29½]in)
Sleeve seam 49cm (19½in)
Figures in square brackets [ ] refer to larger
sizes; where there is only one set of figures, it
applies to all sizes.

MATERIALS

18[18:19]×25g hanks of Rowan Botany in
main shade A (black 62)
2 hanks in shade B (fern 521)
1 hank in each of 2 shades, C (dark blue 54)
and D (tan 603)
1[2:2] hanks in shade E (khaki 407)
1 hank in each of 7 shades, F (dark peach
526), G (kingfisher 528), H (rose pink 69), J
(mauve 522), K (gold 9), L (plum 663) and M
(mustard 664)
Pair each of 2¼mm (US1) and 2¾mm (US2)
knitting needles
A 2¼mm (US1) circular knitting needle

TENSION

34 sts and 41 rows to 10cm (4in) over patt
using 2¾mm (US2) needles

BACK

Using 2¼mm (US1) needles and A, cast on
156[164:172] sts.
Rib row 1 P1, K2, * P2, K2, rep from * to last
st, P1.
Rib row 2 K1, P2, * K2, P2, rep from * to last
st, K1.

Rep these 2 rows for 10cm (4in), ending with
row 1.
Inc row Rib 3[7:11], * M1, rib 5, rep from *
to last 3[7:11] sts, M1, rib to end.
187[195:203] sts.
Change to 2¾mm (US2) needles.
Beg with a K row, cont in st st and work
138[148:158] rows in patt from Chart. Strand
yarns loosely across back of work where
appropriate or use small, separate balls of
yarn for individual motifs. Link one shade to
the next by twisting them around each other
where they meet on the WS to avoid making
gaps.

Shape armholes

Cast off 10 sts at beg of next 2 rows.
167[175:183] sts.
Cont in patt without shaping until row
246[256:266] has been completed, so ending
with a P row.

Shape shoulders and back neck

Cast off 19[20:21] sts at beg of next 2 rows.
Next row Cast off 20[20:21] sts, patt until
there are 24[25:26] sts on right-hand needle,
turn and complete this side first.
Next row Cast off 4[4:5] sts, patt to end.
Cast off rem 20[21:21] sts.
With RS of work facing, rejoin yarn and cast
off centre 41[45:47] sts, patt to end.
44[45:47] sts.
Next row Cast off 20[20:21] sts, patt to end.
Next row Cast off 4[4:5] sts, patt to end.
Cast off rem 20[21:21] sts.

POCKET LININGS
(make 2)

Using 2¼mm (US1) needles and A, cast on 40
sts. Beg with a K row, work 10cm (4in) in st
st, ending with a P row. Cut off yarn and
leave rem sts on a holder.

FRONT

Work as given for back until row 54[58:62]
has been completed.

Place pocket linings

Next row Patt 31[33:35] sts, sl next 40 sts
onto a holder, patt across 40 sts of pocket
lining, patt 45[49:53] sts, sl next 40 sts onto a
holder, patt across 40 sts of pocket lining,
patt to end.
Work as given for back until row
224[230:236] has been completed, so ending
with a P row.

*Overleaf 'Kensington Gardens'
is a masterpiece of knitting
with its pretty pattern.
Details include useful
inset pockets and a
ribbed collar.*

CHART I

A
B
C
D
E
F
G
H
J
K
L
M

261
251
241
231
221
211
201
191
181
171
161
151
141
131
121
111
101
91
81
71
61
51
41
31
21
11
1

SLEEVE
IST SIZE BACK
2ND SIZE BACK
3RD SIZE BACK

Shape neck

Next row Patt 75[79:83] sts, turn and leave rem sts on a spare needle.

Work on these sts for first side of neck.

** Cast off 3 sts at beg of next and foll 2 alt rows. Dec one st at neck edge on next 3 rows, then on every foll alt row until 59[61:63] sts rem.

Cont without shaping until row 246[256:266] (row 247[257:267] for second side of neck) has been completed, so ending at side edge.

Shape shoulder

Cast off 19[20:21] sts at beg of next row and 20[20:21] sts at beg of foll alt row. Work 1 row. Cast off rem 20[21:21] sts.

With RS of work facing rejoin yarn to next st and cast off centre 17 sts, patt to end. 75[79:83] sts.

Work 1 row.

Complete to match first side of neck from ** to end, noting the bracketed exception.

SLEEVES

Using 2¼mm (US1) needles and A, cast on 60 sts.

Work 10cm (4in) in rib as given for back, ending with row 1.

Inc row Rib 10, * M1, rib 2, rep from * to last 10 sts, M1, rib to end. 81 sts.

Change to 2¾mm (US2) needles.

Beg with a K row, cont in st st and patt from Chart, inc one st at each end of every 3rd row until there are 145 sts, then on every foll 5th row until there are 167 sts. Cont in patt without shaping to row 170. Cast off

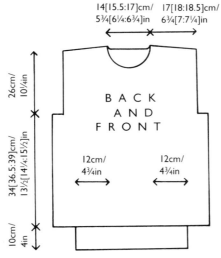

14[15.5:17]cm/ 5¾[6¼:6¾]in   17[18:18.5]cm/ 6¾[7:7¼]in

26cm/ 10¼in

BACK
AND
FRONT

34[36.5:39]cm/ 13½[14¼:15½]in

12cm/ 4¾in   12cm/ 4¾in

10cm/ 4in

55[57:60]cm/21½[22½:23½]in

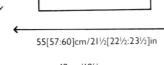

49cm/19¼

SLEEVE

41.5cm/ 16¼in

10cm/ 4in

24cm/9½in

COLLAR

Join shoulder seams. Using the circular needle, A and with RS of work facing, beg at centre front neck cast-off sts, place a marker on needle to denote centre front neck and beg of round, pick up and K44[48:52] sts round to shoulder, 52[56:60] sts across back neck and 44[48:52] sts down to centre front neck. 140[152:164] sts.

Slipping the marker on every round, repeating 2nd row, work 8 rounds rib as given for back

Divide for collar

Keeping rib correct, work backwards and forwards in rows (remove marker after first row) until collar is 10cm (4in) deep. Cast off loosely in rib.

POCKET TOPS
(alike)

Using 2¼mm (US1) needles, A and with RS of work facing, rejoin yarn to 40 pocket sts on holder.

Work 12 rows rib as given for back. Cast off in rib.

TO MAKE UP

Press on WS using a warm iron over a damp cloth. Sew sleeve tops in position, sewing final row-ends to cast-off sts at underarm. Join side and sleeve seams. Sew down pocket linings on WS of work and pocket tops on RS of work. Press seams.

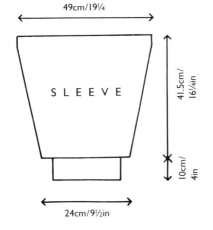

BLOOMSBURY SET

Whether you are dressed up to have tea at the Waldorf or just relaxing at home in your jeans, I always think that a classic knitted twin set is a great asset to any wardrobe.
This short-sleeved sweater, with a deep ribbed hem and collar, has a lacy panel inset at the centre front and fits neatly into the waist. Wear the sweater separately or team it with the matching V-neck cardigan knitted in 4-ply botany wool.

SIZES

To fit 86[91:97]cm (34[36:38]in) bust
Cardigan
Actual size above rib 99[104:109]cm (39[41:43]in)
Length to shoulder 45[47.5:50.5]cm (17¾[18¾:19¾]in)
Sleeve seam 47cm (18½in)
Sweater
Actual size 93[98:103]cm (36½[38½:40½]in)
Length to shoulder 38[40:42]cm (15[15¾:16½]in)
Sleeve seam 13.5cm (5¼in)
Figures in square brackets [ ] refer to larger sizes; where there is only one set of figures, it applies to all sizes.

MATERIALS

Cardigan
14[14:15]×25g hanks of Rowan Botany (neptune 528)
Pair each of 2¼mm (US1) and 2¾mm (US2) knitting needles
Cable needle
5 small buttons
Sweater
9[9:10]×25g hanks of Rowan Botany (neptune 528)
Pair each of 2¼mm (US1) and 2¾mm (US2) knitting needles
Cable needle

TENSION

One patt panel (41 sts) measures 11cm (4¼in)
32 sts and 44 rows to 10cm (4in) over st st using 2¾mm (US2) needles

SPECIAL ABBREVIATIONS

C4L Cable 4 Left thus: sl next 2 sts onto cable needle and leave at front of work, K2, then K2 from cable needle

C4R Cable 4 Right thus: sl next 2 sts onto cable needle and leave at back of work, K2, then K2 from cable needle
p2sso pass 2 slipped sts over

CARDIGAN

LEFT FRONT

Using 2¼mm (US1) needles cast on 73[75:79] sts.
Rib row 1 P1, * K1, P1, rep from * to end.
Rib row 2 K1, * P1, K1, rep from * to end.
Rep these 2 rows for 12cm (4¾in), ending with row 1.
Inc row Rib 7, (inc in next st, rib 3) 3 times, inc in next st, rib 4, inc in next st, rib 3, inc in next st, rib 9, inc in next st, rib 1, inc in next st, rib 9, inc in next st, rib 3, inc in next st, rib 5, (inc in next st, rib 3) 1[3:3] times, inc in next st, rib 8[2:6]. 85[89:93] sts.
Change to 2¾mm (US2) needles.
Cont in st st with lace and cable panel, noting that sts made throughout the patt are returned to their original number by row 10 and these extra sts are not included in any st checks.
Row 1 (RS) K18[22:26], * (P1, K4) twice, P1, skpo, yfwd, K5, (yfwd, K1) 5 times, yfwd, K5, yfwd, K2tog, P1, (K4, P1) twice *, K26.
Row 2 P26, * K1, (P4, K1) twice, P25, K1,
(P4, K1) twice *, P to end.
Row 3 K18[22:26], * P1, (C4L, P1) twice, skpo, yfwd, skpo, K1. (K2tog, yfwd) twice, K3, yfwd, K1, yfwd, K3, (yfwd, skpo) twice, K1, K2tog, yfwd, K2tog, P1, (C4R, P1) twice *, K to end.
Row 4 As row 2.
Row 5 K18[22:26], * P1, (K4, P1) twice, skpo, yfwd, sl 2, K1, p2sso, yfwd, K2tog, yfwd, K5, yfwd, K1, yfwd, K5, yfwd, skpo, yfwd, sl 2, K1, p2sso, yfwd, K2tog, P1, (K4, P1) twice *, K to end.
Row 6 As row 2.
Row 7 K18[22:26], * P1, (C4L, P1) twice, sl 1, K2tog, psso, yfwd, K2tog, yfwd, K1, yfwd, skpo, K1, K2tog, yfwd, sl 2, K1, p2sso, yfwd, skpo, K1, K2tog, yfwd, K1, yfwd, skpo, yfwd, K3tog, P1, (C4R, P1) twice *, K to end.
Row 8 P26, * K1, (P4, K1) twice, P21, K1, (P4, K1) twice *, P to end.
Row 9 K18[22:26], * P1, (K4, P1) twice, K1, K2tog, yfwd, K3, (yfwd, sl 2, K1, p2sso) 3 times, yfwd, K3, yfwd, skpo, K1, P1, (K4, P1) twice *, K to end.
Row 10 P26. * K1, (P4, K1) twice, P19, K1, (P4, K1) twice *, P to end.
Cont to work the cables at each side of the lace panel on next and every foll 4th row, rep the 10 lace panel rows throughout, work a further 4[2:4] rows.

Shape front edge

Dec one st at end of next and every foll 6th row until 20[18:16] sts rem in st st at front edge.
Work 1 row, so ending at side edge.

Shape armhole

Cast off 4 sts at beg of next row.
Work 3 rows.
Next row K3, K3togtbl, patt to last 2 sts, K2tog.
Work 3 rows.
Next row K3, K3togtbl, patt to end.

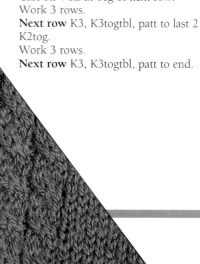

Next row Patt to end.
Next row Patt to last 2 sts, K2tog.
Next row Patt to end.
Next row K3, K3togtbl, patt to end. 8[12:16] sts rem in st st at armhole edge.
** Keeping armhole edge straight, cont to dec one st at front edge on every 6th row as before, until 12[8:5] sts rem in st st at front edge. Now dec one st at front edge on every foll 8th row until 6[4:2] sts rem in st st at front edge.
Work straight until armhole measures 23cm (9in) from beg of armhole shaping, ending at armhole edge.

Shape shoulder
Cast off 19 sts at beg of next row and 18[19:20] sts at beg of foll alt row. Work 1 row. Cast off rem 18[19:20] sts.

R I G H T   F R O N T

Work as given for left front to end of rib, ending with row 1.
Inc row Rib 8[2:6], inc in next st, (rib 3, inc in next st) 1[3:3] times, rib 5, inc in next st, rib 3, inc in next st, rib 9, inc in next st, rib 1, inc in next st, rib 9, inc in next st, rib 3, inc in next st, rib 4, (inc in next st, rib 3) 3 times, inc in next st, rib 7. 85[89:93] sts.
Change to 2¾mm (US2) needles.
Cont in st st with lace and cable panel as folls:
Row 1 K26, work from * to * of row 1 as given for left front, K18[22:26].
Row 2 P18[22:26], work from * to * of row 2 as given for left front, P26.
Cont in this way, working from * to * of each corresponding patt row of left front until the 10th patt row has been completed.
Work a further 4[2:4] rows.

Shape front edge
Dec one st at beg of next and every foll 6th row until 20[18:16] sts rem in st st at front edge.
Work 2 rows, so ending at side edge.

Shape armhole
Cast off 4 sts at beg of next row.
Work 2 rows.
Next row K2tog, patt to last 6 sts, K3tog, K3.
Work 3 rows.
Next row Patt to last 6 sts, K3tog, K3.
Next row Patt to end.
Next row K2tog, patt to end.
Next row Patt to end.
Next row Patt to last 6 sts, K3tog, K3.
8[12:16] sts rem in st st at armhole edge.
Now work as given for left front from ** to end.

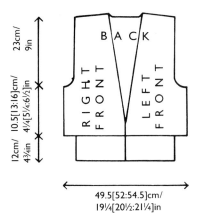

C A R D I G A N

12.5[13.5:15]cm / 5[5¼:6]in   17[18:18.5]cm / 6¾[7:7¼]in

23cm / 9in

12cm / 4¾in   10.5[13:16]cm / 4¼[5¼:6½]in

B A C K

RIGHT FRONT   LEFT FRONT

49.5[52:54.5]cm / 19¼[20½:21¼]in

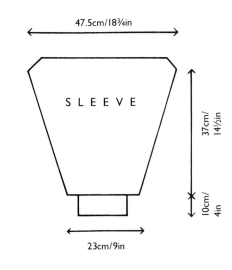

47.5cm/18¾in

S L E E V E

37cm / 14½in

10cm / 4in

23cm/9in

Anna, wearing the complete twin set, looks elegantly sophisticated. The cardigan has a V neckline and lacy panels on both fronts that continue on the back of the garment.

B A C K

Using 2¼mm (US1) needles cast on 143[147:155] sts.
Work 12cm (4¾in) in rib as given for left front, ending with row 1.
Inc row Rib 8[2:6], inc in next st, (rib 3, inc in next st) 1[3:3] times, rib 5, * inc in next st, rib 3, inc in next st, rib 9, inc in next st, rib 1, inc in next st, rib 9, inc in next st, rib 3, inc in next st, rib 4 *, (inc in next st, rib 3) 4 times, (inc in next st, rib 1) twice, (inc in next st, rib 3) 4 times, inc in next st, rib 4, rep from * to * once, (inc in next st, rib 3) 1[3:3] times, inc in next st, rib 9[3:7]. 170[178:186] sts.
Change to 2¾mm (US2) needles.
Cont in st st with lace and cable panel as folls:
Row 1 (RS) K18[22:26], work from * to * of row 1 as given for left front, K52, work from * to * of row 1 as given for left front, K18[22:26].
Row 2 P18[22:26], work from * to * of row 2 as given for left front, P52, work from * to * of row 2 as given for left front, P18[22:26].
Cont in this way, working from each corresponding patt row of left front, until back measures the same as fronts up to beg of armhole shaping, ending with a WS row.

Shape armholes
Cast off 4 sts at beg of next 2 rows.
Work 2 rows.
Dec row K3, K3togtbl, patt to last 6 sts, K3tog, K3.
Work 3 rows.
Rep last 4 rows once more, then work the dec row again. 8[12:16] sts rem in st st at armhole edges. Work straight until back measures the same as fronts up to beg of shoulder shaping, ending with a WS row.

Shape shoulders and back neck
Cast off 19 sts at beg of next 2 rows.
Next row Cast off 18[19:20] sts, patt until there are 22[23:24] sts on right-hand needle, turn and complete this side first.
Next row Cast off 4 sts, patt to end.
Cast off rem 18[19:20] sts.
With RS of work facing, rejoin yarn to next st and cast off centre 32[36:40] sts, patt to end.
Next row Cast off 18[19:20] sts, patt to end.
Next row Cast off 4 sts, patt to end.
Cast off rem 18[19:20] sts.

S L E E V E S

Using 2¼mm (US1) needles cast on 55 sts.
Work 10cm (4in) in rib as given for left front, ending with row 1.
Inc row Rib 9, * inc in next st, rib 1, rep

Design № 10

from * to last 10 sts, inc in next st, rib 9. 74 sts.
Change to 2¾mm (US2) needles.
Beg with a K row, cont in st st, inc one st at each end of 3rd and every foll 4th row until there are 144 sts. Inc one st at each end of next and foll 3 alt rows. 152 sts. Work straight until sleeve measures 47cm (18½in) from cast-on edge, ending with a P row.

Shape top
Cast off 4 sts at beg of next 2 rows.
Work 2 rows.
Dec row K3, K3togtbl, K to last 6 sts, K3tog, K3.
Work 3 rows.
Rep last 4 rows once more, then work the dec row again. Cast off rem 132 sts.

FRONT BAND
Join shoulder seams. Using 2¼mm (US1) needles cast on 7 sts.
Rib row 1 (RS) K2, * P1, K1, rep from * to last st, K1.
Rib row 2 K1, * P1, K1, rep from * to end.
Rib 2 rows.
Buttonhole row (RS) Rib 2, K2tog, yfwd, rib to end.
Rib 15 rows.
Rep last 16 rows 3 times more, then work the buttonhole row again.
Cont in rib until band, slightly stretched, fits up right front, across back neck and down left front.
Cast off in rib.

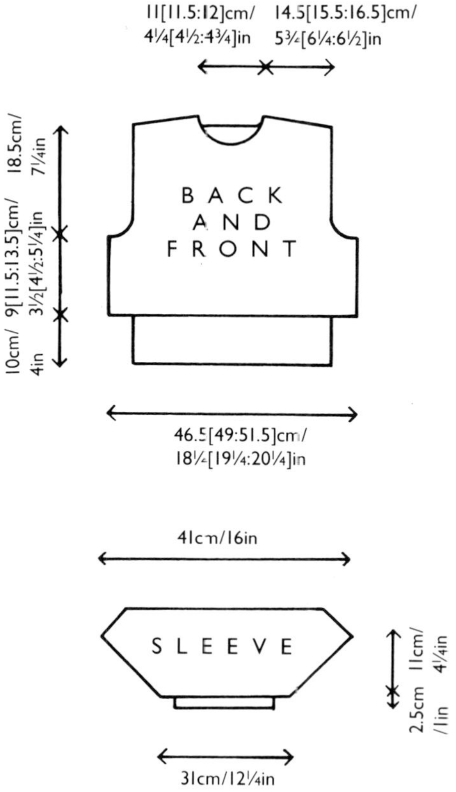

SWEATER

FRONT
Using 2¼mm (US1) needles cast on 133[141:149] sts.
Beg with rib row 2, work 10cm (4in) in rib as given for left front of cardigan, ending with row 2.
Inc row Rib 5[2:6] sts, (inc in next st, rib 5[6:6] sts) 7 times, (inc in next st, rib 3) twice, inc in next st, rib 9, inc in next st, rib 1, inc in next st, rib 9, (inc in next st, rib 3) twice, (inc in next st, rib 5[6:6] sts) 7 times, inc in next st, rib 5[2:6]. 155[163:171] sts.
Change to 2¾mm (US2) needles.
Cont in st st with lace and cable panel as folls:
Row 1 (RS) K57[61:65], work from * to * of row 1 as given for left front of cardigan, K57[61:65].
Row 2 P57[61:65], work from * to * of row 2 as given for left front of cardigan, P57[61:65].
Cont in this way, working from * to * of each corresponding patt row as given for left front of cardigan until the 10 patt rows have been worked.
Work a further 3[4:5] pattern repeats.

Shape armholes
Work as for armhole shaping of cardigan back. 47[51:55] sts rem in st st at armhole edges.

Work straight until the 6th patt from beg of armhole shaping has been completed, so ending with patt row 10.

Shape neck
Next row Patt 63[66:69], turn and leave rem sts on a spare needle
Cont on these sts for first side of neck.
** Cast off 3 sts at beg of next and foll alt row. Dec one st at neck edge on next 5 rows, then on every foll alt row until 47[50:53] sts rem.
Work 3 rows, so ending at armhole edge.

Shape shoulder
Cast off 18[19:20] sts at beg of next row and 14[15:16] sts at beg of foll alt row.
Work 1 row. Cast off.
With RS of work facing, rejoin yarn to next st and cast off next 9[11:13] sts, patt to end.
Patt 1 row.
Now complete to match first side of neck from ** to end.

The sweater of 'Bloomsbury Set' is knitted in a fine pure wool that is perfect for wearing indoors, or for outside on a warmer day.

SWEATER

11[11.5:12]cm/ 4¼[4½:4¾]in   14.5[15.5:16.5]cm/ 5¾[6¼:6½]in

18.5cm/ 7¼in

BACK AND FRONT

10cm/ 4in   9[11.5:13.5]cm/ 3½[4½:5¼]in

46.5[49:51.5]cm/ 18¼[19¼:20¼]in

41cm/16in

SLEEVE   11cm/ 4¼in

2.5cm/ 1in

31cm/12¼in

BACK
Using 2¼mm (US1) needles cast on 133[141:149] sts.
Beg with rib row 2, work 10cm (4in) in rib as given for left front of cardigan, ending with row 2.
Inc row Rib 6[3:7], * inc in next st, rib 7[8:8], rep from * to last 7[3:7] sts, inc in next st, rib to end. 149[157:165] sts.
Change to 2¾mm (US2) needles.
Beg with a K row, cont in st st until back measures same as front up to beg of armhole shaping, ending with a P row.

Shape armholes
Work as for sleeve top shaping of cardigan. 129[137:145] sts.
Work straight until back measures same as front up to beg of shoulder shaping, ending with a P row.

Shape shoulders and back neck
Cast off 18[19:20] sts at beg of next 2 rows.
Next row Cast off 14[15:16] sts, K until there are 19[20:21] sts on right-hand needle, turn and complete this side first.
Next row Cast off 4 sts, P to end.
Cast off rem 15[16:17] sts.
With RS of work facing, rejoin yarn to next st and cast off centre 27[29:31] sts, K to end. 33[35:37] sts.
Next row Cast off 14[15:16] sts, P to end.
Next row Cast off 4 sts, K to end.
Cast off rem 15[16:17] sts.

SLEEVES
Using 2¼mm (US1) needles cast on 77 sts.
Work 2.5cm (1in) in rib as given for left front of cardigan, ending with row 1.
Inc row Rib 6, * inc in next st, rib 2, rep from * to last 8 sts, inc in next st, rib to end. 99 sts.
Change to 2¾mm (US2) needles.
Beg with a K row, cont in st st, inc one st at each end of 3rd and every foll alt row until there are 131 sts. Work straight until sleeve measures 13.5cm (5in) from cast-on edge, ending with a P row.

Shape top
Work as given for sleeve top shaping of cardigan.

COLLAR
Using 2¼mm (US1) needles cast on 145 sts.
Work 8cm (3¼in) in rib as given for front band of cardigan. Cast off in rib.

TO MAKE UP
Press lightly on WS using a warm iron over a damp cloth. Join shoulder seams on sweater, then for both garments, set in sleeves, matching centre of sleeve top to shoulder seam, then join side and sleeve seams. Press seams.
Cardigan
Sew on the front band. Sew on buttons.
Sweater
Sew cast-on edge of collar to neck edge.

WINNING TEAM

I like the idea that knitting can be accessible to everyone. If you have never knitted before you could make this garment using two basic stitches – stocking stitch for the main fabric and moss stitch for the borders. Like most people these days I believe in keeping fit, but in a leisurely fashion. This hooded jacket, drawn in at the waist with a ribbed panel, is perfect for sports or casual wear. Although it is knitted in a cotton yarn, the jacket could easily be worn all year round.

SIZES

To fit 61–66[66/71:71/76:86/91:91/97:97/102]cm (24/26[26/28:28/30:34/36:36/38:38/40]in) chest/bust
Actual size 71[82:92:112:117:121.5]cm (28[32¼:36¼44:46:47¾in)
Length to shoulder 41[46:52:63:66:68]cm (16[18:20½:24¾:26:26¾]in)
Sleeve seam 30[35:40:44.5:44.5:44.5]cm (12[13¾:15¾:17¾:17¾]in)
Figures in square brackets [ ] refer to larger sizes; where there is only one set of figures, it applies to all sizes.

MATERIALS

Colourway 1 – child's jacket
11[11:12]×50g balls of Rowan Cotton Glacé (Clay 738)
Colourway 2 – adult's jacket
16[16:17]×50g balls of Rowan Cotton Glacé (Bleached 726)
Pair each 2¼mm (US1) and 3mm (US3) knitting needles.
8 buttons

TENSION

26 sts and 35 rows to 10cm (4in) over st st using 3mm (US3) needles.

LEFT FRONT

Using 2¼mm (US1) needles cast on 46[54:60:74:80] sts.
Row 1 (K1, P1) to end.
Row 2 [P1, K1) to end.
These 2 rows form Moss st.
Rep them for 2.5[2.5:2.5:4:4:4]cm (1[1:1:1½:1½1½]in), ending with row 2.
Change ot 3mm (US3) needles.
Beg with a K row, cont in st st until work measures 14[15:15.5:22.5:22.5:22.5]cm (5½[6:6¼:8¾:8¾:8¾]in) from cast-on edge, ending with a K row.
Dec row P4[2:2:3:4:3], P2tog, *P1, P2tog, rep from * to last 4[2:2:3:4:3) sts, P to end.
33[37:41:51:53:55] sts.

This jacket can be knitted in a large range of sizes. It features a neat hood that children will love.

Change to 2¼ (US1) needles.
Rib row 1 K1, (P1, K1) to end
Rib row 2 P1, (K1, P1) to end
Rep these 2 rows 6[6:6:8:8:8] times more.
Inc row K5[4:3:5:5:5], * M1, K2, rep from * to last 4[3:2:4:4:4] sts, M1, K to end.
46[53:60:73:76:79] sts.
Change to 3mm (US3) needles.
Beg with a P row, cont in st st until work measures 22.5[27:31.5:40:43:45]cm (8¾[10¾:12¼:15¾:17:17¾]in) from cast-on edge, ending with a P row. (For right front end with a K row.)

Shape armhole
Cast off 4[4:4:8:8:8] sts at beg of next row.
42[49:56:65:68:71] sts.
Work straight until armhole measures 15[15:16:18.5:17:16]cm (6[6:6¼:7¼:6¾:6¼]in) from beg of shaping, ending at front edge.

Shape neck
Cast off 6 sts at beg of next row and 4 sts at beg of foll alt row. Dec one st at neck edge on every row until 25[31:36:44:51:55] sts rem.
5th and 6th sizes only
Dec one st at same edge on every foll alt row until 46[48] sts rem.
All sizes
Work 1[2:2:1:1:2] more rows, so ending at armhole edge.

Shape shoulder
Cast off rem 25[31:36:44:46:48] sts.

RIGHT FRONT

Work as given for left front noting the bracketed exception.

BACK

Using 2¼mm (US1) needles cast on 92[106:120:146:152:158] sts.
Work in Moss st as given for left front for 2.5[2.5:2.5:4:4:4]cm (1[1:1:1½:1½:1½]in), ending with row 2.
Change to 3mm (US3) needles.
Beg with a K row, cont in st st until work measures 14[15:15.5:22.5:22.5:22.5]cm (5½[6:6¼:8¾:8¾:8¾]in) from cast-on edge, ending with a K row.
Dec row P3[1:2:3:3:3], P2tog, * P1, P2tog, rep from * to last 3[1:2:3:3:3] sts, P to end.
63[71:81:99:103:107] sts.
Change to 2¼mm (US1) needles.
Beg with rib row 1 as given for left front, work 14[14:14:18:18:18] rows in rib.
Inc row K4[1:3:4:4:4], * M1, rib 2, rep from * to last 3[2:2:3:3:3] sts, M1, K to end.
92[106:120:146:152:158] sts.
Change to 3mm (US3) needles.

Beg with a P row, cont in st st until back measures same as fronts up to beg of armhole shaping, ending with a P row.

Shape armholes

Cast off 4[4:4:8:8:8] sts at beg of next 2 rows. 84[98:112:130:136:142] sts.
Work straight until back measures the same length as fronts up to shoulders, ending with a P row.

Shape shoulders

Cast off 25[31:36:44:46:48] sts at beg of next 2 rows.
Cast off rem 34[36:40:42:44:46] sts.

SLEEVES

Using 2¼mm (US1) needles cast on 40[44:44:60:60:60] sts.
Beg with rib row 1, work in rib as given for left front for 5[5:5:7.5:7.5:7.5]cm (2[2:2:3:3:3]in), ending with row 2.
Change to 3mm (US3) needles.
Beg with a K row, cont in st st, inc one st at each end of 3rd and every foll 3rd[3rd:3rd:4th:4th:4th] row until there are 94[100:98:118:118:118] sts.

3rd size only
Inc one st at each end of every foll 4th row until there are 106 sts.

All sizes
Work straight until sleeve measures 32[37:42:47.5:47.5:47.5]cm (12½[14½:16½:18¾:18¾:18¾]in) from cast-on edge, ending with a P row. Cast off loosely.

HOOD

Using 3mm (US3) needles cast on 75[81:91:101:111:121] sts.
Beg with a K row, cont in st st for 25.5[27:29:32:34:34]cm (10[10¾:11½:12½:13½:13½]in). Cast off.
Fold cast-off edge in half and join edges together to form top of hood.

Hood Edging

With RS of work facing, rejoin yarn and using

2¼mm (US1) needles, pick up and K153[157:165:173:177:177] sts evenly from front edge.
Moss st row P1, (K1, P1) to end.
Rep this row 6 times more.
Cast off in patt.

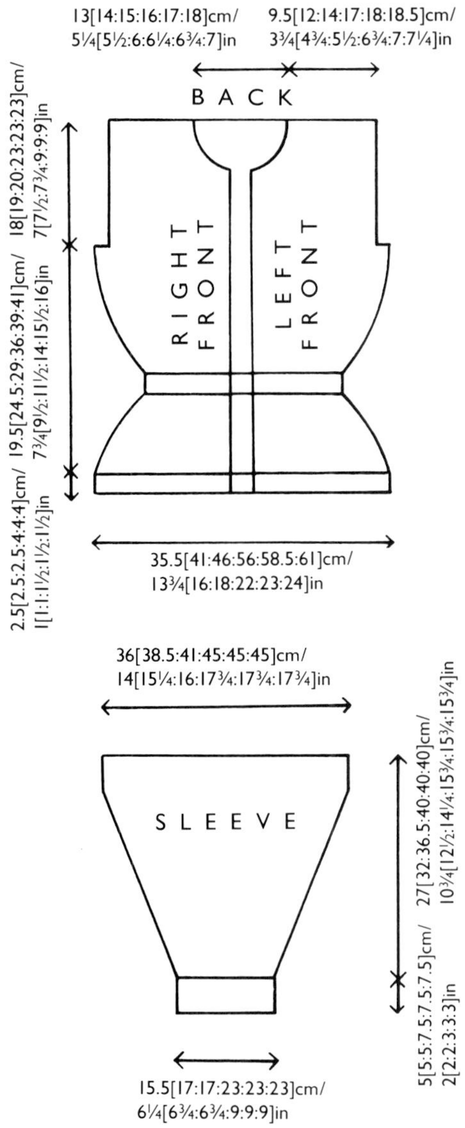

BUTTONHOLE BAND

With RS of work facing, rejoin yarn and using 2¼mm (US1) needles, pick up and K37[39:41:53:55:55] sts up right front to beg of rib, then pick up and K80[84:88:100:100:100] sts up to beg of neck shaping.
117[123:129:153:155:155] sts.
Work 3 rows in Moss st as given for hood edging.
Buttonhole row 1 (RS) Patt 3[3:3:11:13:13], * cast off 2 sts, patt until there are 15[16:17:19:19:19] sts on right-hand needle after cast-off group *, rep from * to * once more, cast off 2 sts, patt until there are 5[5:5:7:7:7] sts on right-hand needle after cast-off group, rep from * to * 4 times, cast off 2 sts, patt to end.
Buttonhole row 2 Patt to end casting on 2 sts over those cast off in previous row.
Patt 2[2:2:4:4:4] more rows.
Cast off in patt.

BUTTON BAND

With RS of work facing, rejoin yarn and using 2¼mm (US1) needles, pick up and K117[123:129:153:155:155] sts down left front.
Work 7[7:7:9:9:9] rows in Moss st.
Cast off in patt.

TO MAKE UP

Press lightly on WS using a warm iron over a damp cloth. Join shoulder seams. Sew sleeve tops in position, matching centre of sleeve to shoulder seam and sewing final rows to cast-off sts at underarm. Join side and sleeve seams. Beginning and ending at centre of front bands, sew cast-on edge of hood to neck edge. Sew on buttons.

13[14:15:16:17:18]cm/ 5¼[5½:6:6¼:6¾:7]in

9.5[12:14:17:18:18.5]cm/ 3¾[4¾:5½:6¾:7:7¼]in

BACK

18[19:20:23:23:23]cm/ 7[7½:7¾:9:9:9]in

RIGHT FRONT

LEFT FRONT

2.5[2.5:2.5:4:4:4]cm/ 1[1:1:1½:1½:1½]in

19.5[24.5:29:36:39:41]cm/ 7¾[9¾:11½:14:15½:16]in

35.5[41:46:56:58.5:61]cm/ 13¾[16:18:22:23:24]in

36[38.5:41:45:45:45]cm/ 14[15¼:16:17¾:17¾:17¾]in

SLEEVE

27[32:36.5:40:40:40]cm/ 10¾[12½:14¼:15¾:15¾:15¾]in

5[5.5:5.7.5:7.5:7.5]cm/ 2[2:2:3:3:3]in

15.5[17:17:23:23:23]cm/ 6¼[6¾:6¾:9:9:9]in

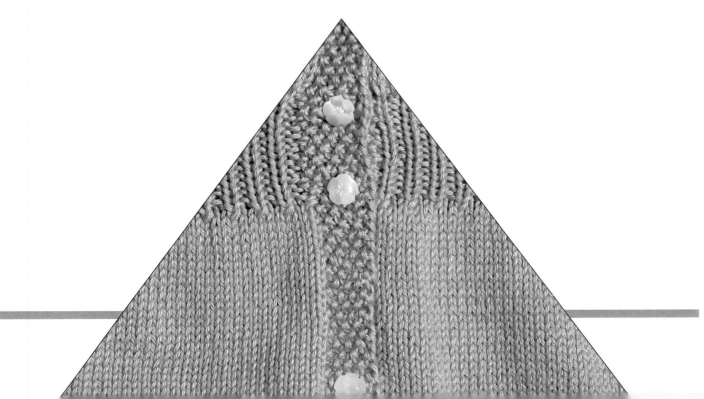

ORIENTAL PAISLEY

*The Paisley pattern has been around for 2000 years and it is still as popular
as ever; it is one of my favourite designs. This cardigan is my interpretation
of its distinctive curved abstract shapes.
Designed to fit a large size range from a small child to a large adult, this
V-neck cardigan uses the same colour range – picking out different
background colours – for both the woman's and child's garments shown here.*

SIZES

To fit 71[76:81:87/92:94/99:102/107]cm
(28[30:32:34/36:37/39:40:42]in) chest/bust
Actual size 83[88:93.5:108:114:119.5]cm
32½[34½:36½:42½:44¾:47]in)
Length to shoulder 48.5[51:53:48.5:51:53]cm
(19[20:20¾:19:20:20¾in)
Sleeve seam 40.5[40.5:40.5:43:43:43]cm
(16[16:16:17:17:17]in)
Figures in square brackets [ ] refer to larger
sizes; one set of figures applies to all sizes

MATERIALS

Colourway 1 – child's cardigan
5[5:6:6:7:8]×50g balls of Rowan Sea Breeze
in main shade A (Forget-Me-Not 557)
1[1:1:2:2:2] balls of Sea Breeze in shade B
(Rosehip 552)
1 ball of Sea Breeze in shade C (Campion
559)
1×50g ball of Rowan Mercerised Cotton in
shade D (Aspen 335)
1 ball of Sea Breeze in shade E (Bronze 560)
1 ball of Mercerised Cotton in shade F (Pippin
339)
1[1:1:2:2:2] balls of Mercerised Cotton in
shade G (Firethorn 337)
Colourway 2 – adult's cardigan
5[5:6:6:7:8]×50g balls of Rowan Sea Breeze
in main shade A (Bronze 560)
1[1:1:2:2:2]×50g balls of Rowan Mercerised
Cotton in shade B (Pippin 339)
1 ball of Mercerised Cotton in shade C
(Firethorn 337)
1 ball of Sea Breeze in shade D (Forget-Me-
Not 557)
1 ball of Mercerised Cotton in shade E (Aspen
335)
1 ball of Sea Breeze in shade F (Rosehip 552)
1[1:1:2:2:2] balls of Sea Breeze in shade G
(Campion 559)
Pair each of 2¼mm (US1) and 2¾mm (US2)
knitting needles
7[7:7:5:5:5] buttons

TENSION

32 sts and 41 rows to 10cm (4in) over patt
using 2¾mm (US2) needles

BACK

Using 2¼mm (US1) needles and A, cast on
115[123:131:151:161:169] sts.
1st row (RS) K1 tbl, (P1 tbl, K1 tbl) to end.
2nd row P1 tbl, (K1 tbl, P1 tbl) to end.
Rep these 2 rows of twisted rib for 5cm (2in),
ending with a 1st row.
Next row Rib 4[8:5:8:4:8], inc in next st, (rib
6[6:7:6:7:7), inc in next st) to last
5[9:5:9:4:8] sts, rib to end.
131[139:147:171:181:189] sts.
Change to 2¾mm (US2) needles.
Beg with a K row, cont in st st and work in
patt from Chart until
178[188:198:178:188:198] rows have been
completed, ending with a P row. Strand
colours loosely across back of work where
appropriate or use small, separate balls of
yarn for individual motifs. Link one shade to
the next by twisting them around each other
where they meet on the WS to avoid gaps.

Shape shoulders and back neck

Cast off 15[16:17:20:21:22] sts at beg of next
2 rows.
Next row Cast off 15[16:17:20:21:22] sts, patt
until there are 19[20:21:25:26:26] sts on
right-hand needle, turn and complete right
side of neck first.
Next row Cast off 4 sts, patt to end.
Cast off rem 15[16:17:21:22:22] sts.
With RS of work facing, rejoin yarn to rem
sts, cast off centre 33[35:37:41:45:49] sts, patt
to end.
Next row Cast off 15[16:17:20:21:22] sts, patt
to end.
Next row Cast off 4 sts, patt to end.
Cast off rem 15[16:17:21:22:22] sts.

LEFT FRONT

Using 2¼mm (US1) needles and A, cast on
57[61:65:75:81:85] sts.
Work 5cm (2in) in twisted rib, ending with a
1st row.
Next row Rib 3[5:4:5:4:6], inc in next st, (rib
6[6:7:6:8:8], inc in next st) to last
4[6:4:6:4:6] sts, rib to end.
65[69:73:85:90:94] sts.
Change to 2¾mm (US2) needles.
Beg with a K row, cont in st st and work from
chart until 108[114:120:84:90:96] rows have
been completed, so ending with a P row.

Shape front edge

Dec one st at end (for right front, read 'beg'
here) of next row and at same edge on every
foll 3rd row until 45[48:51:61:64:66] sts rem.
Cont without shaping until
178[188:198:178:188:198] rows have been
completed from Chart (for right front, work 1
more row here).

Shape shoulder

Cast off 15[16:17:20:21:22] sts at beg of next
and foll alt row. Work 1 row. Cast off rem
15[16:17:21:22:22] sts.

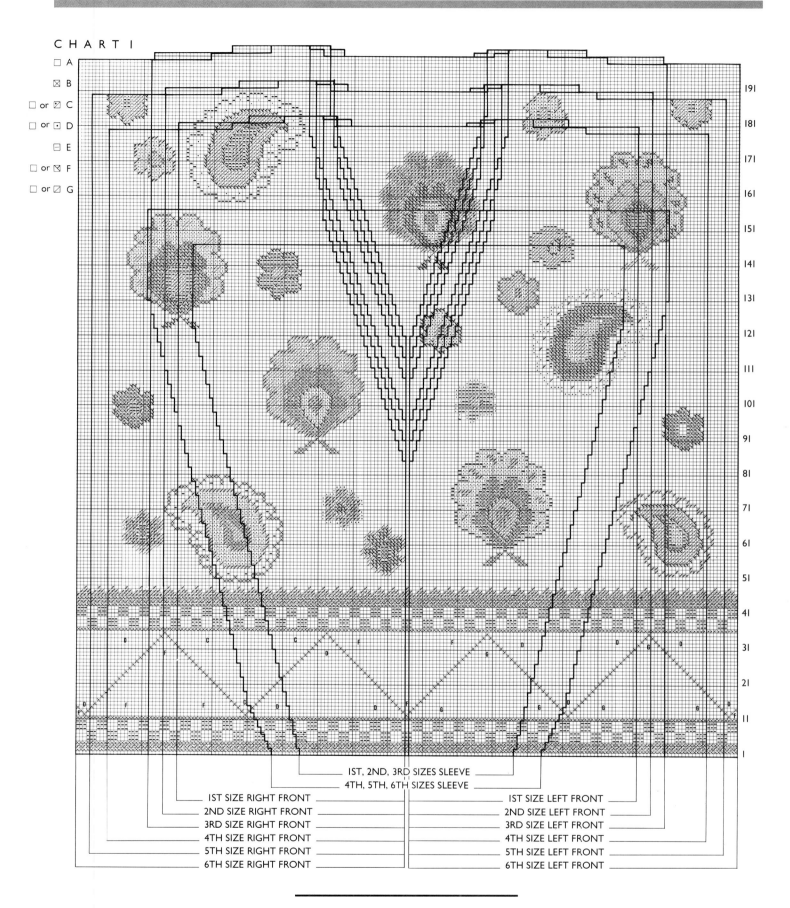

CHART I

☐ A
☒ B
☐ or ☒ C
☐ or ☐ D
☐ E
☐ or ☒ F
☐ or ☑ G

191
181
171
161
151
141
131
121
111
101
91
81
71
61
51
41
31
21
11
1

1ST, 2ND, 3RD SIZES SLEEVE
4TH, 5TH, 6TH SIZES SLEEVE

1ST SIZE RIGHT FRONT   1ST SIZE LEFT FRONT
2ND SIZE RIGHT FRONT   2ND SIZE LEFT FRONT
3RD SIZE RIGHT FRONT   3RD SIZE LEFT FRONT
4TH SIZE RIGHT FRONT   4TH SIZE LEFT FRONT
5TH SIZE RIGHT FRONT   5TH SIZE LEFT FRONT
6TH SIZE RIGHT FRONT   6TH SIZE LEFT FRONT

*The strong spicy colours of the 'Oriental
Paisley' cardigans worn by Elisabeth and
Rahamia will brighten up even the dullest
day. The abstract Paisley motifs are
complimented by a bold geometric patterned
border at the lower edge and cuffs.*

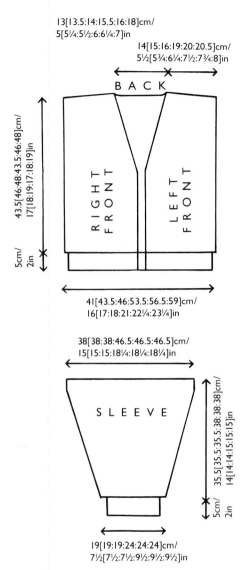

13[13.5:14:15.5:16:18]cm/
5[5¼:5½:6:6¼:7]in

14[15:16:19:20:20.5]cm/
5½[5¾:6¼:7½:7¾:8]in

BACK

RIGHT FRONT

LEFT FRONT

43.5[46:48:43.5:46:48]cm/
17[18:19:17:18:19]in

5cm/
2in

41[43.5:46:53.5:56.5:59]cm/
16[17:18:21:22¼:23¼]in

38[38:38:46.5:46.5:46.5]cm/
15[15:15:18¼:18¼:18¼]in

SLEEVE

35.5[35.5:35.5:38:38:38]cm/
14[14:14:15:15:15]in

5cm/
2in

19[19:19:24:24:24]cm/
7½[7½:7½:9½:9½:9½]in

RIGHT FRONT

Work as given for Left Front, noting the bracketed exceptions.

SLEEVES

Using 2¼mm (US1) needles and A, cast on 53[53:53:67:67:67] sts. Work 5cm (2in) in twisted rib, ending with a 1st row.
Next row Rib 5[5:5:6:6:6], inc in next st, (rib 5, inc in next st) to last 5[5:5:6:6:6] sts, rib to end. 61[61:61:77:77:77] sts.
Change to 2¾mm (US2) needles.
Beg with a K row, cont in st st and work from Chart, inc one st at each end of 3rd and every foll 4th[4th:4th:alt:alt:alt] row until there are 69[69:69:91:91:91] sts, then on every foll 4th row until there are 123[123:123:149:149:149]

sts. Cont without shaping until 146[146:146:156:156:156] rows have been completed from Chart, ending with a P row. Cast off loosely.

FRONT BAND

Join shoulder seams.
Using 2¼mm (US1) needles and A, cast on 9 sts. Cont in twisted rib as given for back welt until band, slightly stretched, fits up left front edge to start of shaping. Slip stitch band in position.
Mark position of 7[7:7:5:5:5] buttonholes with pins as foll: the first to come 1cm (½in) above lower edge, the last 2cm (¾in) below start of front shaping with the others evenly spaced between second and last buttons.
Cont in rib, sewing band in position as

necessary until it fits up left front to shoulder, round back neck and down right front to end of shaping.
Cont with buttonhole band to fit down right front edge making buttonholes as markers are reached as foll: (RS) rib 4, yo, K2 tog, rib to end.
Cast off in rib.
Slip stitch band in position.

TO MAKE UP

Press on WS using a warm iron over a damp cloth. Mark position of underarms 19[19:19:23:23:23]cm (7½[7½:7½:9:9:9]in) down from shoulders on back and fronts. Sew in sleeves between markers, matching centre of sleeve top to shoulder seam. Join side and sleeve seams. Press seams. Sew on buttons.

CHAMONIX CHAMPION

*I like to use pockets in my designs – they are so easy to knit and practical, yet at the same time add interest to an otherwise plain garment. There are two types of pockets in this winter shirt – patch pockets near the lower edge and inset ones higher up the fronts – knitted in stocking stitch and DK used double for extra warmth.
Another feature is the double collar: the top section is worked in chenille that is a shade darker than the rest of the garment.*

SIZES

To fit 86/91[91/97:97/102]cm (34/36[36/38:38/40]in) bust
Actual size 131[137.5:142]cm (51¾[54¼:56]in)
Length to shoulder 73[75:78]cm (28¾[29½:30¾]in)
Sleeve seam (with cuff turned back) 46cm (18in)
Figures in square brackets [ ] refer to larger sizes; where there is only one set of figures, it applies to all sizes.

MATERIALS

50[51:51]×25g hanks of Rowan Lightweight DK in main shade A (Mole 427)
1×50g ball of Rowan Fine Cotton Chenille in shade B (Mole 380)
Pair each of 4mm (US6) and 5mm (US8) knitting needles
12 buttons

TENSION

18 sts and 24 rows to 10cm (4in) over st st using 5mm (US8) needles

NOTE

Both yarns are used double throughout the design

POCKET LININGS
(make 2)

Using 5mm (US8) needles and A, cast on 23 sts and beg with a K row, cont in st st for 15cm (6in), ending with a P row. Cut off yarn and leave rem sts on a holder.

LEFT FRONT

** Using 4mm (US6) needles and A, cast on 56[60:64] sts.
Rib row 1 (RS) P1, K2, * P2, K2, rep from * to last st, P1.
Rib row 2 K1, P2, * K2, P2, rep from * to last st, K1.
Rep these 2 rows for 7cm (2¾in), ending row 2 but for **1st size only** inc 3 sts and for **2nd size only** inc 2 sts evenly across last row. 59[62:64] sts.
Change to 5mm (US8) needles.
Beg with a K row, cont in st st until front measures 42[44:47]cm (16½[17½:18½]in) from cast-on edge, ending with a P row (for right front end with a K row).

Shape armhole
Cast off 5 sts at beg of next row. 54[57:59] sts.
Work straight until armhole measures 11[8:6]cm (4¼[3¼:2¼]in) from beg of shaping, ending with a P row. **

Place pocket lining
Next row K12[15:17], sl next 28 sts onto a holder, K across sts of pocket lining, then K to end.
Work straight until armhole measures 24.5cm (9¾in) from beg of shaping, ending at front edge.

Shape neck
Cast off 4 sts at beg of next row and 3 sts at beg of foll 2 alt rows. Dec one st at neck edge on next 5 rows and one st on foll alt row. 38[41:43] sts.
Work 3 rows, so ending at armhole edge.
Cut off yarn and leave sts on a spare needle for shoulder.

RIGHT FRONT

Work as given for left front from ** to ** noting the bracketed exception.

Place pocket lining
Next row K14, sl next 28 sts onto a holder, K across sts of pocket lining, K to end.
Now complete to match left front.

BACK

Using 4mm (US6) needles and A, cast on 116[124:128] sts.
Work in rib as given for left front for 7cm (2¾in), ending with row 2 but for **1st size only** inc 2 sts evenly across last row. 118[124:128] sts.
Change to 5mm (US8) needles.
Beg with a K row, cont in st st until back measures same as fronts up to beg of armhole shaping, ending with a P row.

Shape armholes

Cast off 5 sts at beg of next 2 rows.
108[114:118] sts.
Work straight until back measures same as fronts up to shoulders, ending with a P row.

Shape shoulders

Next row K38[41:43] sts and place these sts on a spare needle, cast off next 32 sts, K to end and place these last 38[41:43] sts on a spare needle.

S L E E V E S

Using 4mm (US6) needles and A, cast on 44 sts.
Work in rib as given for left front for 16cm (6¼in), ending row 2 but inc 2 sts evenly across last row. 46 sts.
Change to 5mm (US8) needles.
Beg with a K row, cont in st st, inc one st at each end of 3rd and every foll alt row until there are 88 sts, then on every foll 4th row until there are 110 sts. Work straight until sleeve measures 57cm (22½in) from cast-on edge, ending with a P row. Cast off.

P O C K E T T O P S

With RS of work facing, A and using 4mm (US6) needles, rejoin yarn to 28 pocket sts on holder.
Work 4 rows in rib as given for left front.
Buttonhole row 1 (RS) Rib 12, cast off 4, rib to end.
Buttonhole row 2 Rib to end, casting on 4 sts over those cast off in previous row.
Rib 2 more rows. Cast off in rib.

P A T C H P O C K E T S
(make 2)

Using 5mm (US8) needles and A, cast on 18 sts.
Beg with a K row, cont in st st, inc one st at each end of next 7 rows. 32 sts.
Work straight until pocket measures 18cm (7in) from cast-on edge, ending with a P row.
Change to 4mm (US6) needles.
Rep the 2 rib rows of left front twice.
Buttonhole row 1 (RS) Rib 14, cast off 4 sts, rib to end.

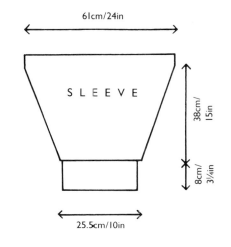

'Chamonix Champion' equals style without any fuss. The long-line, over-size shape makes this shirt-style sweater, knitted in a chunky-weight wool, ideal for relaxing outdoor pursuits. With a smooth fabric and simple lines, the buttons are important decorative details.

18cm/ 7in 21[23:24]cm/ 8¼[9:9½]in

B A C K

R I G H T F R O N T

L E F T F R O N T

31cm/ 12¼in

35[37:40]cm/ 13¾[14½:15¾]in

7cm/ 2¾in

64.5[69:71]cm/25¼[27:28]in

61cm/24in

S L E E V E

38cm/ 15in

8cm/ 3¼in

25.5cm/10in

Buttonhole row 2 Rib to end, casting on 4 sts over those cast off in previous row.
Rib 5 more rows. Cast off in rib.

C O L L A R

Using 4mm (US6) needles and B, cast on 79 sts.
Beg with a P row, work 8cm (3¼in) in reversed st st, ending with a K row. Cast off.

C O L L A R L I N I N G

Using 4mm (US6) needles and A, cast on 79 sts. Beg with a K row, work 8cm (3¼in) st st, ending with a P row. Cast off.

B U T T O N H O L E B O R D E R

With RS of work facing, A and using 4mm (US6) needles, pick up and K116[124:132] sts along right front edge.
Beg with row 2, work 3 rows in rib as given for left front.
Buttonhole row 1 (RS) Rib 4, cast off 3 sts, * rib until there are 12[13:14] sts on right-hand needle after cast-off group, cast off 3 sts, rep from * 6 times more, rib to end.
Buttonhole row 2 Rib to end, casting on 3 sts over those cast off in previous row.
Rib 3 more rows. Cast off in rib.

B U T T O N B O R D E R

Work as given for buttonhole border omitting buttonholes.

S H O U L D E R S E A M S

Graft back and front shoulders together on RS of work as follows:
With wrong sides together take a st from front and back and K them tog, take next 2 sts tog in the same way, then pass first st over second st, cont to cast off in this way until all sts are worked, so forming a seam on the right side of work.

T O M A K E U P

Press lightly on WS using a warm iron over a damp cloth. Sew in sleeves, matching centre of sleeve top to shoulder seam and sewing final rows to cast-off groups at underarms. Join side and sleeve seams, reversing the seam on last 8cm (3¼in). With right sides together, sew side edges and cast-off edges of collar and lining together, turn to right side, then beginning and ending at centre of front borders, sew collar round neck edge. Turn cuffs to RS.
Attach buttons to jacket using the shank method. Press seams.

GROSVENOR HOUSE

*I wanted to show how delicate and feminine a Fair Isle design can look.
Instead of muted dark colours and tweedy yarns I chose soft tones of pastel
shades in cotton yarns for this pretty V-neck sweater with short sleeves and
neat moss stitch collar. With its 'peaches and cream' look I can envisage
wearing this design for afternoon tea with my favourite aunt.*

SIZES

To fit 86[91:97]cm (34[36:38]in) bust
Actual size 96[102:108]cm (37¾[40:42½]in)
Length to shoulder 43.5[45:48.5]cm
(17[17¾:19¼]in)
Sleeve seam 12.5cm (5in)
Figures in square brackets [ ] refer to larger
sizes; where there is only one set of figures, it
applies to all sizes.

MATERIALS

6[6:7]×50g balls of Rowan Cabled
Mercerised Cotton in main shade A (Pale Pink
328)
1×50g ball of Cabled Mercerised Cotton in
shade B (Furnace 314)
1×50g ball of Rowan Sea Breeze in shade C
(Shell 554)
1×50g ball of Cabled Mercerised Cotton in
shade D (Washed Straw 305)
1[1:2]×50g balls of Cabled Mercerised Cotton
in shade E (Lichen 327)
1×50g ball of Cabled Mercerised Cotton in
shade F (Aspen 335)
Pair each of 2¼mm (US1) and 3mm (US3)
knitting needles

TENSION

34 sts and 36 rows to 10cm (4in) over patt
using 3mm (US3) needles

FRONT

Using 2¼mm (US1) needles and A, cast on
101[109:117] sts.
Moss St row K1, * P1, K1, rep from * to end.
Rep this row for 2.5cm (1in), ending with WS
of work facing.
Inc row Patt 3[7:2], * M1, patt 5[5:6], rep
from * to last 3[7:1] sts, M1, patt to end.
121[129:137] sts.
Change to 3mm (US3) needles.
Beg with a K row, cont in st st and work

22[20:20] rows in patt from Chart. Strand
yarns loosely across back of work. Cont to
work the 32-row patt repeat from Chart, inc
one st at each end of next and every foll alt
row until there are 159[163:163] sts, then at
each end of every foll 4th row until there are
163[173:183] sts.
Work 1 row, so ending row 68[74:86].

Shape neck
Next row Patt 81[86:91], turn and leave rem
sts on a spare needle.
Cont on these sts for first side of neck.
** Patt 1 row. Dec one st at neck edge on
next and foll 4th row. 79[84:89] sts.
Work 1 row, (work 2 rows for second side of
neck), so ending at armhole edge.

Shape armhole and neck
Cont to dec one st at neck edge on every 4th
row, cast off 4 sts at beg of next row and 2 sts
at beg of foll 2 alt rows.
Now dec one st at same edge on foll 2 alt
rows. 67[72:77] sts.
Keeping armhole edge straight, cont to dec at
neck edge on every 4th row until 53[56:61]
sts rem. Work straight until row 148[154:166]
(row 149[155:167] for second side of neck)
has been completed, so ending at armhole
edge.

Shape shoulder
Cast off 17[18:20] sts at beg of next row and
18[18:20] sts at beg of foll alt row. Work 1
row. Cast off rem 18[20:21] sts.
With RS of work facing, rejoin yarn to next st,
K2tog, then patt to end. 81[86:91] sts.
Now complete as given for first side of neck
from ** to end noting the bracketed
exceptions.

BACK

Work as given for front until row 68[74:86]
has been completed.
Work straight until row 76[82:94] has been
completed.

Shape armholes
Cast off 4 sts at beg of next 2 rows and 2 sts
at beg of foll 4 rows. Dec one st at each end
of next and foll alt row. 143[153:163] sts.
Work straight until row 148[154:166] has
been completed.

Shape shoulders and neck
Cast off 17[18:20] sts at beg of next 2 rows.
Next row Cast off 18[18:20], patt until there
are 22[24:25] sts on right-hand needle, turn
and cont on these sts for first side of neck.
Next row Cast off 4 sts, patt to end.
Cast off rem 18[20:21] sts.
With RS of work facing, rejoin yarn to next st
and cast off centre 29[33:33] sts, patt to end.
40[42:45] sts.
Next row Cast off 18[18:20] sts, patt to end.
Next row Cast off 4 sts, patt to end.
Cast off rem 18[20:21] sts.

SLEEVES

Using 2¼mm (US1) needles and A, cast on 97
sts.
Work in moss st for 2.5cm (1in), ending with
WS of work facing.
Inc row Patt 5, * M1, patt 8, rep from * to
last 4 sts, M1, patt 4. 109 sts.
Beg with a K row, cont in st st and patt from

*Cream predominates as the main
colour of 'Grosvenor House'
knitted in a 4-ply cotton with
narrow bands of dainty
Fair Isle patterns.*

Chart, inc one st at each end of 5th and every foll alt row until there are 141 sts. Work 1 row, so completing row 36.

Shape top
Cast off 4 sts at beg of next 2 rows and 2 sts at beg of foll 4 rows. Dec one st at each end of next and foll alt row. Work 1 row. Cast off rem 121 sts.

COLLAR

Join shoulder seams. Using 2¼mm (US1) needles and A, cast on 2 sts.
Row 1 K1. P1.
Row 2 Inc in first st, K1.
Row 3 K1, P1, K1.
Rows 4-5 As 3rd row.
Row 6 Inc in first st, P1, K1.
Cont in moss st, inc and work into moss st one st at beg of every foll 4th row until there are 35 sts. Place a marker at shaped edge on last row.

Waiting in the drawing room, Anna browses through a book. Looking expensively chic, she has teamed this sweater with a co-ordinating skirt and jacket: the V neckline, trimmed with a neat collar, and short sleeves are ideal for wearing with a suit. A simple pearl necklace is the only jewellery that is needed.

Work straight until collar, slightly stretched, fits from base of opening to shoulder seam. Place a second marker at shaped edge on last row.
Work straight until collar fits across back neck from second marker to next shoulder seam. Place a 3rd marker at same edge on last row.
Work straight until collar from 3rd marker, is the same depth as between 2nd and 1st markers.
Dec one st at shaped edge on next and every foll 4th row until 2 sts rem. K2tog and fasten off.

TO MAKE UP

Press lightly on WS with a warm iron over a damp cloth. Sew in sleeves matching centre of sleeve top to shoulder seam.
Join side and sleeve seams. Sew shaped edges of collar to front and back neck, matching 2nd and 3rd markers to shoulder seams.

CHART 1

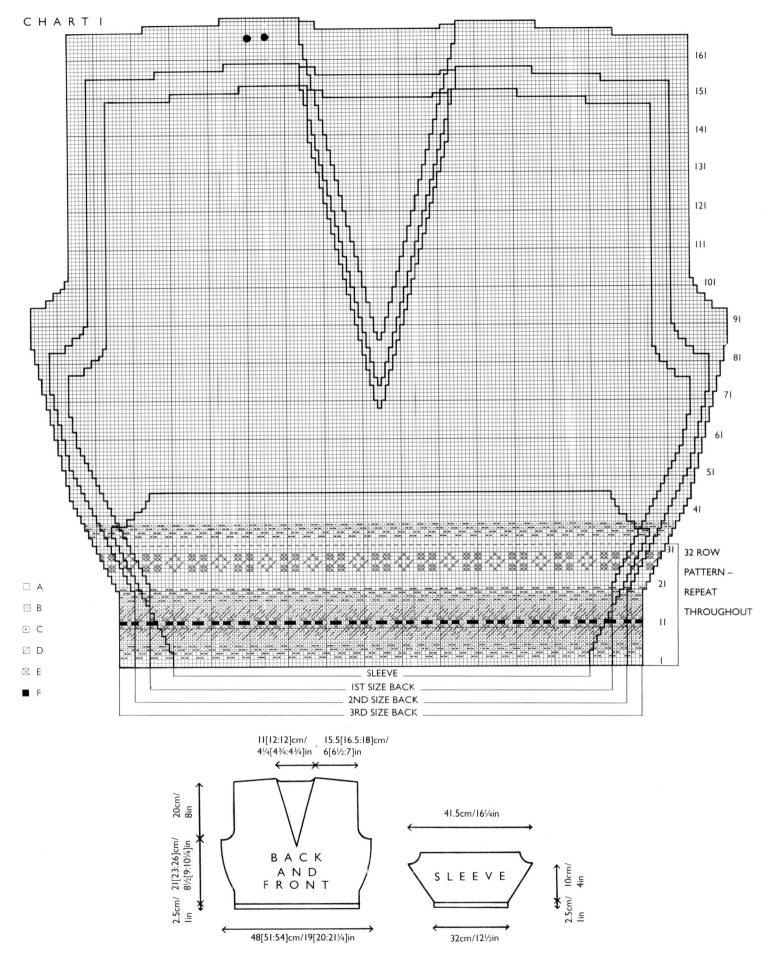

161
151
141
131
121
111
101
91
81
71
61
51
41
31 32 ROW
21 PATTERN –
11 REPEAT
1   THROUGHOUT

□ A
⊟ B
⊡ C
▨ D
⊠ E
■ F

SLEEVE
1ST SIZE BACK
2ND SIZE BACK
3RD SIZE BACK

11[12:12]cm/   15.5[16.5:18]cm/
4¼[4¾:4¾]in   6[6½:7]in

20cm/
8in

21[23:26]cm/
8½[9:10¼]in

2.5cm/
1in

BACK
AND
FRONT

48[51:54]cm/19[20:21¼]in

41.5cm/16¼in

SLEEVE

10cm/
4in

2.5cm/
1in

32cm/12½in

ANTIQUE LACE

*I believe that often the simplest designs are the best. That certainly applies to
the lacy snowflake pattern used here: it is one of the easiest laces to knit, yet
I think that it is one of the prettiest.
In contrast to the over-size shapes that I like for outdoors, I love this little
fitted-to-the-waist cardigan with its short sleeves and dainty glass buttons.
To avoid ribbed bands that would look too heavy with this delicate design, I
have used a soft crochet edging around the neck and down the fronts.*

SIZES

To fit 79/84[86/91:94/99]cm (31/33[34/36:37/
39]in) bust
Actual size 99.5[107.5:115.5]cm
(39¼[42¼:45¼]in)
Length to shoulder 43[45:48]cm
(17[17¾:19]in)
Sleeve seam 14cm (5½in)
Figures in square brackets [ ] refer to larger
sizes; where there is only one set of figures, it
applies to all sizes.

MATERIALS

5[5:6]×50g balls of Rowan Sea Breeze
(Smoke 527)
Pair each of 2¼mm (US1) and 2¾mm (US2)
knitting needles
A 2.00mm (US B/1) crochet hook
7 small buttons

TENSION

30 sts and 46 rows to 10cm (4in) over patt
using 2¾mm (US2) needles

BACK

Using 2¼mm (US1) needles cast on
109[121:133] sts.
Rib row 1 K1, * P1, K1, rep from * to end.
Rib row 2 P1, * K1, P1, rep from * to end.
Rep these 2 rows for 4cm (1½in), ending with
row 1.
Inc row Rib 8[3:9], * M1, rib 4[5:6], rep
from * to last 9[3:10] sts, M1, rib to end.
133[145:153] sts.
Change to 2¾mm (US2) needles.
Cont in Eyelet-hole patt as folls:
Row 1 (RS) K11[5:9], * yfwd, sl 1, K2tog,
psso, yfwd, K9, rep from * to last 14[8:12] sts,
yfwd, sl 1, K2tog, psso, yfwd, K11[5:9].
Row 2 and every alt row P.
Row 3 K9[3:7], * K2tog, yfwd, K3, yfwd,
skpo, K5, rep from * to last 16[10:14] sts,
K2tog, yfwd, K3, yfwd, skpo, K9[3:7].
Row 5 As row 1.

*Anna looks pretty in a pastel-coloured
openwork cardigan that is knitted in a 4-ply
cotton yarn and trimmed with crochet.*

Row 7 K.
Row 9 K5[11:3], * yfwd, sl 1, K2tog, psso,
yfwd, K9, rep from * to last 8[14:6] sts, yfwd,
sl 1, K2tog, psso, yfwd, K5[11:3].
Row 11 K3[9:1], * K2tog, yfwd, K3, yfwd,
skpo, K5, rep from * to last 10[16:8] sts,
K2tog, yfwd, K3, yfwd, skpo, K3[9:1].
Row 13 Inc in first st, K4[10:2], * yfwd, sl 1,
K2tog, psso, yfwd, K9, rep from * to last
8[14:6] sts, yfwd, sl 1, K2tog, psso, yfwd,
K4[10:2], inc in last st.
Row 15 K.
Row 16 P.
These 16 rows establish the position of the
Eyelet-hole patt.
Keeping patt correct. inc one st at each end of
7th[9th:7th] row and every foll
10th[12th:10th] row until there are
149[161:173] sts.
Work 5[1:7] rows straight, so
ending with a WS row.

Shape armholes
Cast off 4 sts at beg of next 2
rows, then dec one st at each end
of every row until 121[133:145] sts rem.
Work straight until armholes measure 20cm
(8in) from beg of shaping, ending with a WS
row.

Shape shoulders and back neck
Cast off 15[16:17] sts at beg of next 2 rows.
Next row Cast off 13[14:16] sts, patt until
there are 16[18:19] sts on right-hand needle,
turn.
Complete this side first.
Next row Cast off 4 sts, patt to end.
Cast off rem 12[14:15] sts.
With RS of work facing, rejoin yarn to next st
and cast off centre 33[37:41] sts, patt to end.
29[32:35] sts.
Next row Cast off 13[14:16] sts, patt to end.
Next row Cast off 4 sts, patt to end.
Cast off rem 12[14:15] sts.

LEFT FRONT

** Using 2¼mm (US1) needles cast on
55[61:67] sts.
Beg with rib row 1, work in rib as given for
back for 4cm (1½in), ending with row 1.
Inc row Rib 5[3:2], * M1, rib 4[5:7], rep

from * to last 6[3:2] sts, M1, rib to end.
67[73:77] sts. **
Change to 2¾mm (US2) needles.
Cont in Eyelet-hole patt as folls:
Row 1 (RS) K11[5:9], * yfwd, sl 1,
K2tog, psso, yfwd, K9, rep from *
to last 8 sts, yfwd, sl 1, K2tog,
psso, yfwd, K5.

Row 2 and every foll alt row P.
Row 3 K9[3:7], * K2tog, yfwd, K3,
yfwd, skpo, K5, rep from * to last 10 sts,
K2tog, yfwd, K3, yfwd, skpo, K3.
Row 5 As row 1.
Row 7 K.
Row 9 K5[11:3], * yfwd, sl 1, K2tog, psso,
yfwd, K9, rep from * to last 2 sts, yfwd, skpo.
Row 11 K3[9:1], * K2tog, yfwd, K3, yfwd,
skpo, K5, rep from * to last 4 sts, K2tog,
yfwd, K2.
Row 13 Inc in first st, K4[10:2], * yfwd, sl 1,
K2tog, psso, yfwd, K9, rep from * to last 2
sts, yfwd, skpo.

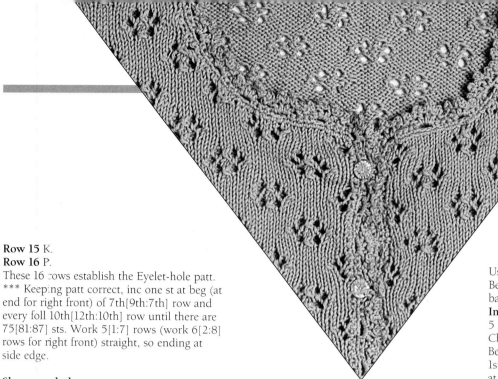

Row 15 K.
Row 16 P.
These 16 rows establish the Eyelet-hole patt.
*** Keeping patt correct, inc one st at beg (at end for right front) of 7th[9th:7th] row and every foll 10th[12th:10th] row until there are 75[81:87] sts. Work 5[1:7] rows (work 6[2:8] rows for right front) straight, so ending at side edge.

Shape armhole
Cast off 4 sts at beg of next row. Work 1 row, then dec one st at armhole edge on every row until 61[67:73] sts rem.
Work straight until armhole measures 13cm (5¼in) from beg of shaping, ending at front edge.

Shape neck
Cast off 9[11:13] sts at beg of next row and 3 sts at beg of foll alt row. Dec one st at neck edge on next 4 rows, then on foll 2 alt rows. Now dec one st at same edge on every foll 4th row until 40[44:48] sts rem.
Work straight until front measures the same as back up to beg of shoulder shaping, ending at armhole edge.

Shape shoulder
Cast off 15[16:17] sts at beg of next row and 13[14:16] sts at beg of foll alt row. Work 1 row. Cast off rem 12[14:15] sts.

RIGHT FRONT

Work as given for left front from ** to **.
Change to 2¾mm (US2) needles.
Cont in Eyelet-hole patt as folls:
Row 1 (RS) K5, *yfwd, sl 1, K2tog, psso, yfwd, K9, rep from * to last 14[8:12] sts, yfwd, sl 1, K2tog, psso, yfwd, K11[5:9].
Row 2 and every foll alt row P.
Row 3 K3, * K2tog, yfwd, K3, yfwd, skpo, K5, rep from * to last 16[10:14] sts, K2tog, yfwd, K3, yfwd, skpo, K9[3:7].
Row 5 As row 1.
Row 7 K.
Row 9 K2tog, yfwd, K9, * yfwd, sl 1, K2tog, psso, yfwd, K9, rep from * to last 8[14: 6] sts, yfwd, sl 1, K2tog, psso, yfwd, K5[11:3].
Row 11 K2, yfwd, skpo, K5, * K2tog, yfwd, K3, yfwd, skpo, K5, rep from * to last 10[16:8] sts, K2tog, yfwd, K3, yfwd, skpo, K3[9:1].
Row 13 K2tog, yfwd, K9, * yfwd, sl 1, K2tog, psso, yfwd, K9, rep from * to last 8[14:6] sts, yfwd, sl 1, K2tog, psso, yfwd, K4[10:2], inc in last st.
Row 15 K.
Row 16 P.
Now complete to match left front from *** to end noting the bracketed exceptions.

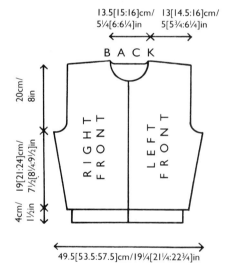

13.5[15:16]cm/ 5¼[6:6¼]in   13[14.5:16]cm/ 5[5¾:6¼]in

BACK

20cm/ 8in

19[21:24]cm/ 7½[8¼:9½]in

RIGHT FRONT   LEFT FRONT

4cm/ 1½in

49.5[53.5:57.5]cm/19¼[21¼:22¾]in

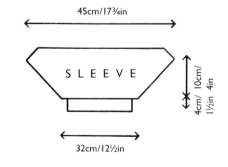

45cm/17¾in

SLEEVE

4cm/ 1½in   10cm/ 4in

32cm/12½in

SLEEVES

Using 2¼mm (US1) needles cast on 67 sts.
Beg with rib row 1, work in rib as given for back for 4cm (1½in), ending with row 1.
Inc row Rib 4, * M1, rib 2, rep from * to last 5 sts, M1, rib to end. 97 sts.
Change to 2¾mm (US2) needles.
Beg with row 1 of Eyelet-hole patt as given for 1st size of back, inc and work into patt one st at each end of 3rd and every foll alt row until there are 135 sts.
Work straight until sleeve measures 14cm (5½in) from cast-on edge, ending with a WS row.

Shape top
Cast off 4 sts at beg of next 2 rows, then dec one st at each end of every row until 107 sts rem.
Cast off these sts.

THE FRONT EDGING

Note that American crochet terms are in round brackets ( ).
Join shoulder seams. With RS of work facing, using the 2.00mm (US B/1) hook, join on yarn at lower edge of right front and work 2 ch, then work 12 dc (sc) up rib, 88[94:100] dc (sc) up to beg of neck shaping, 41 dc (sc) up to shoulder, 42[48:48] dc (sc) across back neck to next shoulder, 41 dc (sc) down to end of neck shaping, 88[94:100] dc (sc) down to top of rib and 12 dc (sc) down rib, so ending at lower edge of left front, turn. 324[342:354] dc (sc).
Next row 2ch, 1dc (sc) into each of first 2dc (sc), * 3ch, miss 2dc (sc), 1dc (sc) into each of next 4dc (sc), rep from * to last 4dc (sc), 3ch, miss 2dc (sc), 1dc (sc) into each of last 2dc (sc), turn.
Next row * 2ch, 1tr (dc) into next 3-ch 1p, (2ch, 1tr (dc) into same 3-ch 1p) 3 times, 2ch, sl st into centre of next 4dc (sc) on previous row, rep from * to end, sl st into top of last dc (sc), turn.
Next row (Sl st into 2-ch sp, sl st into top of next tr (dc), 3ch, sl st into same tr (dc) so forming a picot) 4 times, * sl st into next 2-ch sp, sl st into sl st of previous row (centre of 4dc (sc) group), (sl st into next 2-ch sp, sl st into top of next tr (dc), 1 picot) 4 times, rep from * to end finishing sl st into last 2-ch sp. Fasten off.

TO MAKE UP

Press lightly on WS of work using a warm iron over a damp cloth. Set in sleeves, matching centre of sleeve top to shoulder seam. Join side and sleeve seams. Sew on buttons. Use 3-ch lps on edging as buttonholes. Press seams.

HURLINGHAM CLUB

After spending much of my day working with patterns and colours, it is refreshing for me to design a garment that is perfectly plain, yet still stylish. A stocking stitch tunic in mercerised cotton looks great with leggings or slim trousers – and the scoop neckline makes it suitable for day or evening wear. I deliberately made the fitted sleeves with button cuffs the only detail in this strong simple design.

SIZES

To fit 86[91:97]cm (34[36:38]in) bust
Actual size 112[117:122]cm (44[46:48]in)
Length to shoulder 62[64:65]cm (24½[25:25½]in)
Sleeve seam 38cm (15in)
Figures in square brackets [ ] refer to larger sizes; where there is only one set of figures, it applies to all sizes.

MATERIALS

12[12:13]×50g balls of Rowan Cabled Mercerised Cotton (Cork 331)
Pair each 2¼mm (US1) and 3mm (US3) knitting needles
12 small buttons

TENSION

31 sts and 40 rows to 10cm (4in) over st st using 3mm (US3) needles

FRONT

Using 2¼mm (US1) needles cast on 158[166:174] sts and work 6 rows in K1, P1 rib.
Change to 3mm (US3) needles.
Beg with a K row, work 20 rows st st.
Next row (inc row) K3, M1, K to last 3 sts, M1, K3.
Beg with a P row, cont in st st, inc one st as set at each end of every foll 14th[14th:16th] row until there are 174[182:190] sts. Cont without shaping until work measures 36.5[38.5:39.5]cm (14¼[15¼:15¾]in) from cast-on edge, ending with a P row.

Shape armholes
* Cast off 4 sts at beg of next 2 rows.
Next row K3, K3 tog tbl, K to last 6 sts, K3 tog, K3.
Work 3 rows in st st.
Rep last 4 rows twice more, then work dec row again *. 150[158:166] sts.
Cont without shaping until work measures 16.5[15:13.5]cm (6½[6:5¼]in) from beg of shaping, ending with a P row.

A mercerised cotton yarn adds a subtle sheen to the smooth stocking stitch fabric of this tunic worn by Anna.

Shape neck

Next row K66[70:74], turn and leave rem sts on a spare needle.
Cont on these sts for first side of neck.
Cast off 3 sts at beg of next and foll alt row. Dec one st at neck edge on every row until 53[57:61] sts rem, then on every foll alt row until 49[52:55] sts rem. Now dec one st on every foll 4th row until 46[48:50] sts rem. Work 5 rows straight, so ending at armhole edge.

Shape shoulder

Cast off 16 sts at beg of next and foll alt row. Work one row. Cast off rem 14[16:18] sts. With RS of work facing, rejoin yarn to next st, cast off centre 18 sts, then K to end.
P 1 row, then complete as given for other side of neck.

BACK

Work as given for front to completion of armhole shaping. 150[158:166] sts.
Cont without shaping until back measures same as front up to beg of shoulder shaping, ending with a P row.

Shape shoulders and back neck

Next row Cast off 16 sts, K until there are 38[40:42] sts on right-hand needle, turn and complete this side first.
Next row Cast off 4 sts, P to end.
Next row Cast off 16 sts, K to end.
Next row Cast off 4 sts, P to end.
Cast off rem 14[16:18] sts.
With RS of work facing, rejoin yarn to next st, cast off centre 42[46:50] sts, then K to end.
Next row Cast off 16 sts, P to end.
Next row Cast off 4 sts, K to end.
Rep last 2 rows once more.
Cast off rem 14[16:18] sts.

LEFT SLEEVE

Front Section

Using 2¼mm (US1) needles cast on 39 sts. Beg with a K row, work 4cm (1½in) in st st, ending with a K row.
Next row K to end to form hemline.
Change to 3mm (US3) needles.
Beg with a K row, cont in st st, inc one st (within a border of 3 sts as given on front) at end of 13th row (for right sleeve inc one st at beg of 13th row) and at same edge on every foll 3rd row until there are 56 sts. Work one row, so ending with a P row.
Cut off yarn.
Leave sts on a spare needle.

Back section

Using 2¼mm (US1) needles cast on 17 sts. Beg with a K row, work 4cm (1½in) in st st, ending with a K row.
Next row K to end to form hemline.
Change to 3mm (US3) needles.
Beg with a K row, cont in st st, inc one st (within a border of 3 sts) at beg of 13th row (For right sleeve inc one st at end of 13th row) and at same edge on every foll 3rd row until there are 34 sts. Work one row, so ending with a P row.

Join sections

Next row K to end of back section then K across 56 sts of front section. 90 sts.
** Cont to inc (as before) at each end of next and every foll 3rd row until there are 98 sts,

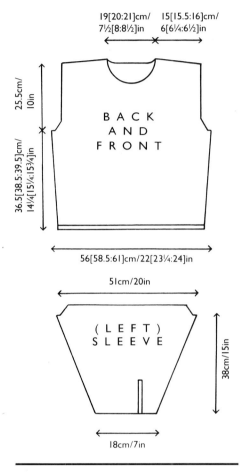

19[20:21]cm/ 7½[8:8½]in   15[15.5:16]cm/ 6[6¼:6½]in

25.5cm/ 10in

36.5[38.5:39.5]cm/ 14¼[15¼:15¾]in

BACK AND FRONT

56[58.5:61]cm/22[23¼:24]in

51cm/20in

(LEFT) SLEEVE

38cm/15in

18cm/7in

Understated in an outdoor setting, 'Hurlingham Club' has surprising details including elegant fitted sleeves and cuffs with buttoned openings.

then at each end of every foll alt row until there are 158 sts.
Cont without shaping until sleeve measures 38cm (15in) from hemline, ending with a P row.

Shape top

Work as given for front armhole shaping from * to *. Work 3 more rows in st st. Cast off rem 134 sts.

BUTTONHOLE BAND

Using 2¼mm (US1) needles and with RS of work facing, pick up and K 52 sts up left side of opening between hemline and top of vent.
1st-3rd rows Beg with a P row, work 3 rows in st st.
4th row (buttonhole row) K3, yfwd, K2 tog, (K7, yfwd, K2 tog) 5 times, K2.
5th-7th rows As 1st-3rd.
8th row P to end to mark foldline.
9th-11th rows As 1st-3rd.
12th row As 4th.
13th-15th rows As 1st-3rd
Cast off.

RIGHT SLEEVE

Back section

Work as given for back section of left sleeve noting the bracketed exception.
Cut off yarn. Leave sts on a spare needle.

Front section

Work as given for front section of left sleeve noting the bracketed exception.
Do not cut off yarn.

Join sections

Next row K to end of front section, then K across 34 sts of back section. 90 sts.
Complete as given for left sleeve from ** to end.

BUTTONHOLE BAND

Work as given for left sleeve buttonhole band, but work along right side of opening.

NECK EDGING

Join right shoulder seam. Using 2¼mm (US1) needles and with RS of work facing, join yarn to left shoulder seam and pick up and K53 sts down left side of neck, 18 sts from centre front, 53 sts up right side of neck, 8 sts down right back neck, 42[46:50] sts across back neck and 8 sts up left back neck. 182[186:190] sts.
Work 6 rows in K1, P1 rib.
Cast off in rib.

TO MAKE UP

Press on WS using a warm iron over a damp cloth. Join left shoulder and neckband seam. Set in sleeves, then join side and sleeve seams. Turn buttonhole bands to WS at foldline and slip stitch in position. Turn hem at cuff edges to WS and slip stitch in position. Press seams. Sew on buttons at sleeve openings.

SMITH'S LAWN

Easy to make and easy to wear, this man's polo shirt is knitted in a soft and comfortable blend of wool and cotton. Once again I have used the merest of details – a striped edging to the ribbed bands – to maintain a casual elegance to the garment. For a smarter appearance you could knit the shirt in one colour only; worn under a jacket it would look exclusive.

SIZES

To fit 86/91[91/97:97/102]cm (34/36[36/38:38/40]in) chest
Actual size 121[127:131]cm (47½[50:51½]in)
Length to shoulder 64[65.5:66.5]cm (25[25¾:26¼]in)
Sleeve seam 46[48.5:50.5]cm (18[19¼:19¾]in)
Figures in square brackets [ ] refer to larger sizes; where there is only one set of figures, it applies to all sizes

MATERIALS

16[17:18]×40g balls of Rowan Wool and Cotton in main shade A (Alabaster 909)
1×40g ball of Wool and Cotton in shade B (Wedgewood 923)
Pair each of 2¾mm (US2) and 3¼mm (US3) knitting needles
4 buttons

TENSION

28 sts and 36 rows to 10cm (4in) over st st using 3¼mm (US3) needles

BACK

Using 2¾mm (US2) needles and A, cast on 144[152:156] sts.
Rib row 1 P1, K2, * P2, K2, rep from * to last st, P1.
Rib row 2 K1, P2, * K2, P2, rep from * to last st, K1.
Cont in rib, work 2 rows B, 2 rows A, 2 rows B, then cont in A only until rib measures 9cm (3½in) from cast-on edge, ending with row 1. Cut off B.
Inc row Rib 10[1:11], * M1, rib 5[6:5], rep from * to last 9[1:10] sts, M1, rib to end. 170[178:184] sts.
Change to 3¼mm (US3) needles.
Beg with a K row, cont in st st until work measures 41.5[42.5:43]cm (16¼[16¾:17]in) from cast-on edge, ending with a P row.

Shape armholes

Cast off 4 sts at beg of next 2 rows and 2 sts at beg of foll 8 rows. 146[154:160] sts.
Work straight until armholes measure 22.5[23:23.5]cm (8¾[9:9¼]in) from beg of shaping, ending with a P row.

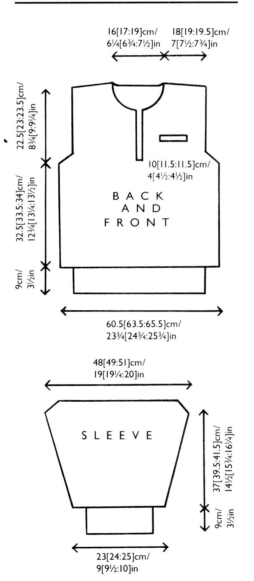

The shirt-style of this sweater, with its four-button opening at the neck, makes it popular for both casual and sportswear. The wool and cotton mixed yarn is a good choice for a variable climate.

Shape shoulders and back neck

Cast off 17[17:18] sts at beg of next 2 rows.
Next row Cast off 17[18:18] sts, K until there are 21[22:23] sts on right-hand needle, turn and complete this side of neck first.
Next row Cast off 4 sts, P to end.
Cast off rem 17[18:19] sts.
With RS of work facing, rejoin A to rem sts, cast off centre 36[40:42] sts, K to end.
Next row Cast off 17[18:18] sts, P to end.
Next row Cast off 4 sts, K to end.
Cast off rem 17[18:19] sts.

POCKET LINING

Using 3¼mm (US3) needles and A, cast on 28[32:32] sts and work in st st for 9.5[10:10.5]cm (3¾[4:4¼]in). Cut off yarn and leave sts on a holder.

FRONT

Work as given for back up to beg of armhole shaping, ending with a P row.

Shape armholes and divide for front opening

Next row Cast off 4 sts, K until there are 78[82:85] sts on right-hand needle, turn and leave rem sts on a spare needle.
Cont on these sts for first side of neck.
Work 1 row.
** Cast off 2 sts at beg of next and foll 3 alt rows. 70[74:77] sts.
Work 11[9:9] rows straight, so ending at armhole edge.

Place pocket lining

Next row K22[24:27], sl next 28[32:32] sts on a holder, K across sts of pocket lining, then K to end.
Work straight until armhole measures 16.5cm (6½in) from beg of shaping, ending at front edge.

Shape neck

Cast off 4 sts at beg of next row and 3 sts at beg of foll 2 alt rows. Dec one st at neck edge on next 5[9:9] rows, then on every alt row until 51[53:55] sts rem.
Work straight until front measures the same as back up to beg of shoulder shaping, ending at armhole edge.

Warren, wearing 'Smith's Lawn' and Anna, in 'Hurlingham Club' (page 73) are a well-matched couple in the fashion stakes.

Shape shoulder

Cast off 17[17:18] sts at beg of next row and 17[18:18] sts at beg of foll alt row. Work 1 row. Cast off rem 17[18:19] sts.
With RS of work facing, rejoin A and cast off centre 6 sts, K to end. 82[86:89] sts.
Next row Cast off 4 sts, P to end.
Work 1 row.
Now complete to match first side of neck from ** to end, omitting pocket.

SLEEVES

Using 2¾mm (US2) needles and A, cast on 52[56:60] sts and work 9cm (3½in) in rib with stripes, as given for back, ending with row 1.
Inc row Rib 4[6:3], * M1, rib 4[4:6], rep from * to last 4[6:3] sts, M1, rib to end. 64[68:70] sts.
Change to 3¼mm (US3) needles.
Beg with a K row, cont in st st inc one st at each end of 3rd and every foll 4th row until there are 126[132:142] sts.

1st and 2nd sizes only
Inc one st at each end of every foll alt row until there are 134[138] sts.

All sizes
Work straight until sleeve measures 46[48.5:50.5]cm (18[19¼:19¾]in) from cast-on edge, ending with a P row.

Shape top
Cast off 4 sts at beg of next 2 rows and 2 sts at beg of next 8 rows. Cast off rem 110[114:118] sts.

POCKET TOP

With RS of work facing, A and using 2¾m (US2) needles, rejoin yarn to 28[32:32] pocket sts on holder.
Working in rib as given for back, work (2 rows A and 2 rows B) twice and 2 rows A. Using A, cast off in rib.

BUTTON BORDER

With RS of work facing, A and using 2¾mm (US2) needles, pick up and K48 sts evenly along right front opening.
Beg with rib row 2, using A only, work 8 rows in rib as for back.
Cast off in rib.

BUTTONHOLE BORDER

With RS of work facing, A and using 2¾mm (US2) needles, pick up and K48 sts evenly along left front opening.
Beg with rib row 2, using A only, work 3 rows in rib as given for back.
Buttonhole row 1 (RS) Rib 3, * cast off 2, rib

until there are 11 sts on right-hand needle after cast-off group, rep from * twice more, cast off 2, rib to end.
Buttonhole row 2 Rib to end casting on 2 sts over those cast off in previous row.
Rib 3 more rows.
Cast off in rib.

COLLAR

Join shoulder seams. With RS of work facing, A and using 2¾mm (US2) needles, beg at centre of button band, pick up and K44[47:48] sts up right front neck, 56[58:60] sts across back neck and 44[47:48] sts down

left front neck, ending at centre of buttonhole band. 144[152:156] sts.
Beg with rib row 2, using A only, work 6.5cm (2½in) in rib as given for back, then work (2 rows B and 2 rows A) twice.
Using A only, cast off in rib.

TO MAKE UP

Press on WS using a warm iron over a damp cloth. Set in sleeves, then join side and sleeve seams. Sew down pocket lining on WS of work and pocket top on RS of work. Sew buttonhole band over button band at base of opening. Press seams. Sew on buttons.

ETON COLLEGE

Rowan Wool and Cotton is one of my favourite yarns. It feels soft and luxurious next to the skin, is ideal for wearing all year round and gives marvellous definition for stitch patterns such as those incorporated in this Aran-style sweater.
As Wool and Cotton is lighter than Aran-type yarn, this sweater is perfect for indoor or outdoor wear, for him or for her, with or without a jacket – a classic companion.

SIZES

To fit 102[107:112]cm (40[42:44]in) bust/chest
Actual size 122.5[128:133]cm (48¼[50½:52½]in)
Length to shoulder 64.5[67:69.5]cm (25¼[26½:27¼]in)
Sleeve seam 50.5cm (19¾in)
Figures in square brackets [ ] refer to larger sizes; where there is only one set of figures, it applies to all sizes

MATERIALS

20[21:22]×40g balls of Rowan Wool and Cotton (Kashmir 910 or Natural 908)
Pair each of 2¾mm (US2) and 3¼mm (US3) knitting needles
Cable needle

TENSION

31 sts and 40 rows to 10cm (4in) over patt using 3¼mm (US3) needles

SPECIAL ABBREVIATIONS

C3R Cable 3 Right thus: sl next 2 sts onto cable needle and leave at back of work, K1tbl, then P1 and K1tbl from cable needle
C4F Cable 4 Front thus: sl next 2 sts onto cable needle and leave at front of work, K2tbl, then K2tbl from cable needle
C4R Cable 4 Right thus: sl next 2 sts onto cable needle and leave at back of work, K2, then K2 from cable needle
C4L Cable 4 Left thus: sl next 2 sts onto cable needle and leave at front of work, K2, then K2 from cable needle
Cr3R Cross 3 Right thus: sl next st onto cable needle and leave at back of work, K2tbl, then P1 from cable needle
Cr3L Cross 3 Left thus: sl next 2 sts onto cable needle and leave at front of work, P1, then K2tbl from cable needle
Cr3F Cross 3 Front thus: sl next 2 sts onto cable needle and leave at front of work, K1, then K2tbl from cable needle

BACK

Using 2¾mm (US2) needles cast on 147[155:163] sts.

Anna is wearing a version of 'Eton College' that has been knitted in a flattering soft shade of pinky-beige. Vertical lines of cables divide the front of the sweater into panels with a diamond lattice design at the centre front and zig-zag stitchwork et either side.

Row 1 K3, * P1, (K1tbl, P1) twice, K3, rep from * to end.
Row 2 P3, * K1, (P1tbl, K1) twice, P3, rep from * to end.
Rows 3-6 Rep rows 1 and 2 twice.
Row 7 K3, * P1, C3R, P1, K3, rep from * to end.
Row 8 As row 2.
These 8 rows form the rib patt.

Rep them 3 times more, then work row 1 again.
Inc row Rib 11[14:18], * M1, rib 3, rep from * to last 10[15:19] sts, M1, rib to end. 190[198:206] sts.
Change to 3¼mm (US3) needles.
Cont in patt as folls:
Row 1 (RS) K1[5:9], P1, (K5, P1) twice, * K12, (P1, K1) 3 times, P2, (K5, P1) twice, rep from * once more, K2, P6, C4F, P10, C4F, P6, K2, ** (P1, K5) twice, P2, (K1, P1) 3 times, K12, rep from ** once more, (P1, K5) twice, P1, K1[5:9].
Row 2 K1[5:9], P1, (K1, P4) twice, K1, * P12, (K1, P1) 3 times, K1, P2, (K1, P4) twice, K1, rep from * once more, P3, K6, P4, K10, P4, K6, P3, ** K1, (P4, K1) twice, P2, K1, (P1, K1) 3 times, P12, rep from ** once more, K1, (P4, K1) twice, P1 K1[5:9].
Row 3 K1[5:9], P1, K1, C4R, P1, C4R, K1, P1, * K10, P1, (K1, P1) 3 times, K2, P1, K1, C4R, P1, C4R, K1, P1, rep from * once more, K2, P5, Cr3R, Cr3F, P8, Cr3R, Cr3F, P5, K2, ** P1, K1, C4L, P1, C4L, K1, P1, K2, P1, (K1, P1) 3 times, K10, rep from ** once more, P1, K1, C4L, P1, C4L, K1, P1, K to end.
Row 4 P2[6:10], K1, (P4, K1) twice, * P10, K1, (P1, K1) 3 times, (P4, K1) 3 times, rep from * once more, P3, K5, P3, K1, P2, K8, P3, K1, P2, K5, P3, ** (K1, P4) 3 times, K1, (P1, K1) 3 times, P10, rep from ** once more, K1, (P4, K1) twice, P to end.
Row 5 K1[5:9], P1, (K5, P1) twice, * K8, P1, (K1, P1) 3 times, K4, P1, (K5, P1) twice, rep from * once more, K2, P4, Cr3R, K1, P1, Cr3F, P6, Cr3R, K1, P1, Cr3F, P4, K2, ** P1, (K5, P1) twice, K4, P1, (K1, P1) 3 times, K8, rep from ** once more, P1, (K5, P1) twice, K to end.
Row 6 P2[6:10], K1, (P4, K1) twice, * P8, K1, (P1, K1) 3 times, P6, K1, (P4, K1) twice, rep from * once more, P3, K4, P3, K1, P1, K1, P2, K6, P3, K1, P1, K1, P2, K4, P3, ** K1, (P4, K1) twice, P6, K1, (P1, K1) 3 times, P8, rep from ** once more, K1, (P4, K1) twice, P to end.
Row 7 K1[5:9], P1, (K5, P1) twice, * K6, P1, (K1, P1) 3 times, K6, P1, (K5, P1) twice, rep from * once more, K2, P3, Cr3R, (K1, P1) twice, Cr3F, P4, Cr3R, (K1, P1) twice, Cr3F, P3, K2, ** P1, (K5, P1) twice, K6, P1, (K1, P1)

3 times, K6, rep from ** once more, P1, (K5, P1) twice, K to end.

Row 8 K1[5:9], P1, K1, (P4, K1) twice, * P6, K1, (P1, K1) 3 times, P8, K1, (P4, K1) twice, rep from * once more, P3, K3, P3, K1, (P1, K1) twice, P2, K4, P3, K1, (P1, K1) twice, P2, K3, P3, ** K1, (P4, K1) twice, P8, K1, (P1, K1) 3 times, P6, rep from ** once more, K1, (P4, K1) twice, P1, K to end.

Row 9 K1[5:9], P1, K1, C4R, P1, C4R, K1, P1, * K4, P1, (K1, P1) 3 times, K8, P1, K1, C4R, P1, C4R, K1, P1, rep from * once more, K2, P2, Cr3R, (K1, P1) 3 times, Cr3F, P2, Cr3R, (K1, P1) 3 times, Cr3F, P2, K2, ** P1, K1, C4L, P1, C4L, K1, P1, K8, P1, (K1, P1) 3 times, K4, rep from ** once more, P1, K1, C4L, P1, C4L, K1, P1, K to end.

Row 10 P2[6:10], K1, (P4, K1) twice, * P4, K1, (P1, K1) 3 times, P10, K1, (P4, K1) twice, rep from * once more, P3, K2, P3, K1, (P1, K1) 3 times, P2, K2, P3, K1, (P1, K1) 3 times, P2, K2, P3, ** K1, (P4, K1) twice, P10, K1, (P1, K1) 3 times, P4, rep from ** once more, K1, (P4, K1) twice, P to end.

Row 11 K1[5:9], P1, (K5, P1) twice, * K2, P1, (K1, P1) 3 times, K10, P1, (K5, P1) twice, rep from * once more, K2, P1, Cr3R, (K1, P1) 4 times, Cr3F, Cr3R, (K1, P1) 4 times, Cr3F, P1, K2, ** P1, (K5, P1) twice, K10, P1, (K1, P1) 3 times, K2, rep from ** once more, P1, (K5, P1) twice, K to end.

Row 12 P2[6:10], K1, (P4, K1) twice, * P2, K1, (P1, K1) 3 times, P12, K1, (P4, K1) twice,

rep from * once more, (P3, K1) twice, (P1, K1) 4 times, P5, K1, (P1, K1) 4 times, P2, K1, P3, ** K1, (P4, K1) twice, P12, K1, (P1, K1) 3 times, P2, rep from ** once more, K1, (P4, K1) twice, P to end.

Row 13 K1[5:9], (P1, K5) twice, * P2, (K1, P1) 3 times, K12, (P1, K5) twice, rep from * once more, P1, K2, P1, K3, P1, (K1, P1) 4 times, C4F, (K1, P1) 5 times, (K2, P1) twice, ** (K5, P1) twice, K12, (P1, K1) 3 times, P2, rep from ** once more, (K5, P1) twice, K to end.

Row 14 K1[5:9], P1, K1, (P4, K1) twice, * P2, K1, (P1, K1) 3 times, P12, K1, (P4, K1) twice, rep from * once more, P3, K1, P2, K1, (P1, K1) 4 times, P5, K1, (P1, K1) 4 times, P3, K1, P3, ** K1, (P4, K1) twice, P12, K1, (P1, K1) 3 times, P2, rep from ** once more, K1, (P4, K1) twice, P1, K to end.

Row 15 K1[5:9], P1, K1, C4R, P1, C4R, K1, P1, * K2, P1, (K1, P1) 3 times, K10, P1, K1, C4R, P1, C4R, K1, P1, rep from * once more, K2, P1, Cr3L, (K1, P1) 4 times, Cr3R, Cr3L, (K1, P1) 4 times, Cr3R, P1, K2, ** P1, K1, C4L, P1, C4L, K1, P1, K10, P1, (K1, P1) 3 times, K2, rep from ** once more, P1, K1, C4L, P1, C4L, K1, P1, K to end.

Row 16 P2[6:10], K1, (P4, K1) twice, * P4, K1, (P1, K1) 3 times, P10, K1, (P4, K1) twice, rep from * once more, P3, K2, P2, K1, (P1, K1) 3 times, P3, K2, P2, K1, (P1, K1) 3 times, P3, K2, P3, ** K1, (P4, K1) twice, P10, K1, (P1, K1) 3 times, P4, rep from ** once more, K1, (P4, K1) twice, P to end.

Row 17 K1[5:9], P1, (K5, P1) twice, * K4, P1, (K1, P1) 3 times, K8, P1, (K5, P1) twice, rep from * once more, K2, P2, Cr3L, (K1, P1) 3 times, Cr3L, P2, Cr3L, (K1, P1) 3 times, Cr3R, P2, K2, ** P1, (K5, P1) twice, K8, P1, (K1, P1) 3 times, K4, rep from ** once more, P1, (K5, P1) twice, K to end.

Row 18 P2[6:10], K1, (P4, K1) twice, * P6, K1, (P1, K1) 3 times, P8, K1, (P4, K1) twice, rep from * once more, P3, K3, P2, K1, (P1, K1) twice, P3, K4, P2, K1, (P1, K1) twice, P3, K3, P3, ** K1, (P4, K1) twice, P8, K1, (P1, K1) 3 times, P6, rep from ** once more, K1, (P4, K1) twice, P to end.

Row 19 K1[5:9], P1, (K5, P1) twice, * K6, P1, (K1, P1) 3 times, K6, P1, (K5, P1) twice, rep from * once more, K2, P3, Cr3L, (K1, P1) twice, Cr3R, P4, Cr3L, (K1, P1) twice, Cr3R, P3, K2, ** P1, (K5, P1) twice, K6, P1, (K1, P1) 3 times, K6, rep from ** once more, P1, (K5, P1) twice, K to end.

Row 20 K1[5:9], P1, K1, (P4, K1) twice, * P8, K1, (P1, K1) 3 times, P6, K1, (P4, K1) twice, rep from * once more, P3, K4, P2, K1, P1, K1, P3, K6, P2, K1, P1, K1, P3, K4, P3, ** K1, (P4, K1) twice, P6, K1, (P1, K1) 3 times, P8, rep from ** once more, K1, (P4, K1) twice, P1, K to end.

Row 21 K1[5:9], P1, K1, C4R, P1, C4R, K1, P1, * K8, P1, (K1, P1) 3 times, K4, P1, K1, C4R, P1, C4R, K1, P1, rep from * once more, K2, P4, Cr3L, K1, P1, Cr3R, P6, Cr3L, K1, P1, Cr3R, P4, K2, ** P1, K1, C4L, P1, C4L, K1, P1, K4, P1, (K1, P1) 3 times, K8, rep from ** once, P1, K1, C4L, P1, C4L, K1, P1, K to end.

Row 22 P2[6:10], K1, (P4, K1) twice, * P10, K1, (P1, K1) 3 times, (P4, K1) 3 times, rep from * once more, P3, K5, P2, K1, P3, K8, P2, K1, P3, K5, P3, ** (K1, P4) 3 times, K1, (P1, K1) 3 times, P10, rep from ** once more, K1, (P4, K1) twice, P to end.

Row 23 K1[5:9], P1, (K5, P1) twice, * K10, P1, (K1, P1) 3 times, K2, P1, (K5, P1) twice, rep from * once more, K2, P5, Cr3L, Cr3R, P8, Cr3L, Cr3R, P5, K2, ** P1, (K5, P1) twice, K2, P1, (K1, P1) 3 times, K10, rep from ** once more, P1, (K5, P1) twice, K to end.

Row 24 P2[6:10], K1, (P4, K1) twice, * P12, K1, (P1, K1) 3 times, P2, K1, (P4, K1) twice, rep from * once more, P3, K6, P4, K10, P4, K6, P3, ** K1, (P4, K1) twice, P2, K1, (P1, K1) 3 times, P12, rep from ** once more, K1, (P4, K1) twice, P to end.

These 24 rows form the patt.
Cont in patt until back measures 39[41.5:44]cm (15½[16¼:17½]in) from cast-on edge, ending with a WS row.

Shape armholes
Cast off 8 sts at beg of next 2 rows.
174[182:190] sts.
Work straight until armholes measure 25.5cm (10in) from beg of shaping, ending with a WS row.

Shape shoulders and back neck
Cast off 19[20:20] sts at beg of next 2 rows.
Next row Cast off 19[20:21] sts, patt until there are 24[24:25] sts on right-hand needle, turn and complete this side first.
Next row Cast off 4 sts, patt to end.
Cast off rem 20[20:21] sts.
With RS of work facing, rejoin yarn to next st and cast off centre 50[54:58] sts, patt to end.
43[44:46] sts.
Next row Cast off 19[20:21] sts, patt to end.
Next row Cast off 4 sts, patt to end.
Cast off rem 20[20:21] sts.

FRONT
Work as given for back until armholes measure 19.5[18.5:17.5]cm (7¾[7¼:6¾]in) from beg of shaping, ending with a WS row.

Shape neck
Next row Patt 78[80:84] sts, turn and leave rem sts on a spare needle.
Cont on these sts for first side of neck.
Cast off 4 sts at beg of next and foll alt row, then dec one st at neck edge on next 11[9:9] rows. Now dec one st at same edge on every foll alt row until 58[60:62] sts rem.
Work straight until front measures the same length as back up to beg of shoulder shaping, ending at armhole edge.

The same sweater, 'Eton College', is shown in a different colour and scene. Here Anna looks elegantly sophisticated in cream. The long line of the sweater teams well with the shorter-length pleated skirt.

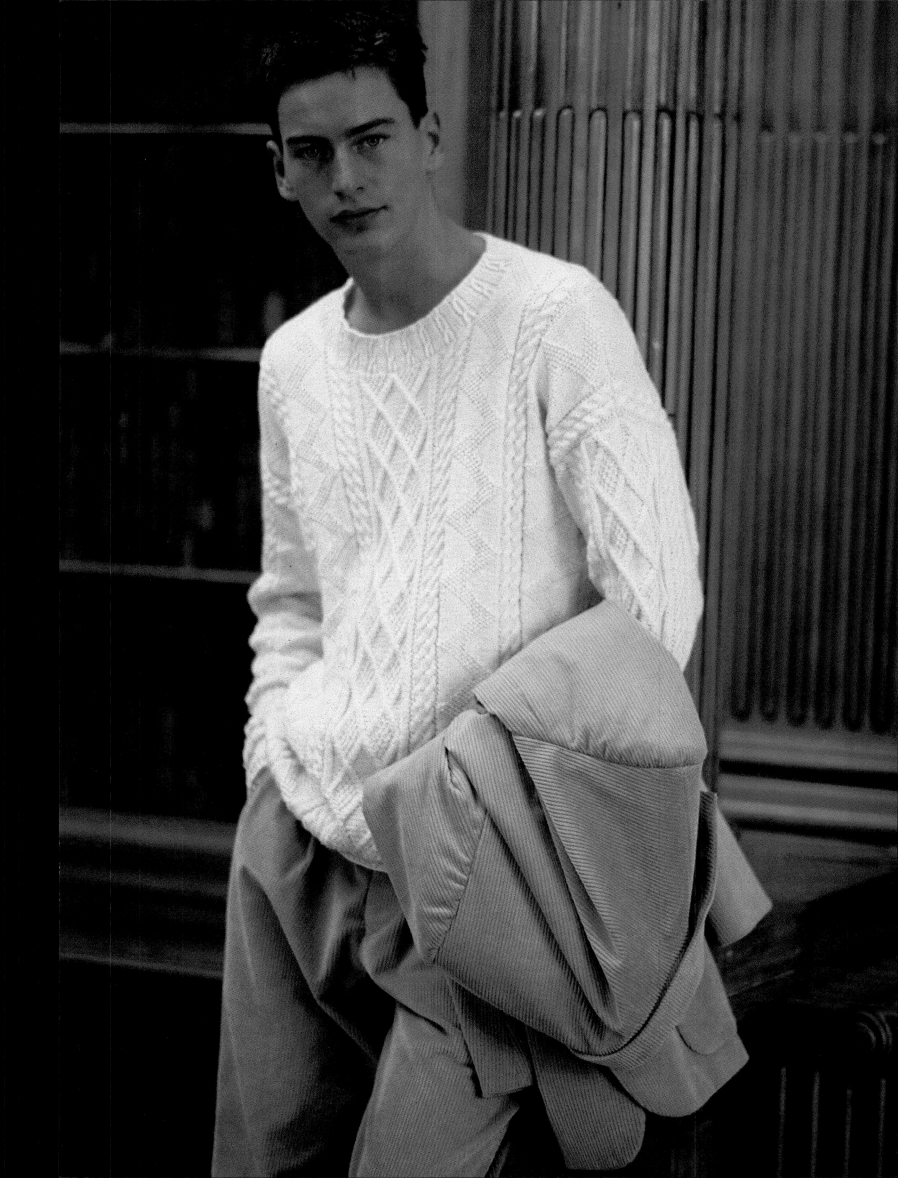

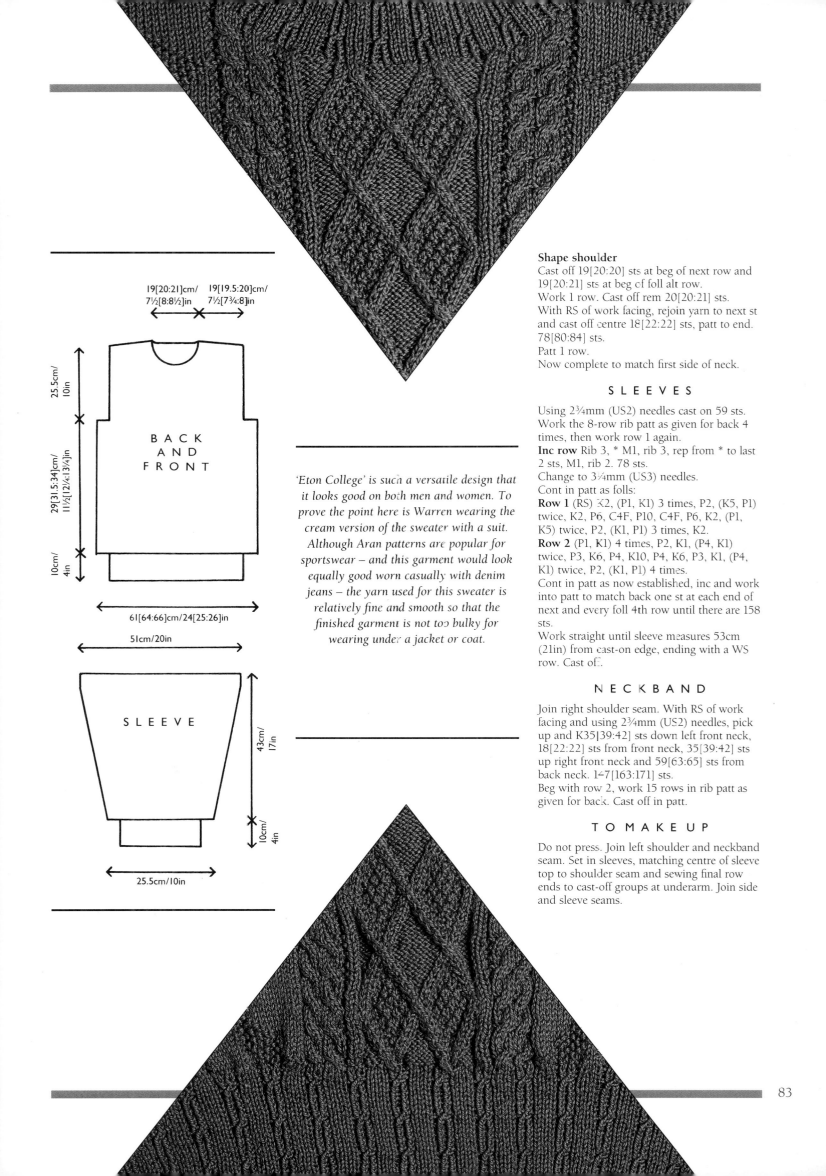

19[20:21]cm/ **19[19.5:20]cm/**
7½[8:8½]in **7½[7¾:8]in**

25.5cm/
10in

BACK AND FRONT

29[31.5:34]cm/
11½[12¼:13¾]in

10cm/
4in

61[64:66]cm/24[25:26]in

51cm/20in

SLEEVE

43cm/
17in

10cm/
4in

25.5cm/10in

'Eton College' is such a versatile design that it looks good on both men and women. To prove the point here is Warren wearing the cream version of the sweater with a suit. Although Aran patterns are popular for sportswear – and this garment would look equally good worn casually with denim jeans – the yarn used for this sweater is relatively fine and smooth so that the finished garment is not too bulky for wearing under a jacket or coat.

Shape shoulder

Cast off 19[20:20] sts at beg of next row and 19[20:21] sts at beg of foll alt row.
Work 1 row. Cast off rem 20[20:21] sts.
With RS of work facing, rejoin yarn to next st and cast off centre 18[22:22] sts, patt to end. 78[80:84] sts.
Patt 1 row.
Now complete to match first side of neck.

SLEEVES

Using 2¾mm (US2) needles cast on 59 sts.
Work the 8-row rib patt as given for back 4 times, then work row 1 again.
Inc row Rib 3, * M1, rib 3, rep from * to last 2 sts, M1, rib 2. 78 sts.
Change to 3¼mm (US3) needles.
Cont in patt as folls:
Row 1 (RS) K2, (P1, K1) 3 times, P2, (K5, P1) twice, K2, P6, C4F, P10, C4F, P6, K2, (P1, K5) twice, P2, (K1, P1) 3 times, K2.
Row 2 (P1, K1) 4 times, P2, K1, (P4, K1) twice, P3, K6, P4, K10, P4, K6, P3, K1, (P4, K1) twice, P2, (K1, P1) 4 times.
Cont in patt as now established, inc and work into patt to match back one st at each end of next and every foll 4th row until there are 158 sts.
Work straight until sleeve measures 53cm (21in) from cast-on edge, ending with a WS row. Cast off.

NECKBAND

Join right shoulder seam. With RS of work facing and using 2¾mm (US2) needles, pick up and K35[39:42] sts down left front neck, 18[22:22] sts from front neck, 35[39:42] sts up right front neck and 59[63:65] sts from back neck. 147[163:171] sts.
Beg with row 2, work 15 rows in rib patt as given for back. Cast off in patt.

TO MAKE UP

Do not press. Join left shoulder and neckband seam. Set in sleeves, matching centre of sleeve top to shoulder seam and sewing final row ends to cast-off groups at underarm. Join side and sleeve seams.

CHAMPAGNE & PEARLS

I remember having great fun making the originals of these beaded flowers as part of a machine-knitting project that I worked on at Brighton Polytechnic. This time I have appliquéd the flowers on to the neckline and shoulders of a long-line fitted cardigan. It is easy to make extra flowers or arrange them to suit yourself. I have purposely kept the colours pale and neutral throughout for a soft, elegant look.

SIZES

To fit 81[86:91]cm (32[34:36]in) bust
Actual size 86[91:97]cm (34[36:38]in)
Length to shoulder 61[63:66]cm (24[24¾:26]in)
Sleeve seam 47cm (18½in)
Figures in square brackets [ ] refer to larger sizes; where there is only one set of figures, it applies to all sizes.

MATERIALS

23[24:24]×20g balls of Rowan Edina Ronay Silk and Wool (Camel 851)
Pair each of 2¼mm (US1) and 3mm (US3) knitting needles
8 small buttons
Approximately 460 small beads for the flowers

TENSION

28 sts and 36 rows to 10cm (4in) over st st using 3mm (US3) needles

BACK

Using 2¼mm (US1) needles cast on 120[128:136] sts.
Beg with a K row, work 13 rows st st, so ending with a K row.
Next row K to end to form hemline.
Change to 3mm (US3) needles.
Beg with a K row, work 10[14:20] rows st st, so ending with a P row.
1st dec row K30[32:34], K3togtbl, K54[58:62], K3tog, K30[32:34].
Work 9 rows st st.
2nd dec row K29[31:33], K3togtbl, K52[56:60], K3tog, K29[31:32].
Work 9 rows st st.
3rd dec row K28[30:32], K3togtbl, K50[54:58], K3tog, K28[30:32].
Work 9 rows st st.
4th dec row K27[29:31], K3togtbl, K48[52:56], K3tog, K27[29:31].
Work 9 rows st st.
5th dec row K26[28:30], K3togtbl, K46[50:54], K3tog, K26[28:30].
Work 9 rows st st.
6th dec row K25[27:29], K3togtbl, K44[48:52], K3tog, K25[27:29].
Work 9 rows st st.
7th dec row K24[26:28], K3togtbl,

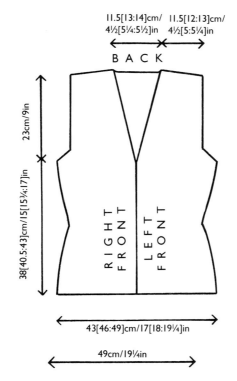

11.5[13:14]cm/ 4½[5¼:5½]in   11.5[12:13]cm/ 4½[5:5¼]in

BACK

23cm/9in

38[40.5:43]cm/15[15¾:17]in

RIGHT FRONT   LEFT FRONT

43[46:49]cm/17[18:19¼]in

49cm/19¼in

SLEEVE

47cm/18½in

20.5cm/8in

The knitted flowers appliquéd to the neck and shoulders of this cardigan make a stunning feature. The flowers are easy to make in stocking stitch with beads adding extra sparkle.

K42[46:50], K3tog, K24[26:28]. 92[100:108] sts.
Work 12 rows st st, so ending with a K row.
Place markers for increase as folls:
Next row P25[27:29], place a loop of contrasting yarn onto right-hand needle to form marker, P43[47:51], place a loop of contrasting yarn on right-hand needle, P24[26:28].
Inc row K to marker, M1, sl marker, K1, M1, K to next marker, M1, sl marker, K1, M1, K to end. (4 sts increased)
Slipping marker on every row, work 7 rows st st.
Rep last 8 rows 5 times more, then work the inc row again. 120[128:136] sts.
Remove markers.
Work 5[9:13] rows st st, so ending with a P row.

Shape armholes

Next row K3, K3togtbl, K to last 6 sts, K3tog, K3.
Next row P.
Rep last 2 rows 5 times more. 96[104:112] sts.
Work straight until armholes measure 23cm (9in) from beg of shaping, ending with a P row.

Shape shoulders and back neck

Cast off 10[10:12] sts at beg of next 2 rows.
Next row Cast off 11[12:12] sts, K until there are 15[16:16] sts on right-hand needle, turn and complete this side first.
Next row Cast off 4 sts, P to end.
Cast off rem 11[12:12] sts.
With RS of work facing, rejoin yarn to next st, cast off centre 24[28:32] sts, K to end.
Next row Cast off 11[12:12] sts, P to end.
Next row Cast off 4 sts, K to end.
Cast off rem 11[12:12] sts.

LEFT FRONT

* Using 3mm (US3) needles cast on 24 sts. Cut off yarn and leave aside for front band.
Using 2¼mm (US1) needles cast on 54[58:62] sts.
Beg with a K row, work 13 rows st st, so ending with a K row.
Next row K to end to form hemline. *
Change to 3mm (US3) needles.
K 1 row, then onto same needle work across

the 24 sts of front band thus: P1, K11, sl1 P-wise, K11. 78[82:86] sts.
Next row P23, K1, P to end.
Next row K54[58:62], P1, K11, sl1 P-wise, K11.
Cont to work front band as now set, work 7[11:17] more rows, so ending with a WS row.
1st dec row K30[32:34], K3togtbl, work to end.
Work 9 rows st st.
2nd dec row K29[31:33], K3togtbl, work to end.
Work 9 rows st st.
3rd dec row K28[30:32], K3togtbl, work to end.
Work 9 rows.
4th dec row K27[29:31], K3togtbl, work to end.
Work 9 rows.
5th dec row K26[28:30], K3togtbl, work to end.
Work 9 rows.
6th dec row K25[27:29], K3togtbl, work to end.
Work 9 rows.
7th dec row K24[26:28], K3togtbl, work to end. 64[68:72] sts.
Work 12 rows, so ending with a RS row.
Place marker for increases as folls:
Next row Work to last 24[26:28] sts, place marker on right-hand needle, P to end.
Inc row K to marker, M1, sl marker, K1, M1, work to end. (2 sts increased)
Slipping the marker on every row, work 7 rows.
Rep last 8 rows 5 times more, then work the inc row again. 78[82:86] sts.
Remove markers.
Work 5[9:13] rows, so ending with a WS row.
Shape armhole and front neck
Next row K3, K3togtbl, K46[50:54], K2togtbl, work to end.
Next row Work to end.
Cont to dec 2 sts at armhole edge on next and foll 4 alt rows as now set, dec one st within the 24-st front band on the 5th row. 64[68:72] sts.
Work 1 row.

Keeping armhole edge straight, cont to dec one st within the 24-st front band on next and every foll 8th[6th:6th] row until 56[58:65] sts rem.
3rd size only
Dec one st within the 24-st front band on every foll 4th row until 60 sts rem.
All sizes
Work straight until front measures the same as back up to beg of shoulder shaping, ending at armhole edge.

Shape shoulder
Cast off 10[10:12] sts at beg of next row and 11[12:12] sts at beg of foll 2 alt rows.
Cont on rem 24 sts until band fits across back neck ending at centre back. Cast off.
Mark position of 8 buttonholes with pins as folls: the first to come 3 rows from cast-on edge of band, the last to come just below beg of neck shaping with the others evenly spaced between.

RIGHT FRONT

Work as given for left front from * to *.
Change to 3mm (US3) needles and work across the 24 sts of front band thus: K11, sl1 P-wise, K11, P1, then onto same needle K across sts of right front. 78[82:86] sts.
Next row P54[58:62], K1, P23.
Buttonhole row 1 K5, cast off 2, K until there are 4 sts on right-hand needle after cast off group, sl1 P-wise, K4, cast off 2 sts, K until there are 5 sts on right-hand needle after cast off group, P1, K to end.
Buttonhole row 2 Work to end casting on 2 sts over each buttonhole on previous row.
Cont to work front band and buttonholes to correspond with markers as now set, work 6[10:16] rows, so ending with a WS row.
1st dec row Work 45[47:49], K3tog, K to end.
Work 9 rows.
Working decreasings as now set, work to match left front until the 7th dec row has been completed. 64[68:72] sts.
Work 12 rows, so ending with a RS row.
Place marker for increases as folls:
Next row P25[27:29], place marker on right-

hand needle, work to end.
Inc row Work to marker, M1, sl marker, K1, M1, K to end. (2 sts increased)
Slipping the marker on every row, work 7 rows.
Now work as given for left front up to beg of armhole and neck shaping, ending with a WS row.

Shape armhole and neck
Next row Work 24, K2tog, K to last 6 sts, K3tog, K3.
Next row Work to end.
Now complete to match left front.

SLEEVES

Using 2¼mm (US1) needles cast on 58 sts.
Beg with a K row, work 13 rows st st, so ending with a K row.
Next row K to end to form hemline.
Change to 3mm (US3) needles.
Beg with a K row, work 2 rows st st.
Inc row K3, M1, K to last 3 sts, M1, K3.
Cont to inc in this way on every foll 4th row until there are 136 sts.
Work straight until sleeve measures 47cm (18½in) from hemline, ending with a P row.

Shape top
Next row K3, K3togtbl, K to last 6 sts, K3tog, K3.
Next row P.
Rep these 2 rows 5 times more. 112 sts.
Cast off loosely.

TO MAKE UP

Press lightly on WS using a warm iron over a damp cloth. Join shoulder seams. Join centre back neck band seam, then sew in place. Fold band in half to WS and slip stitch in position. Set in sleeves, then join side and sleeve seams. Fold hems to WS and slip stitch in position. Neaten lower edge of front bands. Sew on buttons.

A Flower
Petal Thread 10 beads onto yarn and using

3mm (US3) needles cast on 1 st.
Next row All into st work (K1, P1 and K1).
P 1 row.
Next row K1, bring yarn forward to RS of work, slide a bead down the yarn close to the last stitch worked, slip the next stitch purlwise from left-hand needle, pass the bead in front of the slipped stitch tightly, then take yarn to back of work, K1.
Beg with 4th row, foll Chart 1, shaping sides and positioning beads as shown until the 24 rows have been completed. 11 sts.
Cut off yarn leaving a long end, thread end through rem sts.

CHART I

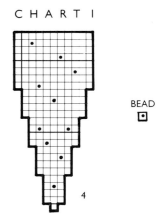

BEAD

4

Make 4 more petals in the same way.
Centre Thread 7 beads onto yarn and using 3mm (US3) needles cast on 25 sts.
Work 3 rows st st, positioning beads as shown on Chart 2. Cast off.

CHART 2

To form the flower coil centre strip and sew edges together. Using the long end, gather the 11 sts of one petal together, then sew to centre. Sew remaining 4 petals to centre in the same way.
Make 7 more flowers.
Position and overlap 4 flowers on each shoulder and down fronts, then sew centres and points of petals carefully in place.

The 'Champagne and Pearls' cardigan is a couture garment. Knitted in a luxurious mixture of silk and wool it has such stylish details – including shaped darts and hemmed borders – that are seldom found in hand-knits.

I love the elegance of formal evening dress. Here I have taken tips from the men for a dress shirt with a feminine bias. The plain stocking stitch fabric looks and feels extra smooth as it is knitted in a special blend of silk and wool. I have used pockets and double cuffs with gilt cuff links as small, but important details.

POLO LOUNGE

SIZES

To fit 81[86:91]cm (32[34:36]in) bust
Actual size 86[91:97]cm (34[36:38]in)
Length to shoulder 46[48.5:51]cm (18[19¼:20]in)
Sleeve seam (excluding cuff) 43cm (17in)
Figures in square brackets [ ] refer to larger sizes; where there is only one set of figures, it applies to all sizes

MATERIALS

17[18:19] × 20g balls of Rowan Edina Ronay Silk and Wool (Ecru 857)
Pair each of 2¼mm (US1) and 3mm (US3) knitting needles
8 small buttons
A pair of cuff links

TENSION

28 sts and 36 rows to 10cm (4in) over st st using 3mm (US3) needles

BACK

Using 2¼mm (US1) needles cast on 100[108:116] sts.
Beg with a K row, work 9 rows st st, so ending with a K row.
Next row K to end to form hemline.
Change to 3¼mm (US3) needles.
Beg with a K row, work 6[8:10] rows st st, so ending with a P row.
1st dec row K27[29:31], K3togtbl, K40[44:48], K3tog, K27[29:31].
Work 5[7:5] rows st st.
2nd dec row K26[28:30], K3togtbl, K38[42:46], K3tog, K26[28:30].
Work 5[7:5] rows st st.
3rd dec row K25[27:29], K3togtbl, K36[40:44], K3tog, K25[27:29].
Work 4[6:5] rows st st.
3rd size only
4th dec row K28, K3togtbl, K42, K3tog, K28.
Work 6 rows st st.

Dressed for a special occasion, Elisabeth wears this fitted button-through shirt with gilt button trimmings. The slight texture of the moss stitch collar, front bands and double cuffs emphasizes the smoothness and simplicity of the stocking stitch fabric.

All sizes
88[96:100] sts.
Place markers for increases as folls:
Next row P26[28:29], place a loop of contrasting yarn on right-hand needle to form marker, P37[41:43], place a loop of contrasting yarn on right-hand needle, P25[27:28].
Inc row K to marker, M1, sl marker, K1, M1, K to next marker, M1, sl marker, K1, M1, K to end. (4 sts increased.)
Work 7 rows st st.
Rep last 8 rows 6[6:7] times more, then work the inc row again. 120[128:136] sts.
Remove markers.
Work 1[3:1] rows st st.

Shape armholes
Cast off 2 sts at beg of next 2 rows.
Next row K3, K3togtbl, K to last 6 sts, K3tog, K3.
Next row P.
Rep last 2 rows 3 times more.
100[108:116] sts.
Cont without shaping until armholes measure 23cm (9in) from beg of shaping, ending with a P row.

Shape shoulders and back neck
Cast off 11[11:12] sts at beg of next 2 rows.
Next row Cast off 11[12:12] sts, K until there 16[17:18] sts on right-hand needle, turn and complete this side first.
Next row Cast off 4 sts, P to end.
Cast off rem 12[13:14] sts.
With RS of work facing, rejoin yarn to next st, cast off centre 24[28:32] sts, then K to end.
Next row Cast off 11[12:12] sts, P to end.
Next row Cast off 4 sts, K to end.
Cast off rem 12[13:14] sts.

LEFT FRONT

* Using 2¼mm (US1) needles cast on 50[54:58] sts.
Beg with a K row, work 9 rows st st, so ending with a K row.
Next row K to end to form hemline. *
Change to 3mm (US3) needles.
Beg with a K row, work 6[8:10] rows st st.
1st dec row K27[29:31], K3togtbl, K20[22:24].
Work 5[7:5] rows st st.

2nd dec row K26[28:30], K3togtbl, K19[21:23].
Work 5[7:5] rows st st.
3rd dec row K25[27:29], K3togtbl, K18[20:22].
Work 4[6:5] rows st st.
3rd size only
4th dec row K28, K3togtbl, K21.
Work 6 rows st st.
All sizes
44[48:50] sts.
Place marker for increases as folls:
Next row P19[21:22], place marker on right-hand needle, P25[27:28].
Inc row K to marker, M1, sl marker, K1, M1, K to end. (2 sts increased.)
Work 7 rows st st.
Rep last 8 rows 6[6:7] times more, then work the inc row again. 60[64:68] sts.
Remove marker.
Work 1[3:1] rows (for right front work 2[4:2] rows), so ending at side edge.

Shape armhole
Cast off 2 sts at beg of next row.
Next row P.
Next row K3, K3togtbl, K to end.
Rep last 2 rows 3 times more.
50[54:58] sts.
Work 13[9:5] rows straight, so ending at armhole edge.

Place mock pocket
Next row K8[9:10], sl next 28[30:32] sts on a holder, turn and cast on 28[30:32] sts, turn and K to end.
Cont without shaping until armhole measures 17.5[16:15]cm (6¾[6¼:6]in) from beg of shaping, ending at front edge.

Shape neck
Cast off 4 sts at beg of next and foll alt row.
Dec one st at neck edge on next 6[6:7] rows, then on every foll alt row until 34[36:38] sts rem.
Cont without shaping until armhole measures the same as back armhole up to beg of shoulder shaping, ending at armhole edge.

Shape shoulder
Cast off 11[11:12] sts at beg of next row and 11[12:12] sts at beg of foll alt row.
Work 1 row.
Cast off rem 12[13:14] sts.

RIGHT FRONT

Work as given for left front from * to *.
Change to 3mm (US3) needles.
Beg with a K row, work 6[8:10] rows st st, so
ending with a P row.
1st dec row K20[22:24], K3tog, K27[29:31].
Work 5[7:5] rows st st.
Working decreasings as set, work to match
left front until the 3rd[3rd:4th] dec row has
been completed. 44[48:50] sts.
Work 4[6:6] rows.
Place marker for increases as folls:
Next row P26[28:29], place marker on right-
hand needle, P18[20:21].
Work as given for left front to armhole,
noting the bracketed exception.

Shape armhole

Cast off 2 sts at beg of next row.
Next row K to last 6 sts, K3tog, K3.
Next row P.
Rep last 2 rows 3 times more. 50[54:58] sts.
Work 14[10:6] rows, ending with a P row.

Place mock pocket

Next row K14[15:16], sl next 28[30:32] sts
on a holder, turn and cast on 28[30:32] sts,
turn and K to end.
Now complete to match left front.

SLEEVES

Using 3mm (US3) needles cast on 64 sts.
Beg with a K row, work 6 rows st st, so
ending with a P row.
Inc row K3, M1, K to last 3 sts, M1, K3.
Cont to inc in this way on every foll 4th row
until there are 136 sts. Cont without shaping
until sleeve measures 43cm (17in) from
cast-on edge, ending with a P row.

Shape top

Cast off 2 sts at beg of next 2 rows.
Next row K3, K3togtbl, K to last 6 sts, K3tog,
K3.
Next row P.
Rep these 2 rows 3 times more.
Cast off loosely.

CUFFS
(alike)

Using 2¼mm (US1) needles cast on 71 sts
and work in moss st as follows:
Patt row K1, (P1, K1) to end.
Rep this row 9 times more.
Buttonhole row 1 Patt 6, cast off 2, patt to
last 8 sts, cast off 2, patt to end.
Buttonhole row 2 Patt to end, casting on 2
sts at each cast-off group.
Work 40 rows moss st, then work the
buttonhole row again.
Work 10 rows moss st. Cast off.

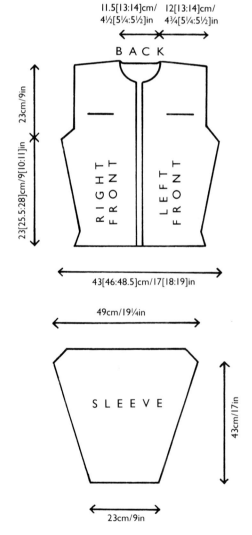

11.5[13:14]cm/
4½[5¼:5½]in

12[13:14]cm/
4¾[5¼:5½]in

BACK

23cm/9in

23[25.5:28]cm/9[10:11]in

RIGHT FRONT

LEFT FRONT

43[46:48.5]cm/17[18:19]in

49cm/19¼in

SLEEVE

43cm/17in

23cm/9in

*Looking very distinguished in cream and
black, Elisabeth (standing) in 'Polo Lounge'
and Anna (seated) in 'Glittering Prize'
(page 114) enjoy a few moments of quiet
reflection in the library.*

POCKET TOPS
(alike)

Using 2¼mm (US1) needles and with RS of
work facing, rejoin yarn to 28[30:32] pocket
sts on holder and moss st as folls:
Row 1 (K1, P1) to end.
Row 2 (P1, K1) to end.
Rep these 2 rows 3 times more. Cast off.

BUTTON BAND

Join shoulder seams. Using 2¼mm (US1)
needles cast on 7 sts.
Cont in moss st as given for cuffs until band,
slightly stretched, fits up left front from
hemline to beg of neck shaping, slip stitching
band in position as it is worked. Cast off.
Mark position of 6 buttonholes with pins as
folls: the first to come 1cm (½in) above lower
edge, the last to come 1cm (½in) below cast-
off edge with the others evenly spaced
between.

BUTTONHOLE BAND

Work as given for button band making
buttonholes at markers as follows:
Buttonhole row 1 (RS) Patt 2, cast off 2, patt
to end.
Buttonhole row 2 Patt to end, casting on 2
sts over those cast-off in previous row.
Slip stitch band in position.

COLLAR

Using 2¼mm (US1) needles cast on 111 sts
and work 2 rows moss st as given for cuffs.
Shape side edges thus:
Next row Patt 1, M1, patt to last st, M1, patt
1.
Patt 1 row.
Keeping patt correct, cont to inc one st at
each end within the edge st on next and every
foll alt row until there are 143 sts. Patt 1 row.
Cast off in patt.

TO MAKE UP

Press on WS using a warm iron over a damp
cloth. Set in sleeves, then join side and sleeve
seams. Fold hem to WS and slip stitch in
position.
Leaving 4cm (1½in) free from seam on back
of sleeve, begin sewing cuff to sleeve edge at
the 8th st of cuff and finishing at seam leaving
last 8 sts of cuff free. Fold back cuffs and
insert cuff links.
Sew cast-on edge of collar to neck, beginning
and ending at centre of front bands. Sew on
the buttons.
Sew cast-on edge of mock pocket to base of
moss st on WS, then sew down ends of
pocket tops on RS. Sew on button at centre of
each pocket. Press seams.

VELVET OPERA

The flowing pattern of leaves and flowers in a Turkish carpet inspired me to achieve the same effect in knitting. Keeping the colours true to the original – very rich, warm and close in tone – I have used chenille yarns against an Aran-weight background for a plush raised effect. Such a bold fabric needs to be used extravagantly. This dramatic evening coat displays it to perfection and makes a stunning cover-up for all your party wear.

SIZES

To fit 86/91[91/97:97/102]cm (34/36[36/38:38/40]in) bust
Actual size 158[162:167]cm (62[64:66]in)
Length to shoulder 91[94:96]cm (36[37:38]in)
Sleeve seam (excluding cuff) 40cm (15¾in)
Figures in square brackets [ ] refer to larger sizes; where there is only one set of figures, it applies to all sizes.

MATERIALS

44[45:45]×25g hanks of Rowan Lightweight DK in main shade A (brown 80) – used double throughout
5×100g hanks of Rowan Chunky Chenille in shade B (Wild Cherry 370)
1×100g hank of Chunky Chenille in shade C (Teak 351)
1×100g hank of Chunky Chenille in shade D (Chestnut 373)
1×100g hank of Chunky Chenille in shade E (Driftwod 352)
2×50g balls of Rowan Fine Cotton Chenille in shade F (Maple 396) – used double throughout
Pair each of 4mm (US6) and 5mm (US8) knitting needles

TENSION

18 sts and 23 rows to 10cm (4in) over patt using 5mm (US8) needles

NOTE

All yarns are used as a single strand throughout the design with the exceptions of Lightweight DK and Fine Cotton Chenille which are used double throughout

BACK

Using 4mm (US6) needles and A, cast on 106[110:114] sts.
Beg with a K row, work 12 rows st st, so ending with a P row.
Next row P to end to form hemline.
P 1 row.
Change to 5mm (US8) needles.
Beg with a K row, cont in st st and working from Chart, inc one st at each end of

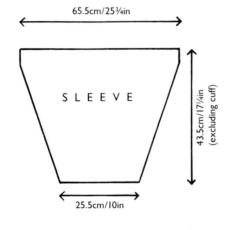

15.5cm/   23[24:25.5]cm/
6in   9[9½:10]in

BACK

33cm/13in

58[61:64]cm/23[24:25]in

RIGHT FRONT   LEFT FRONT

69[71:74]cm/27[28:29]in

65.5cm/25¾in

SLEEVE

43.5cm/17¼in (excluding cuff)

25.5cm/10in

Anna, generously wrapped in a fabulous knitted fabric, is on her way to a party. She makes a bold statement in this patterned coat with a shawl collar and double cuffs.

17th[21st:21st] row. Then inc one st at each end of every foll 12th row until there are 124[128:132] sts.
Work straight until row 134[140:146] has been completed.
Strand yarns loosely across back of work where appropriate or use small, separate balls of yarn for individual motifs. Link one shade to the next by twisting them around each other where they meet on the WS to avoid making gaps.

Shape armholes

Cast off 6 sts at beg of next 2 rows.
112[116:120] sts.
Work straight until row 210[216:222] has been completed.

Shape shoulders

Cast off 15[15:16] sts at beg of next 2 rows and 15[16:16] sts at beg of foll 2 rows. Cast off 12[13:14] sts at beg of next 2 rows. Cast off rem 28 sts.

LEFT FRONT

Using 4mm (US6) needles and A, cast on 71[73:75] sts.
Beg with a K row, work 12 rows st st, so ending with a P row.
Next row P to end to form hemline.
P 1 row.
Change to 5mm (US8) needles.
Beg with a K row, cont in st st and working from Chart, inc one st at beg (at end for right front) of 17th[21st:21st] row and on every foll 12th row until there are 80[82:84] sts.
Work 21[23:25] rows straight (work 22[24:26] rows straight for right front).
3rd size only
Shape front edge
Dec one st at end of next and foll alt row.
Work 1 row.
All sizes
Row 134[140:146] now completed (row 135[141:147] for right front).

Shape armhole and front edge
1st and 2nd sizes only
Cast off 6 sts at beg of next row.
Work 7[1] rows.
3rd size only
Cast off 6 sts, patt to last 2 sts, work 2tog.
Work 1 row.

CHART I

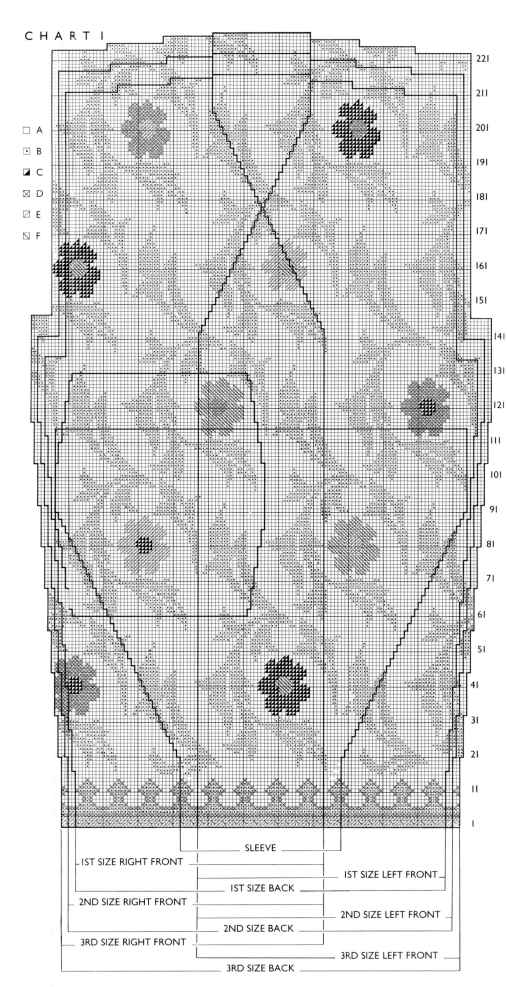

221
211
201
191
181
171
161
151
141
131
121
111
101
91
81
71
61
51
41
31
21
11
1

□ A
⊡ B
◪ C
⊠ D
▨ E
◩ F

— SLEEVE —

⌐ IST SIZE RIGHT FRONT ┐
| IST SIZE LEFT FRONT |
| IST SIZE BACK |
⌐ 2ND SIZE RIGHT FRONT ┐
| 2ND SIZE LEFT FRONT |
| 2ND SIZE BACK |
⌐ 3RD SIZE RIGHT FRONT ┐
| 3RD SIZE LEFT FRONT |
| 3RD SIZE BACK |

All sizes

Dec one st at front edge on next and every foll alt row until 42[44:46] sts rem. Work straight until row 210[216:222] has been completed (row 211[217:223] for right front).

Shape shoulder

Cast off 15[15:16] sts at beg of next row and 15[16:16] sts at beg of foll alt row. Work 1 row. Cast off rem 12[13:14] sts.

RIGHT FRONT

Work as given for Left Front noting the bracketed exceptions.

SLEEVES

Using 5mm (US8) needles and A, cast on 46 sts.
Beg with a K row, work 14 rows st st, so ending with a P row.
Beg with a K row and row 15 of Chart, cont in st st and patt, inc one st at each end of 7th and every foll alt row until there are 118 sts. Work straight until row 114 has been completed. Cast off.

COLLAR

(2 pieces alike)
Using 5mm (US8) needles and A, cast on 4 sts.
Using B to work leaf background design (omitting flower design), beg with a K row and row 61 of Chart, inc one st at each end of 3rd and every foll alt row until there are 74 sts. Work 39 rows straight, so ending with row 170.

CUFFS

Using 5mm (US8) needles and A, cast on 50 sts.
Beg with a K row and row 61 of Chart, inc one st at each end of 3rd and every foll 6th row until there are 60 sts.
Work straight until row 104 has been completed. Dec one st at each end of next and every foll 6th row until 50 sts rem. Work 1 row. Cast off.

LEFT FRONT FACING

With RS of work facing, A and 4mm (US6) needles, pick up and K106 sts from beg of front shaping down to hemline.
K 1 row to form hemline.
Beg with a K row, inc one st at beg of next and foll 4 alt rows. 111 sts.
Work 1 row. Cast off.

RIGHT FRONT FACING

With RS of work facing, A and 4mm (US6) needles, pick up and K106 sts from hemline up to beg of front shaping.
K 1 row to form hemline.
Beg with a K row, inc one st at end of next and foll 4 alt rows. 111 sts.
Work 1 row. Cast off.

TO MAKE UP

Press lightly on WS using a warm iron over a damp cloth. Join shoulder seams. Sew sleeve tops in position, matching centre of sleeve to

The party is over and Anna – still in her party clothes – relaxes. Underneath 'Velvet Opera' she is wearing a knitted dress – 'Bronze Belle' (page 117) – with a beaded bodice and in a subtle shade of purple to tone with the patterned coat.

shoulder seam and sewing final rows to cast-off sts at underarm. Join side and sleeve seams.
Join cast-off edges of collar together. Place seam at centre back neck and sew collar in place, beginning and ending at beg of front shaping. Fold collar in half to WS and slipstitch in position. Fold front facings to WS and slipstitch in position, sewing shaped edge to collar. Make hem at lower edge.
Fold the 14 rows in A to WS of sleeve and slipstitch in position. Sew side edges of cuff together, then sew cuff to lower edge of sleeve, fold cuff in half to WS and slipstitch in position. Double cuff back to RS and sew in place.

HAMPTON COURT

*Less formal and more fashionable than a cardigan, the bolero jacket – with
its curving fronts – is such a useful item of knitwear. I have several boleros
in my wardrobe; most are very plain, but the prettier ones with embroidery
or patterns are always admired.
Although the yarns are much finer, the flower pattern that I have used on the
fronts of this design is taken from the same source as 'Royal Peacock'. The
colours in the flowers have been linked into a small Fair Isle border around
the edges and cuffs of the bolero.*

SIZES

To fit 86[91:97]cm (34[36:38]in) bust
Length to shoulder 36.5[39:41]cm
(14¼(15½:16]in)
Sleeve seam 49cm (19¼in)
Figures in square brackets [ ] refer to larger
sizes; where there is only one set of figures, it
applies to all sizes

MATERIALS

14[14:15]×20g balls of Rowan Edina Ronay
Silk and Wool in main shade A
(Donkey 856)
1×25g hank of Rowan Botany in shade B
(dark brown 80)
1×25g hank of Botany in shade C (neptune
528)
2×10g hanks of Rowan Mulberry Silk in
shade D (Russet 874)
1×25g hank of Botany in shade E (airforce
65)
1×25g hank of Botany in shade F (purple
652)
1×25g hank of Botany in shade G (mauve
118)
1×20g ball of Silk and Wool in shade H
(Coral 855)
1×25g hank of Botany in shade J (rust 526)
Pair each of 2¼mm (US1) and 3mm (US3)
knitting needles
A 2¼mm (US1) circular needle

TENSION

28 sts and 36 rows to 10cm (4in) over st st
using 3mm (US3) needles

BACK

Using 3mm (US3) needles and A, cast on
108[114:120] sts.

---

*Team this long-sleeved bolero with a shirt
for extra warmth on cooler spring days. The
curved shape of the fronts is echoed in the
flower motifs that are boldly outlined in a
dark colour.*

Beg with a K row, cont in st st and patt from
Chart, inc one st at each end of 7th[7th:9th]
row and every foll 4th[6th:6th] row until
there are 118[126:136] sts. Now inc one st at
each end of every foll 6th[6th:8th] row until
there are 128[134:140] sts. Use separate, small
balls of yarn for each individual motif. Link
one strand to the next by twisting them
around each other where they meet
on the WS to avoid making gaps.
Work straight until row
60[68:76] has been
completed.

Shape armholes
Cast off 4 sts at beg of next 2 rows,
then dec one st at each end of every
row until 108[114:120] sts rem.
Work straight until row 132[140:148] has
been completed.

Shape shoulders
Cast off 12[13:13] sts at beg of next 2 rows,
12[13:14] sts at beg of foll 2 rows and
13[13:14] sts at beg of next 2 rows. Cast off
rem 34[36:38] sts.

LEFT FRONT

Using 3mm (US3) needles and A, cast on
24[27:30] sts.
Beg with a K row, cont in st st and patt from
Chart, work 1 row, so ending at front edge.

Shape front edge and side edge
Cast on 4 sts at beg of next and foll alt row
and 3 sts at beg of foll alt row. Inc one st at
front edge on next 10 rows and **at the same
time** inc one st at side edge on 1st[1st:3rd]
row and the 2[1:1] foll 4th[6th:6th] rows.
48[50:53] sts.
** Working 2[1:1] more increases at side edge
as before, inc one st at front edge on foll 3 alt
rows. 53[54:57] sts.
Cont to inc one st at side edge on every 6th
row, inc one st at front edge on foll 4th row,
then on foll 6th row. 56[58:60] sts (56[58:61]
sts for right front).
This completes the front shaping.

Cont to inc at side edge as before until there
are 60[63:64] sts.
3rd size only
Inc one st at side edge on 2 foll 8th rows.
66 sts.
All sizes
Work straight until row 60[68:76] (row
61[69:77] for right front) has been completed.

Shape armhole
Cast off 4 sts at beg of next row. Work 1 row.
Dec one st at armhole edge on every row until
50[53:56] sts rem.
Work 6[4:2] rows (5[3:1] rows for right front)
straight, so ending with row 74[80:86].

Shape neck
Dec one st at front edge on next and every
foll 4th row until 37[39:41] sts rem.

Work straight until row 132[140:148] (row 133[141:149] for right front) has been completed.

Shape shoulder

Cast off 12[13:13] sts at beg of next row and 12[13:14] sts at beg of foll alt row. Work 1 row. Cast off rem 13[13:14] sts.

RIGHT FRONT

Using 3mm (US3) needles and A, cast on 24[27:30] sts.
Beg with a K row, cont in st st and patt from Chart, work 2 rows, so ending at front edge.

Shape front edge and side edge

Cast on 4 sts at beg of next and foll alt row. Work 1 row.
Cast on 3 sts at beg of next row, then inc one st at front edge on foll 10 rows and **at the same time** inc one st at side edge on 1st[1st:3rd] row and the 2[1:1] foll 4th[6th:6th] rows. 48[50:53] sts.
Now complete as given for left front from ** to end, noting the bracketed exceptions.

SLEEVES

Using 2¼mm (US1) needles and A, cast on 49 sts.
Beg with a K row, work 9 rows st st, so ending with a K row.
Next row K to end to form hemline.
Change to 3mm (US3) needles.
K 1 row.
Cont in st st and Border patt as folls:
Row 1 P1B, * 2A, 3B, rep from * to last 3 sts, 2A, 1B.
Row 2 K1G, * 2B, 3G, rep from * to last 3 sts, 2B, 1G.
Row 3 As row 1.
Cont with A only, inc one st at each end of

next and every foll 4th row until there are 107 sts, then at each end of every foll 6th row until there are 119 sts.
Work straight until sleeve measures 49cm (19¼in) from hemline, ending with a P row.

Shape top

Cast off 4 sts at beg of next 2 rows, then dec one st at each end of every row until 99 sts rem. Cast off rem sts.

THE EDGING

Join shoulder and side seams. With RS of work facing, A and using the 2¼mm (US1) circular needle, join yarn to left side seam and pick up and K108[114:120] sts across lower edge of back, 134[138:141] sts round shaped front edge up to shoulder, 34[35:38] sts across back neck to next shoulder and 134[138:141] sts down shaped front edge to side seam. 410[425:440] sts.
Place a loop of contrasting yarn on right-hand needle to denote end of round.
Slipping the marker on every round, K 1 round.
Cont in Edging patt as folls:
Round 1 * K2A, 3B, rep from * to end.
Round 2 * K2B, 3G, rep from * to end.
Round 3 As round 1.
Cont with A only, K 1 round.
Next round P to end to form foldline.
K 6 more rounds. Cast off.

TO MAKE UP

Press lightly on WS of work using a warm iron over a damp cloth. Set in sleeves, matching centre of sleeve top to shoulder seams. Join sleeve seams. Fold hems and facing to WS and slipstitch in position. Press seams.

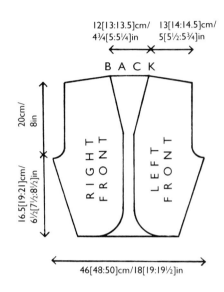

12[13:13.5]cm/
4¾[5:5¼]in   13[14:14.5]cm/
5[5½:5¾]in

BACK

20cm/
8in

16.5[19:21]cm/
6½[7½:8½]in

RIGHT FRONT   LEFT FRONT

46[48:50]cm/18[19:19½]in

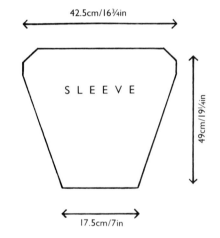

42.5cm/16¾in

SLEEVE

49cm/19¼in

17.5cm/7in

CHART I

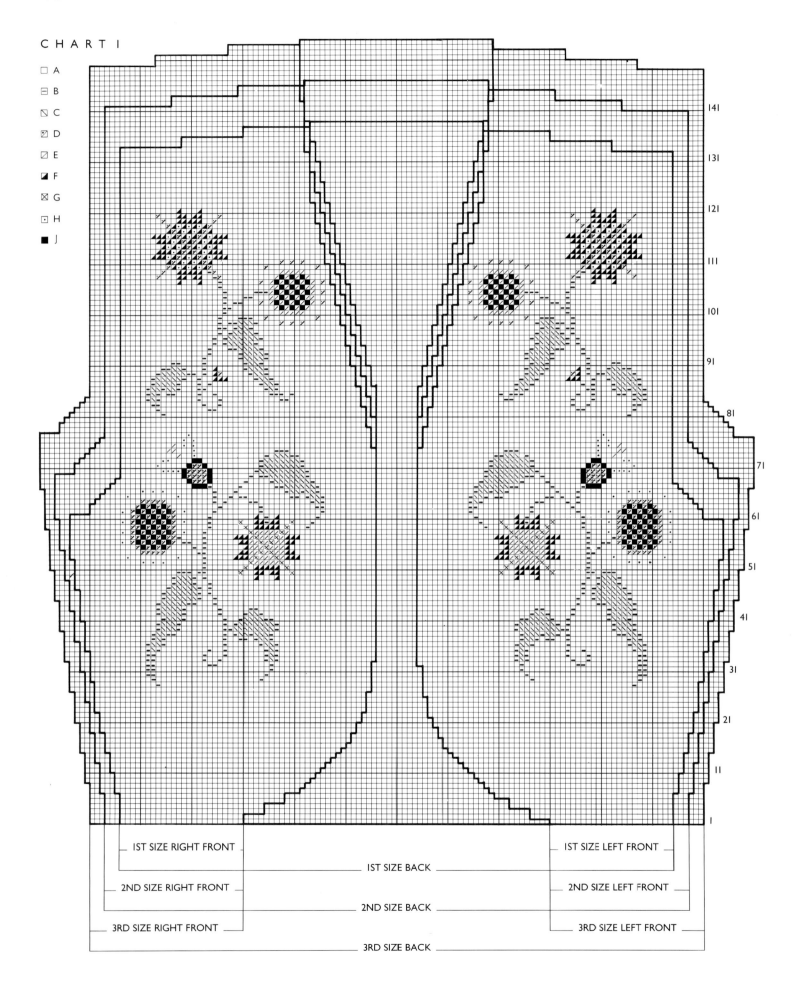

□ A
⊟ B
◨ C
☑ D
◪ E
◤ F
⊠ G
⊡ H
■ J

141
131
121
111
101
91
81
71
61
51
41
31
21
11
1

IST SIZE RIGHT FRONT

IST SIZE BACK

2ND SIZE RIGHT FRONT

2ND SIZE BACK

3RD SIZE RIGHT FRONT

3RD SIZE BACK

IST SIZE LEFT FRONT

2ND SIZE LEFT FRONT

3RD SIZE LEFT FRONT

GALA PERFORMANCE

I taught myself to crochet when I was experimenting with fabrics for evening wear. I soon realized that beautiful openwork patterns resembling lace can be crocheted quickly and simply.
Cotton is the traditional yarn for crochet work. Here I have used a soft cotton worked in a daisy pattern for a fitted evening top that fastens down the front with numerous dainty buttons.

SIZES

To fit 81/86cm (32/34in) bust
Actual size 93cm (36½in)
Length to centre back neck 61cm (24in)
Sleeve seam 41.5cm (16¼in)

MATERIALS

7×50g balls of Rowan Sea Breeze (559)
A 1.75mm (US5 steel) crochet hook
14 small buttons

TENSION

14 blks or sps and 14 rows to 10cm (4in) over patt using 1.75mm (US5 steel) crochet hook

BACK

Note that American crochet terms are in round brackets ( ).
Using 1.75mm (US5 steel) hook make 207ch.
Row 1 Follow row 1 of Chart 1 thus: 1tr (dc) into 9th ch from hook, (2ch, miss next 2 ch, 1tr (dc) into next ch so making 1 sp) 4 times, 1tr (dc) into each of next 3ch – 1 blk, * (2ch, miss next 2ch, 1tr (dc) into next ch so making 1 sp) 7 times, 1tr (dc) into each of next 3 ch – 1 blk, rep from * 6 times more, (2ch, miss next 2 ch, 1tr (dc) into next ch so making 1 sp) 5 times, turn. 59 sps and 8 blks.
Row 2 5ch to count as 1tr (dc) and 2ch, miss first sp, 1tr (dc) into next tr so making 1 sp over first sp, (2ch, miss next sp, 1tr (dc) into next tr (dc)) 3 times, 2tr (dc) into next sp, 1tr (dc) into next tr (dc) so making 1 blk over 1 sp, 2ch, miss next 2 tr (dc), 1tr (dc) into next tr (dc) so making 1 sp over 1 blk, 2tr (dc) into next sp, 1tr (dc) into next tr (dc) so making 1 blk over 1 sp, * work 5 sps over next 5 sps, 1 blk over next sp, 1 sp over next blk and 1 blk over next sp, rep from * 6 times more, 3 sps over next 3 sps, 2ch, 1tr (dc) into 3rd of the 8ch so making 1 sp over last sp, turn.
Row 3 * 3 sps, 1 blk, 5ch, miss 1 blk, 1tr tr (d tr) into next sp, 5ch, miss next blk, 1 blk, rep from * 7 times more, 3 sps, turn.
Row 4 2 sps, * 1 blk, 4ch, miss 1 blk and next 4ch, 1dc (sc) into next ch, 1dc (sc) into tr tr (d tr), 1dc (sc) into next ch, 4ch, miss next 4 ch and 1 blk, 1 blk, 1 sp, rep from * 7 times more, 1 sp, turn.
Row 5 1 sp, 1 blk, * 6ch, miss 1 blk and next

To compliment the pretty lacy fabric the outer edges of this jacket are finished with a crochet border trimmed with picots. The buttons are fastened through loops in the edging.

3ch, 1dc (sc) into next ch, 1dc (sc) into each of next 3dc (sc), 1dc (sc) into next ch, 6ch, miss next 3ch and 1 blk, 1blk, rep from * 7 times more, 1 sp, turn.
Row 6 2 sps, * 1tr (dc) into each of next 3ch, 7ch, miss next 3ch and 1dc (sc), 1dc (sc) into each of next 3dc (sc), 7ch, miss next dc (sc) and 3ch, 1tr (dc) into each of next 3ch and 1tr (dc), 1 sp, rep from * 7 times more, 1 sp, turn.
Row 7 3 sps, 1tr into each of next 3ch, 4ch, miss next 4ch and 1dc (sc), 1tr tr (d tr) into next dc (sc), 4ch, miss next dc (sc) and 4ch, 1 tr (dc) into each of next 3ch and 1tr (dc), * 5ch, 1tr tr (d tr) into next sp, 5ch, miss next 3tr (dc), 1tr (dc) into each of next tr (dc) and 3ch, 4ch, miss next 4ch and 1dc (sc), 1 tr tr (d tr) into next dc (sc), 4ch, miss next dc (sc) and 4ch, 1tr (dc) into each of next 3ch and 1tr

(dc), rep from * 6 times more, 3 sps, turn.
Row 8 4 sps, 1 tr (dc) into each of next 3ch, 2ch, miss next ch, tr tr (d tr) and ch, 1tr (dc) into each of next 3ch and 1tr (dc), * 4ch, miss next blk and 4ch, 1dc (sc) into next ch, 1dc (sc) into tr tr (d tr), 1dc (sc) into next ch, 4ch, miss next 4ch and 3tr (dc), 1 tr (dc) into each of next 1tr (dc) and 3ch, 2ch, miss next ch, tr tr (d tr) and ch, 1tr (dc) into each of next 3ch and 1tr (dc), rep from * 6 times more, 4 sps, turn.
Row 9 5 sps, 1 blk, * 6ch, miss 1 blk and 3ch, 1 dc (sc) into next ch, 1dc (sc) into each of next 3dc (sc), 1dc (sc) into next ch, 6ch, miss 3ch and 1 blk, 1 blk, rep from * 6 times more, 5 sps, turn.
Row 10 4 sps, 1 blk, 1 sp, * 1tr (dc) into each of next 3ch, 7ch, miss next 3ch and 1dc (sc), 1dc (sc) into each of next 3dc (sc), 7ch, miss next dc (sc) and 3ch, 1tr (dc) into each of next 3ch and 1tr (dc), 1 sp, rep from * 6 times more, 1 blk, 4 sps, turn.
Row 11 3 sps, 1 blk, * 5ch, miss 1 blk, 1tr tr (d tr) into next sp, 5ch, miss next blk, 1tr (dc) into each of next tr (dc) and 3ch, 4ch, miss next 4ch and 1dc (sc), 1tr tr (d tr) into next dc (sc), 4ch, miss next dc (sc) and 4ch, 1 tr (dc) into each of next 3ch and 1tr (dc), rep from * 6 times more, 5ch, miss next blk, 1tr tr (d tr) into next sp, 5ch, miss next blk, 1 blk, 3 sps, turn.
Row 12 2 sps, 1 blk, * 4ch, miss next blk and 4ch, 1dc (sc) into next ch, 1dc (sc) into next dc (sc), 1dc (sc) into next ch, 4ch, miss next 4ch and 1 blk, 1tr (dc) into next tr (dc) and 3ch, 2ch, miss 1ch, tr tr (d tr) and 1 ch, 1 tr (dc) into each of next 3ch and 1 tr (dc), rep from * 6 times more, 4ch, miss next blk and 4ch, 1dc (sc) into next ch, 1dc (sc) into next tr tr (d tr), 1dc (sc) into next ch, 4ch, miss next 4 ch and blk, 1 blk, 2 sps, turn.
Rows 5 to 12 form the Diamond patt with sps at each side.
Cont in patt until row 16 has been completed.
Next row 3ch, miss first sp, 1tr (dc) into next tr (dc) so decreasing one sp at beg of row, patt to last 2 sps, 2ch, leaving last 1p of each on hook, work 1tr (dc) into next tr (dc) and 1 tr (dc) into 3rd of the 5ch, yoh and draw through all 3 lps on hook so decreasing one sp at end of row.
Keeping diamond patt correct, cont to dec

C H A R T I

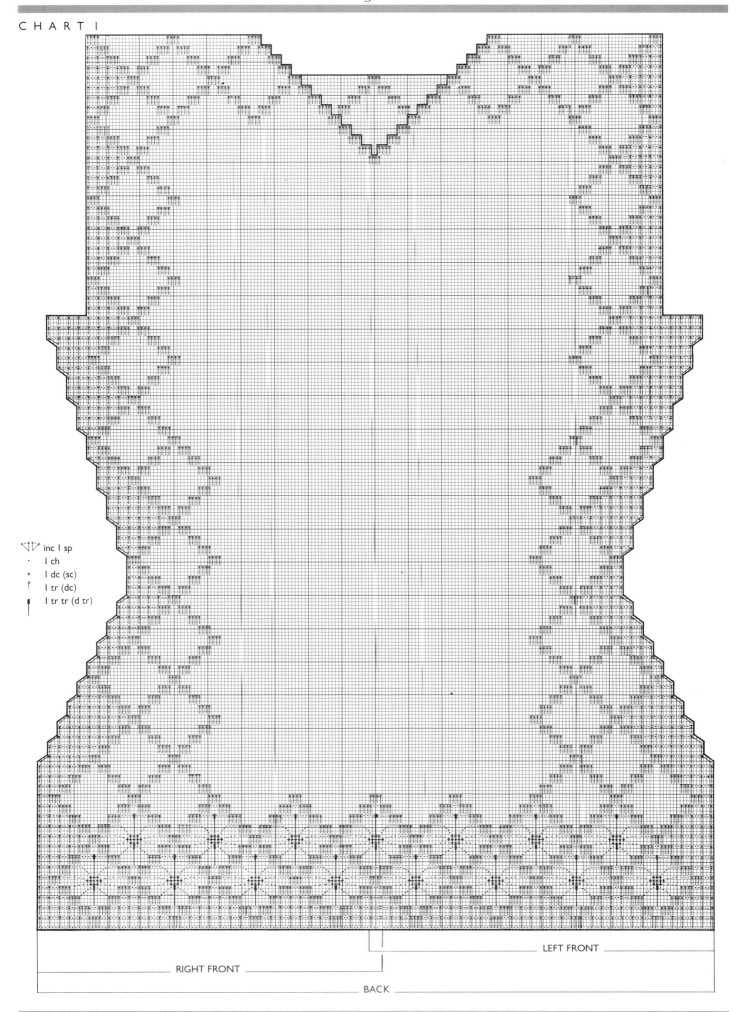

⟨⇂⇂⟩ inc I sp
· I ch
+ I dc (sc)
† I tr (dc)
‡ I tr tr (d tr)

LEFT FRONT

RIGHT FRONT

BACK

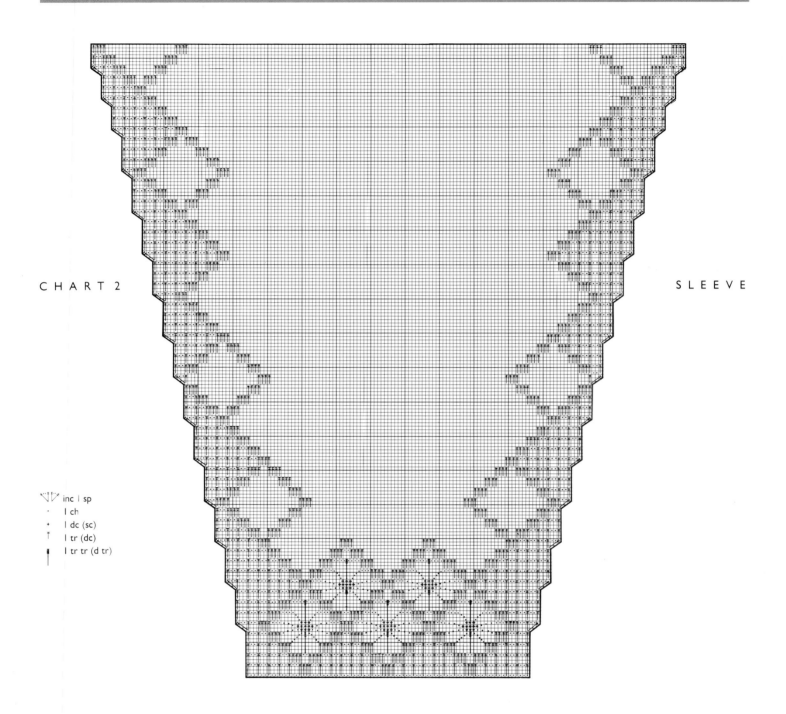

CHART 2

SLEEVE

inc 1 sp
· 1 ch
+ 1 dc (sc)
┬ 1 tr (dc)
┃ 1 tr tr (d tr)

one sp at each end of 8 foll alt rows.
Patt 4 more rows. (6 complete diamonds
rem.)
Next row 5ch, 1tr (dc) into first tr (dc) so
increasing one sp at beg of row, patt to end,
2ch, work 1tr (dc) into same place as last tr
(dc) so increasing one sp at end of row.
Inc one sp at each end of 7 foll 3rd rows. (7
diamonds with 6 sps at each side.)
Patt 2 more rows.

Shape armholes
Next row S1 st into each of first 13 sts, 5ch,
patt to last 4 sps, turn.
Patt 23 more rows.

Shape back neck
Next row Patt until 3rd blk (end of second
diamond) has been completed, turn.

Next row S1 st into each of first 4 sts, 3ch,
patt to end, turn.
Dec one blk at neck edge on next 2 rows.
Fasten off.
With WS facing, rejoin yarn to 4th tr (dc) of
3rd blk so leaving 2 diamonds for back neck,
3ch, patt to end.
Dec one blk at neck edge on next 3 rows.
Fasten off.

LEFT FRONT
Using 1.75mm (US5 steel) hook make 110ch.
Cont in patt from Chart 1 as folls:
Row 1 (RS) 1 tr (dc) into 9th ch from hook,
(2ch, miss next 2ch, 1tr (dc) into next ch) 4
times, 1tr (dc) into each of next 3ch, * (2ch,
miss next 2ch, 1tr (dc) into next ch) 7 times,
1tr (dc) into each of next 3ch, rep from *

twice more, (2ch, miss 2ch, 1tr (dc) into next
ch) 4 times, turn.
30 sps and 4 blks.
Row 2 3 sps, 1 blk, 1 sp, 1 blk, * 5 sps, 1 blk,
1 sp, 1 blk, rep from * twice more, 4 sps,
turn.
Cont in patt as now established until row 16
has been completed.
Dec one sp at beg (at end for right front) of
next and foll 8 alt rows.
Patt 4 rows.
Inc one sp at same edge on next and 7 foll
3rd rows.
Patt 2 rows.

Shape armhole
Next row Patt to last 4 sps, turn.
Patt 15 more rows.

Shape neck

Next row Sl st over first blk, 3 ch, patt to end.

Dec one blk at neck edge on next 11 rows. Fasten off.

RIGHT FRONT

Using 1.75mm (US5 steel) hook make 11Cch.
Cont in patt from Chart 1 as folls:

Row 1 (RS) 1tr (dc) into 9th ch from hook, (2ch, miss 2ch, 1tr (dc) into next ch) 3 times, 1tr (dc) into each of next 3ch, * (2ch, miss 2ch, 1tr (dc) into next ch) 7 times, 1tr (dc) into each of next 3 ch, rep from * twice more, (2ch, miss 2ch, 1tr (dc) into next ch) 5 times. 30 sps and 4 blks.

Row 2 4 sps, 1 blk, 1 sp, 1 blk, * 5 sps, 1 blk, 1 sp, 1 blk, rep from * twice more, 3 sps, turn.

Work as given for left front up to beg of armhole, noting the bracketed exception.

Shape armhole

Next row Sl st into each of first 13 sts, 5ch, patt to end.
Patt 15 more rows.

Shape neck

Next row Patt to last blk, turn.
Dec one blk at neck edge on next 11 rows.
Fasten off

SLEEVES

Using 1.75mm (US5 steel) hook make 87ch.
Row 1 Follow row 1 of Chart 2 thus: 1tr (dc) into 9th ch from hook, (2ch, miss next 2ch 1tr (dc) into next ch) 4 times, 1tr (dc) into each of next 3ch, * (2ch, miss next 2ch, 1tr (dc) into next ch) 7 times, 1tr (dc) into each of next 3ch, rep from * once more, (2ch, miss 2ch, 1tr (dc) into next ch) 5 times, turn. 24 sps and 3 blks.
Row 2 5ch to count as 1tr (dc) and 2ch, miss first sp, 1tr (dc) into next tr (dc), (2ch, miss next sp, 1tr (dc) into next tr (dc)) 3 times, 2tr (dc) into next sp, 1tr (dc) into next tr, 2ch, miss next 2tr (dc), 1tr (dc) into next tr (dc),

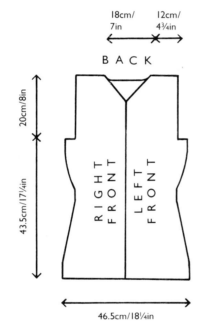

18cm/ 7in   12cm/ 4¾in

BACK

20cm/8in

43.5cm/17¼in

RIGHT FRONT   LEFT FRONT

46.5cm/18¼in

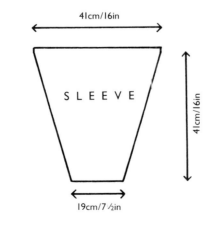

41cm/16in

SLEEVE

41cm/16in

19cm/7½in

2tr (dc) into next sp, 1tr (dc) into next tr (dc), * work 5 sps over next 5 sps, 1 blk over next sp, 1 sp over next blk, 1 blk over next sp, rep from * once more, 4 sps, turn.
Cont in patt, follow Chart 2, positioning diamond patt as indicated, inc 1 sp at each end of 3rd and every foll 4th row until row 53 has been completed. Now inc 1 sp at each end of the 2 foll 3rd rows, then patt 2 more rows, so ending with row 61. Fasten off.

THE EDGING

Join shoulder seams.
With RS of work facing and using the 1.75mm (US5 steel) hook, join on yarn at lower edge of right front and work 162dc (sc) up to beg of neck shaping, 48dc (sc) up to shoulder, 72dc (sc) round back neck to next shoulder, 48dc (sc) down left front to end of neck shaping and 162dc (sc) down to lower edge, turn. 492dc (sc).
Next row 2ch, 1dc (sc) into each of next 122 dc (sc), * 3ch, miss 2dc (sc), 1dc (sc) into each of next 4dc (sc), rep from * to last 4dc (sc), 3ch, miss 2dc (sc), 1dc (sc) into each of last 2dc (sc), turn.
Next row * 2ch, 1tr (dc) into next 3-ch lp, (2ch, 1tr (dc) into same 3-ch lp) 3 times, 2ch, 1dc (sc) into centre of 4dc (sc) group on previous row, rep from * 61 times more, turn.
Next row Sl st into 2-ch sp, sl st into top of next tr (dc), 3ch, sl st into same tr (dc) so forming a picot) 4 times, * sl st into next 2-ch sp, sl st into dc (sc) of previous row (centre of 4dc (sc) group), (sl st into next 2-ch sp, sl st into top of next tr (dc), 1 picot) 4 times, rep from * to end finishing sl st into last 2-ch sp. Fasten off.

TO MAKE UP

Do not press. Set in sleeves, matching centre of sleeve top to shoulder seams and sewing final rows to shaping at underarm. Join side and sleeve seams. Sew on buttons. Use 3-ch lps on edging as buttonholes.

SILK STAR

Silk is fabulous for evening wear. Here I have chosen a black Mulberry Silk background and studded it with starfish (for their softer, more fluid shapes) in jewel colours of cottons and silks. The sweater is a popular cropped shape with a deep scoop neckline edged in crochet with an exotic lacy border at the lower edge.

SIZES

To fit 86[91:97]cm (34[36:38]in) bust
Actual size 92[98:102]cm (36¼[38½:40] in)
Length to shoulder (excluding edging) 32.5[35.5:38]cm (12¾[14:15]in)
Sleeve seam 46cm (18in)
Figures in square brackets [ ] refer to larger sizes; where there is only one set of figures, it applies to all sizes.

MATERIALS

32×10g hanks of Rowan Mulberry Silk in main shade A (Boka 885)
1×50g ball of Rowan Cabled Mercerised Cotton in shade B (Mistral 332)
1×50g ball of Cabled Mercerised Cotton in shade C (Deep Blue 309)
1×50g ball of Cabled Mercerised Cotton in shade D (Mauve Pink 333)
1×50g ball of Cabled Mercerised Cotton in shade E (Cerise 326)
2×10g hanks of Mulberry Silk in shade F (Jade 884)
2×10g hanks of Mulberry Silk in shade G (Nightshade 880)
Pair of 3mm (US3) knitting needles
A 3.00mm (US D/3) crochet hook

TENSION

27 sts and 35 rows to 10cm (4in) over patt using 3mm (US3) needles

BACK

Using 3mm (US3) needles and A, cast on 106[114:120] sts.
Beg with a K row, cont in st st and work from Chart, inc one st at each end of 3rd and every foll 4th[4th:6th] row until there are 124[132:138] sts.
Cont in patt until row 42[52:62] has been completed.

Wearing this star-studded evening top Elisabeth will be certain to attract masses of attention. The yarn and colours are dazzlingly brilliant while the details – such as the scalloped crochet neckline – are soft and pretty.

Use separate, small balls of yarn for individual motifs. Link one shade to the next by twisting them around each other where they meet on WS to avoid making gaps.

Shape armholes

Cast off 4 sts at beg of next 2 rows and 2 sts at beg of foll 2 rows. Dec one st at each end of next and foll 6 alt rows. 98[106:112] sts.
Work straight until row 114[124:134] has been completed.

Shape shoulders and back neck

Cast off 10[11:11] sts at beg of next 2 rows.
Next row Cast off 11[11:12] sts, patt until there are 15[16:16] sts on right-hand needle, turn and complete this side first.
Next row Cast off 4 sts, patt to end.
Cast off rem 11[12:12] sts.
With RS of work facing, rejoin yarn to next st and cast off centre 26[30:34] sts, patt to end.
Next row Cast off 11[11:12] sts, patt to end.
Next row Cast off 4 sts, patt to end.
Cast off rem 11[12:12] sts.

FRONT

Work as given for back up to beg of armhole shaping, ending with row 42[52:62].

Shape armholes

Cast off 4 sts at beg of next 2 rows and 2 sts at beg of foll 2 rows.

3rd size only
Dec one st at each end of next row. Patt 1 row.

1st and 2nd sizes only
Dec one st at each end of next and foll 4[2] alt rows. Patt 1 row.

All sizes
102[114:124] sts.

Shape neck

Next row K2tog, patt 41[46:50], turn and leave rem sts on a spare needle.
Cont on these sts for first side of neck.
Cont to dec at armhole edge on foll 1[2:2] alt rows, cast off 3 sts at beg of next and foll 2 alt rows. 32[36:40] sts.

2nd and 3rd sizes only
Cont to work 1[3] more decreases at armhole edge as before and **at the same time** for **all sizes** dec one st at neck edge on next 4[5:5] rows.
Work 9[9:13] rows straight.
Inc one st at neck edge on next and every foll 10th[10th:14th] row until there are 32[34:35] sts.
Work straight until row 114[124:134] (row 115[125:135] for second side of neck) has been completed.

Shape shoulder

Cast off 10[11:11] sts at beg of next row and 11[11:12] sts at beg of foll alt row. Work 1 row. Cast off rem 11[12:12] sts.
With RS of work facing, rejoin yarn to next st and cast off centre 16[18:20] sts, patt to last 2 sts, K2tog. 42[47:51] sts.
Patt 1 row.
Cont to work 1[3:3] more decreases at armhole edge as before, cast off 3 sts at beg of next and foll 2 alt rows. 32[35:39] sts.

For **3rd size only** cont to work 2 more decreases at armhole edge as before and **at the same time** for **all sizes** dec one st at neck edge on next 4[5:5] rows. 28[30:32] sts. Work 8[8:12] rows straight. Now complete to match first side of neck noting the bracketed exception.

SLEEVES

Using 3mm (US3) needles and A, cast on 48 sts. Beg with a K row, cont in st st and work from Chart, inc one st at each end of 3rd and every foll 4th row until there are 94 sts. Now inc one st at each end of every foll 6th row until there are 110 sts. Work straight to row 160.

Shape top

Cast off 4 sts at beg of next 2 rows and 2 sts at beg of foll 2 rows. Dec one st at each end of next and foll 6 alt rows. Work 1 row. Cast off rem 84 sts.

TO MAKE UP

Sleeve edging

Note that American crochet terms are in round brackets ( ). With RS facing, A and using 3.00mm (US D/3) hook, work a row of dc (sc) evenly around lower edge of sleeve. Fasten off.

Neck edging

Join shoulder seams. With RS facing, A and using 3.00mm (US D/3) hook, join on yarn at neck edge and work 2ch to count as first dc (sc), then work 127[135:143] dc (sc) evenly all round front neck and 40[44:48] dc (sc) across back neck, sl st into top of the 2ch. 168[180:192] dc (sc).
Next round 2ch, 1dc (sc) into each dc (sc) to end, sl st into top of the 2ch.
Next round 2ch, 1dc (sc) into next dc (sc), * 3ch, miss 2dc (sc), 1dc (sc) into each of next 4dc (sc), rep from * to last 4dc (sc), 3ch, miss 2dc (sc), 1dc (sc) into each of last 2dc (sc), sl st into top of the 2ch.
Next round * 2ch, 1tr (dc) into next 3-ch lp,

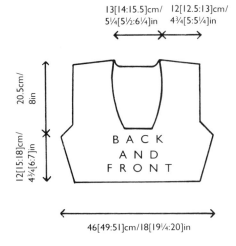

13[14:15.5]cm/
5¼[5½:6¼]in

12[12.5:13]cm/
4¾[5:5¼]in

20.5cm/
8in

12[15:18]cm/
4¾[6:7]in

BACK
AND
FRONT

46[49:51]cm/18[19¼:20]in

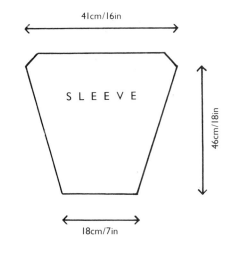

41cm/16in

SLEEVE

46cm/18in

18cm/7in

(2ch, 1tr (dc) into same 3-ch lp) 3 times, 2ch, sl st into centre of next 4 dc (sc) group, rep from * to end, finishing last sl st into same place as last sl st on previous round.
Next round (Sl-st into next 2-ch sp, sl st into top of next tr (dc), 3ch, sl st into top of same tr so forming a picot) 4 times, * (sl st into next 2-ch sp) twice, sl st into top of next tr (dc), 1 picot, (sl st into next 2-ch sp, sl st into top of next tr (dc), 1 picot) 3 times, rep from * to end, sl st into last 2-ch sp, sl st into first 2-ch sp. Fasten off.

Lower edging

Set in sleeves, matching centre of sleeve top to shoulder seams. Join side and sleeve seams. With RS facing, A and using 3.00mm (US D/3) hook, join on yarn to lower edge at side seam and work 2ch to count as 1dc (sc), then work 209[227:239]dc (sc) evenly all round lower edge, sl st into top of the 2ch.
Next round 2ch, 1dc (sc) into each dc (sc) to end, sl st into top of the 2ch.
Next round 5ch to count as 1tr (dc) and 2ch, miss 2dc (sc), 1tr (dc) into next dc (sc), * 2ch, miss 2dc (sc), 1tr (dc) into next dc (sc), rep from * to last 2dc (sc), 2ch, sl st into 3rd of the 5ch.
Next round 5ch to count as 1tr tr (d tr), 2tr tr (d tr) into 2-ch sp, 1 tr tr (d tr) into next tr (dc), * 5ch, miss next 2-ch sp, 1tr tr (d tr) into next tr (dc), 2tr tr (d tr) into next 2-ch sp, 1tr tr (d tr) into next tr (dc), rep from * to end finishing 5ch, miss last 2-ch sp, sl st into top of the 5ch.
Next round Sl st into top of next tr tr (d tr), * into 5-ch lp work 1tr (dc), 1ch, (1d tr (tr), 1ch) twice, 1tr tr (d tr), 1ch, (1d tr (tr), 1ch) twice and 1tr (dc), sl st into centre of 4tr tr (d tr) group, rep from * to end finishing last sl st into same place as first sl st.
Next round * (Sl st into top of next d tr (tr), 1 picot, sl st into next 1-ch sp) twice, sl st into top of tr tr (d tr), 1 picot, (sl st into next 1-ch sp, sl st into top of next d tr (tr), 1 picot) twice, sl st into sl st of previous round (centre of 4tr tr (d tr) group), rep from * to end. Fasten off.

CHART I

- ☐ A
- ⊡ B
- ◢ C
- ◩ D
- ⊠ E
- ⊟ F
- ◪ G

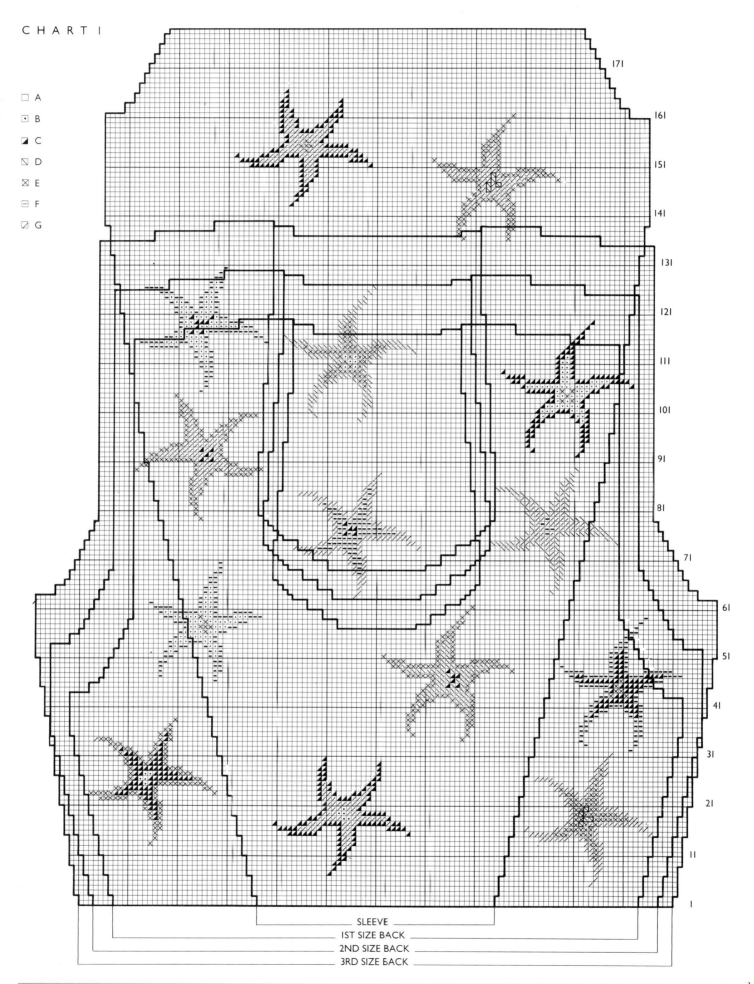

171
161
151
141
131
121
111
101
91
81
71
61
51
41
31
21
11
1

SLEEVE
1ST SIZE BACK
2ND SIZE BACK
3RD SIZE BACK

BROCADE DANDY

Italy has a long history of producing luxurious textiles. Around the mid nineteenth century the Venetian nobility used these extravagant fabrics to make beautiful ballgowns. After seeing a heavy silk brocade dress from this period, I was inspired to create my own version of the fabric for a fitted waistcoat that looks equally good on a man or a woman.

SIZES

To fit 86/91[91/97:102/107]cm (34/36[36/38:40/42]in) bust/chest
Actual size 99[104.5:110]cm (39[41:43¼]in)
Back length to shoulder 46[47:48.5]cm (18[18½:19]in)
Figures in square brackets [ ] refer to larger sizes; where there is only one set of figures, it applies to all sizes

MATERIALS

Colourway shown on woman
8[10:12] × 20g balls of Rowan Edina Ronay Silk and Wool in main colour A (Black)
9[10:11] × 10g hanks of Rowan Mulberry Silk in contrast colour B (Natural)
Colourway shown on man
8[10:12] × 20g balls of Rowan Edina Ronay Silk and Wool in main colour A (Pine)
2[3:3] × 50g balls of Rowan Fine Cotton Chenille in contrast colour B (Privet)
Pair each of 2¼mm (US1) and 3mm (US3) knitting needles
2¼mm (US1) circular knitting needle
7 buttons

TENSION

31 sts and 34 rows to 10cm (4in) over charted patt using 3mm (US3) needles

BACK

Using 3mm (US3) needles and A, cast on 132[140:148] sts. Using a small, separate ball of B for each vertical stripe, cont in patt as foll:
1st row (RS) K6[3:7] A, 1 B, (6 A, 1 B) to last 6[3:7] sts, 6[3:7] A.
2nd row As 1st, but P instead of K.
These 2 rows set patt. Cont in patt, inc one st at each end of 17th and every foll 8th row until there are 148[156:164] sts, working extra stripes into patt as necessary.
Cont without shaping until 92 rows have been completed, so ending with a WS row.

A subtle, yet striking, waistcoat patterned in two yarns of the same colour, but contrasting textures. Velvety chenille against smooth, shiny silk imitates the plush effect of brocade.

This is the same design as the man's waistcoat, but it looks dramatically different with the bold contrast of white silk against a black silk and wool background.

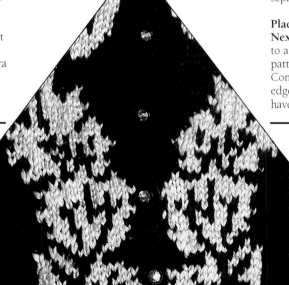

Shape armholes
Cast off 8 sts at beg of next 2 rows and 3 sts at beg of foll 4 rows. Dec one st at each end of every row 4 times, every foll alt row twice and every foll 4th row twice. 104[112:120] sts. Cont without shaping until 166[170:174] rows in all have been completed from beg, so ending with a WS row.

Shape shoulders and back neck
Cast off 11[13:14] sts at beg of next 2 rows.
Next row Cast off 11[13:14] sts, patt until there are 16[16:18] sts on right-hand needle, turn and complete right side of neck first.
Next row Cast off 4 sts, patt to end.
Cast off rem 12[12:14] sts.
With RS of work facing, rejoin yarn to rem sts, cast off centre 28 sts, patt to end.
Next row Cast off 11[13:14] sts, patt to end.
Next row Cast off 4 sts, patt to end.
Cast off rem 12[12:14] sts.

POCKET LININGS
(make 2)

Using 2¼mm (US1) needles and A, cast on 31 sts. Beg with a K row, work 30 rows in st st. Cut off yarn. Leave sts on a holder.

LEFT FRONT

Using 3mm (US3) needles and A, cast on 4 sts. Beg with a K row, cont in st st and patt from Chart, shaping as indicated, until 56th row has been completed. Read odd-numbered (K) rows from right to left and even-numbered (P) rows from left to right. Use separate balls of B for each main area of patt.

Place pocket lining
Next row Patt 20[24:28] sts, sl next 31 sts on to a holder, patt across 31 sts of pocket lining, patt to end.
Cont in patt, shaping side, armhole and front edges as indicated, until 186[190:194] rows have been completed. Cast off rem 12[12:14] sts.

RIGHT FRONT

Work as given for Left Front until 188[192:196] rows have been completed and placing pocket lining on 57th row as foll:
57th row Patt 21 sts, sl next 31 sts on to a holder, patt across 31 sts of pocket lining, patt to end.

POCKET TOPS

Using 2¼mm (US1) needles and with RS of work facing, sl 31 sts from holder on to left-hand needle. Join in A and B. Work 4 rows in patt from the appropriate side of the Chart. Cont in A only, K 1 row.
Next row K to end to mark foldline.
Beg with a K row, work a further 6 rows in st st. Cast off.

LOWER EDGES
LEFT FRONT

Using 2¼mm (US1) needles, A and with RS of work facing, pick up and K32 sts from centre front to lower point, one st at centre and 44[48:52] sts from point to side edge. 77[81:85] sts.
Next row (WS) K to end to form foldline.
Next row K31, sl 1, K2 tog, psso, K to end.
Next row P to end.
Next row K30, sl 1, K2 tog, psso, K to end.
Cont as set, dec at centre as before, until 67[71:75] sts rem. Cast off loosely.

RIGHT FRONT

Work as given for Left Front, picking up sts as foll: 44[48:52] sts from side edge to point, one st from centre and 32 sts from point to centre front.

BACK

Using 2¼mm (US1) needles, A and with RS of work facing, pick up and K132[140:148] sts along lower edge.

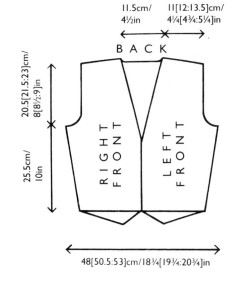

11.5cm/ 4½in   11[12:13.5]cm/ 4¼[4¾:5¼]in

BACK

RIGHT FRONT   LEFT FRONT

20.5[21.5:23]cm/ 8[8½:9]in

25.5cm/ 10in

48[50.5:53]cm/18¾[19¾:20¾]in

Next row (WS) K to end to form foldline.
Beg with a K row, work 10 rows in st st. Cast off loosely.

ARMHOLE EDGING

Join shoulder seams.
Using 2¼mm (US1) needles, A and with RS of work facing, pick up and K130[136:142] sts along armhole edge.
Next row (WS) K to end to form foldline.
Beg with a K row, work 8 rows in st st. Cast off loosely.

FRONT BAND

Using 2¼mm (US1) circular needle, A and with RS of work facing, pick up and K60[63:66] sts up Right Front edge to beg of shaping, 68 sts to shoulder, 40 sts across back neck, 68 sts down Left Front to beg of shaping and 60[63:66] sts to lower edge. 296[302:308] sts. Work in rows.
1st row (WS) P to end.
Woman's version: 2nd row (buttonhole row) K2[3:2], (K2 tog, yo, K7[7:8]) 6 times, K2 tog, yo, K to end.
Man's version: 2nd row (buttonhole row) K238[243:244], yo, K2 tog, (K7[7:8], yo, K2 tog) 6 times, K2[3:2].
3rd row P to end.
4th row P to end to form foldline.
5th row P to end.
6th row As 2nd.
Beg with a P row, work 9 rows in st st. Cast off loosely.

TO MAKE UP

Press on WS using a warm iron over a damp cloth. Join armhole edging, side and lower edging seams. Turn all edgings to WS at foldline and slip stitch in position, easing cast-off edge around the curved edges. Sew down pocket linings on WS of work and edges of pocket tops on RS of work. Press seams. Sew on buttons.

CHART I

□ A

⊡ B

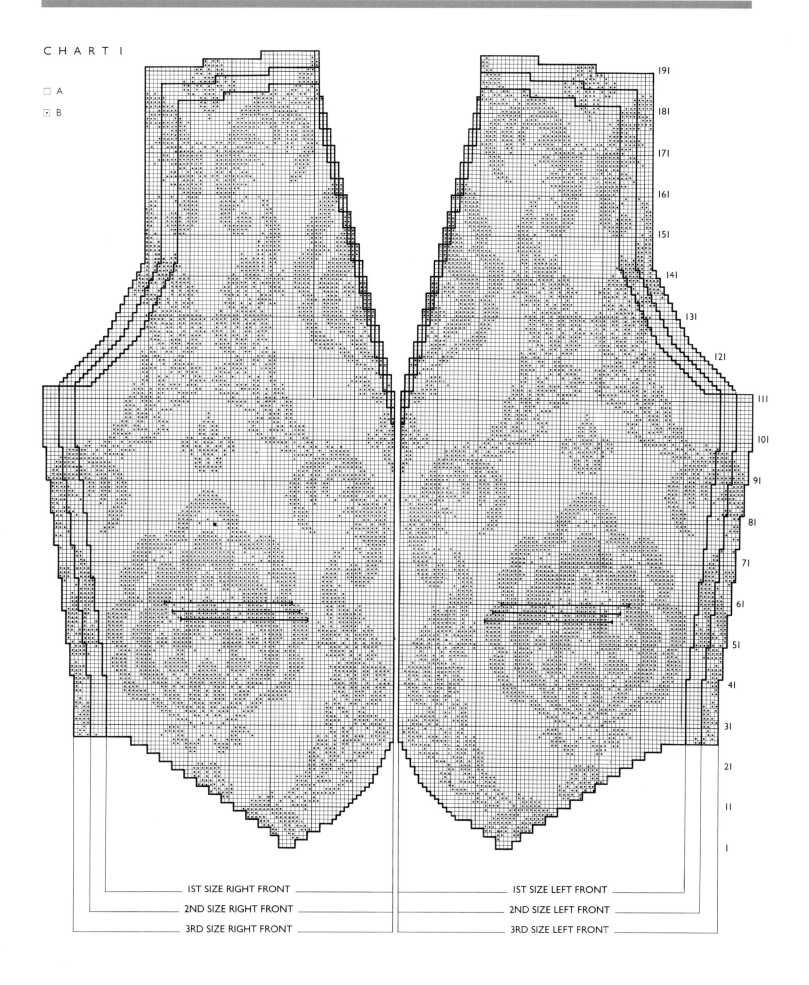

191

181

171

161

151

141

131

121

111

101

91

81

71

61

51

41

31

21

11

1

1ST SIZE RIGHT FRONT ————————

2ND SIZE RIGHT FRONT ————————

3RD SIZE RIGHT FRONT ————————

1ST SIZE LEFT FRONT ————————

2ND SIZE LEFT FRONT ————————

3RD SIZE LEFT FRONT ————————

GLITTERING PRIZE

*Beadwork adds an expensive couture touch to knitting, yet it is easy to do
and the results always look good. This evening top is my own version of a 'a
little black outfit'; I think that it looks stunningly simple and very wearable.
The beads are placed in a basic lattice pattern and follow through onto the
beaded button bands and edgings.*

SIZES

To fit 81[86:91:97]cm (32[34:36:38]in) bust
Actual size 85[91:96:101]cm
(33½[36:37¾:39¾]in)
Length to centre back neck 56[58:60:62]cm
(22[23:23½:24½]in)
Figures in square brackets [ ] refer to larger
sizes; where there is only one set of figures, it
applies to all sizes.

MATERIALS

7[7:8:8]×50g balls of Rowan Cabled
Mercerised Cotton (Bleached 302 or Black
319)
Approximately 200g of beads
Pair each 2¼mm (US1) and 3mm (US3)
knitting needles
14[15:15:15] faceted beads for buttons

TENSION

31 sts and 49 rows to 10cm (4in) over patt
using 3mm (US3) needles

BACK

Thread approximately half of the beads onto
yarn or as many beads as you are comfortable
working with.
Using 2¼mm (US1) needles cast on
133[141:149:157] sts.
Beg with a K row, work 11 rows st st, so
ending with a K row.
Next row K to end to form hemline.
Change to 3mm (US3) needles.
Work 2 rows st st.
Following Chart 1 for position of bead
pattern, work bead as folls:
Work to position of bead, bring yarn forward
to RS of work, slide a bead down the yarn
close to the last stitch worked, slip the next
stitch purlwise from the left-hand needle,
pass the bead in front of the slipped stitch
tightly, then take yarn back and K next st in
the usual way.
Cont in st st working the 16-row bead patt
throughout.
Dec one st at each end of 13th[19th:25th:31st]
row, then on every foll 4th row until
95[103:111:119] sts rem.
Work 11 rows straight, so ending with a P
row.
Inc one st at each end of next and every foll
4th row until there are 133[141:149:157] sts.
Work 9[11:15:17] rows straight, so ending
with a P row.

*In classic black (right) or gleaming white
(above – with 'Brocade Dandy') with
matching beads, this design wins the
'Glittering Prize'.*

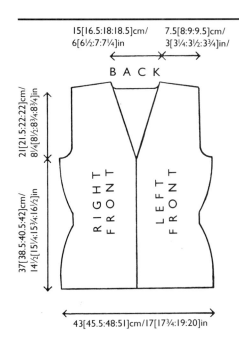

15[16.5:18:18.5]cm/
6[6½:7:7¼]in

7.5[8:9:9.5]cm/
3[3¼:3½:3¾]in/

BACK

21[21.5:22:22]cm/
8¼[8½:8½:8¾]in

37[38.5:40.5:42]cm/
14½[15¼:15¾:16½]in

RIGHT FRONT

LEFT FRONT

43[45.5:48:51]cm/17[17¾:19:20]in

Shape armholes

Cast off 6 sts at beg of next 2 rows. Dec one
st at each end of next 5 rows, then at each
end of foll 4 alt rows. Dec one st at each end
of every foll 4th row until 95[103:111:119] sts
rem. Work straight until armholes measure
19[20:20:20]cm (7½[8:8:8]in) from beg of
shaping, ending with a P row.

Shape shoulders and back neck

Next row Patt 38[40:44:47] sts, turn and
complete this side first.
Cast off 4 sts at beg of next and foll 2 alt
rows. Dec one st at neck edge on next
2[2:4:5] rows.
4th size only
Work one row.
All sizes
Cast off 12[13:14:15] sts at beg of next row.
Work 1 row. Cast off rem 12[13:14:15] sts.
With RS of work facing, rejoin yarn to next st
and cast off centre 19[23:23:25] sts, patt to
end. 38[40:44:47] sts. Work 1 row. Now
complete to match first side of neck.

LEFT FRONT

Thread approximately half of the rem beads
onto yarn or as many beads as you are
comfortable working with.
Using 2¼mm (US1) needles cast on
66[70:74:78] sts. Beg with a K row, work 11
rows st st, so ending with a K row.
Next row K to end to form hemline.
Change to 3mm (US3) needles.
Work 2 rows st st.
Cont in st st working the 16-row bead patt
but shape side by decreasing one st at beg (at
end for right front) of 13th[19th:25th:31st]
row and every foll 4th row until 47[51:55:59]
sts rem. Work 11 rows straight. Inc one st at
side edge on next and every foll 4th row until
there are 66[70:74:78] sts. Work 9[11:11:9]
rows straight (for right front work
10[12:12:10] rows), so ending at side edge.
3rd size only
Dec one st at front edge.
Work 3 rows, so ending at side edge.
4th size only
Dec one st at front edge on next and foll 4th
row. Work 3 rows, so ending at side edge.

All sizes
Shape armhole
Cast off 6 sts, patt to last 2 sts, work 2tog.
Decreasing one st at front edge on every foll

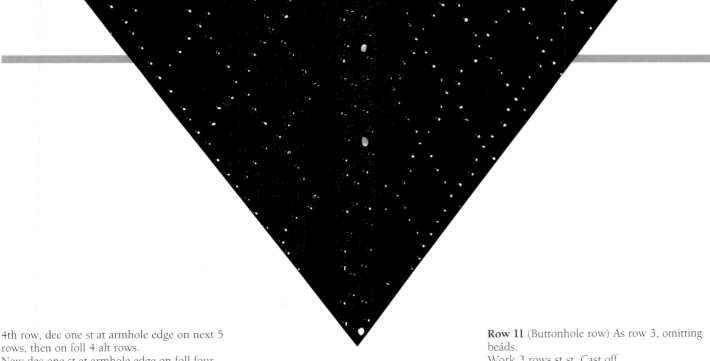

4th row, dec one st at armhole edge on next 5 rows, then on foll 4 alt rows.
Now dec one st at armhole edge on foll four 4th rows. 39[43:46:49] sts.
Keeping armhole edge straight, cont to dec at front edge on every 4th row until 24[26:28:30] sts rem.
Work straight until front measures the same as back up to beg of shoulder shaping, ending at armhole edge.

Shape shoulder
Cast off 12[13:14:15] sts at beg of next row.
Work 1 row. Cast off rem 12[13:14:15] sts.

RIGHT FRONT

Thread the rem beads onto yarn or as many beads as you are comfortable working with.
Work as given for left front noting the bracketed exceptions.

RIGHT FRONT EDGING AND FACING

Join shoulder seams. With RS of work facing and using 2¼mm (US1) needles, beg at hemline, join on yarn and pick up and K137[141:141:146] sts up right front edge to beg of shaping, 84[86:86:88] sts to shoulder seam and 29[33:33:36] sts across to centre back neck. 250[260:260:270] sts.

P 1 row.
Following the bead patt on Chart 2, work as folls:
Row 1 Work in bead patt.
Row 2 P.
Row 3 (Buttonhole row) Patt 4, yfwd, K2tog, (patt 8, yfwd, K2tog) 13[14:14:14] times, patt to end.
Row 4 P.
Row 5 Patt to end.
This completes the bead patt.
Row 6 P.
Row 7 P to end to form foldline.
Rows 8-10 Beg with a P row, work in st st.

Row 11 (Buttonhole row) As row 3, omitting beads.
Work 3 rows st st. Cast off.

LEFT FRONT EDGING AND FACING

With RS of work facing and using 2¼mm (US1) needles, beg at centre back neck, join on yarn and pick up and K29[33:33:36] sts across back neck, 84[86:86:88] sts down left front edge to end of shaping and 137[141:141:146] sts down to hemline.
250[260:260:270] sts.
Work as given for right front edging and facing, omitting the buttonholes.

ARMHOLE FACINGS
(alike)

With RS of work facing and using 2¼mm (US1) needles, pick up and K152[154:154:156] sts evenly all round armhole edge.
Next row K to end to form foldline.
Beg with a K row, work 8 rows st st. Cast off.

TO MAKE UP

Do not press. Join side seams. Join facing at centre back neck. Fold front, lower edge and armhole facings to WS and slipstitch in position. Sew on buttons.

CHART 2

□ • BEAD

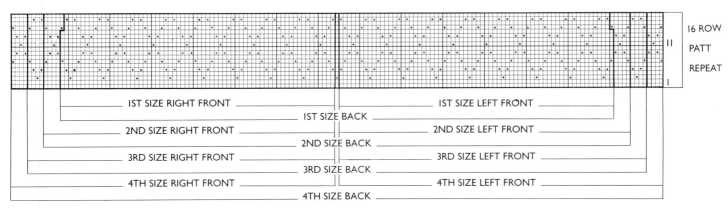

BRONZE BELLE

I use a lot of beads in my evening wear designs; they always make a garment look so glamorous. The choice of beads is astounding – I can spend hours browsing in my favourite bead shops.
For this figure-hugging dress knitted in Rowan Cabled Mercerised Cotton, I have chosen a chevron pattern of small self-coloured beads across the bodice.
The same dress – in a different colour – is worn with 'Windsor Glow' (see page 121), but the beads are smaller.

SIZES

To fit 81/86cm (32/34in) bust
Actual size 86cm (34in)
Length to shoulder 91cm (36in)

MATERIALS

7×50g balls of Rowan Cabled Mercerised Cotton (Pippin 339 or Rich Purple 310)
Approximately 3270 beads
Pair of 3mm (US3) knitting needles
3.00mm (US D/3) crochet hook

TENSION

31 sts and 40 rows to 10cm (4in) over st st using 3mm (US3) needles
31 sts and 48 rows to 10cm (4in) over bead patt using 3mm (US3) needles

BACK

Thread approximately 355 beads onto yarn or as many beads as you are comfortable working with.
Using 3mm (US3) needles cast on 123 sts.
Rows 1 and 2 Work in st st.
Following Chart 1 for position of bead pattern, work bead as folls: work to position of bead, bring yarn forward to RS of work, slide a bead down the yarn close to the last stitch worked, slip the next stitch purlwise from left-hand needle, pass bead in front of slipped stitch tightly, then take yarn to back of work and K next st.
Cont in st st working the beaded border patt, inc one st at each end of 13th row. Avoid placing a bead on outer edges.
These 19 rows complete the border patt.
Beg with a P row, work 5 rows st st.
Next row (inc row) K3, M1, K to last 3 sts, M1, K3.

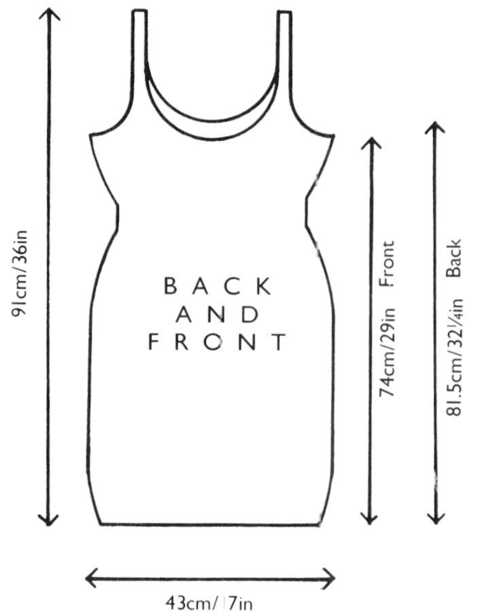

Beg with a P row, cont in st st, inc one st at each end of every foll 12th row until there are 133 sts. Cont without further shaping until work measures 35cm (13¾in) from cast-on edge, ending with a P row.
1st dec row K36, K3togtbl, K55, K3tog, K36. Work 15 rows.
2nd dec row K35, K3togtbl, K53, K3tog, K35.
Work 13 rows.
3rd dec row K34, K3togtbl, K51, K3tog, K34. Work 11 rows.
4th dec row K33, K3togtbl, K49, K3tog, K33. Work 9 rows.
5th dec row K32, K3togtbl, K47, K3tog, K32. Work 7 rows.
6th dec row K31, K3togtbl, K45, K3tog, K31, 109 sts.
Work 15 rows st st, so ending with a P row.
Next row (inc row) K31, M1, K1, M1, K45, M1, K1, M1, K31.
Work 11 rows.
Next row (inc row) K32, M1, K1, M1, K47, M1, K1, M1, K32. 117 sts.
Work 5 rows, so ending with a P row.
Cut off yarn and thread as many beads as you are comfortable to work with on this ball (approximately 1340 beads are required to complete back). Rejoin yarn, beg row 1 of Chart 2, cont in st st working the bead patt, inc one st at each end of 7th and every foll 6th row until there are 133 sts.
Work straight until row 60 has been completed.

Shape armholes

Cast off 8 sts at beg of next 2 rows, 4 sts at beg of foll 2 rows and 3 sts at beg of next 2 rows. Dec one st at each end of next and foll 7 alt rows, then at each end of every foll 4th row until 77 sts rem.

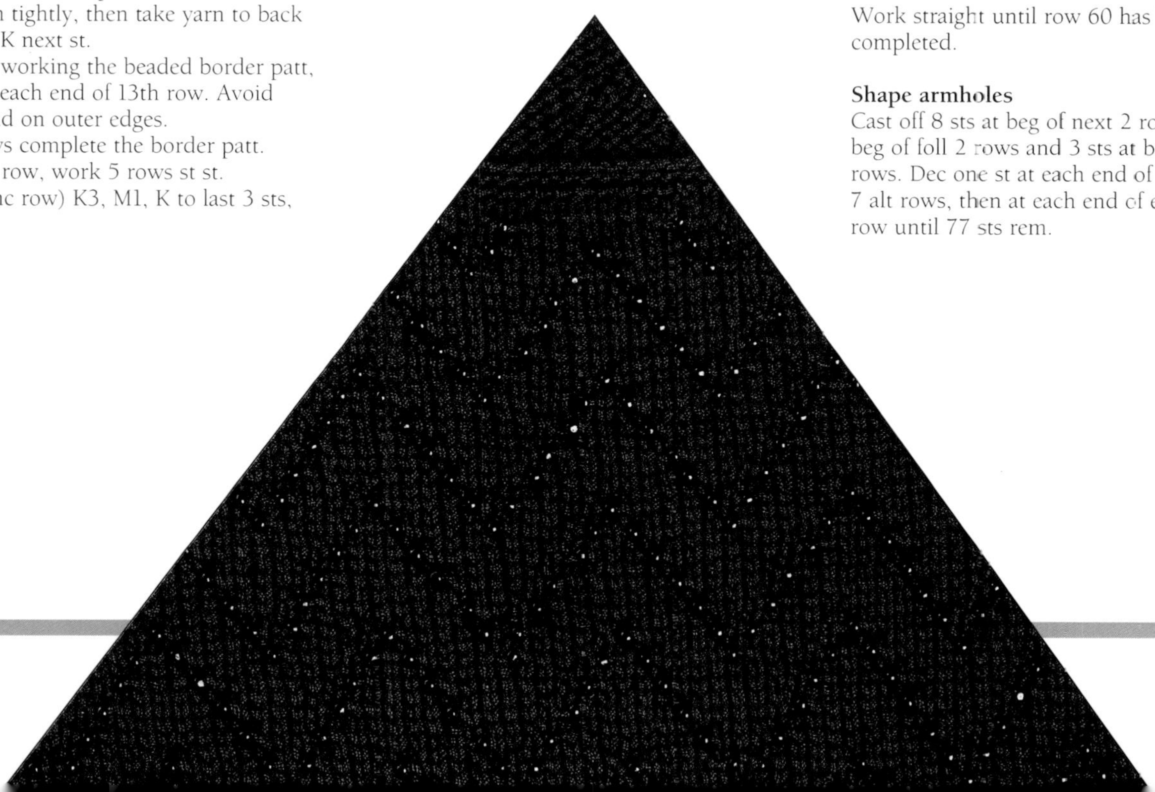

91cm/36in

BACK
AND
FRONT

74cm/29in Front

81.5cm/32¼in Back

43cm/17in

CHART 1

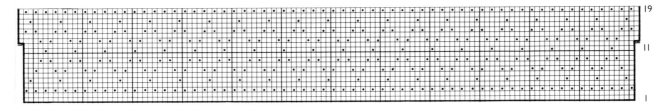

19

11

1

CHART 2

☐ BEAD

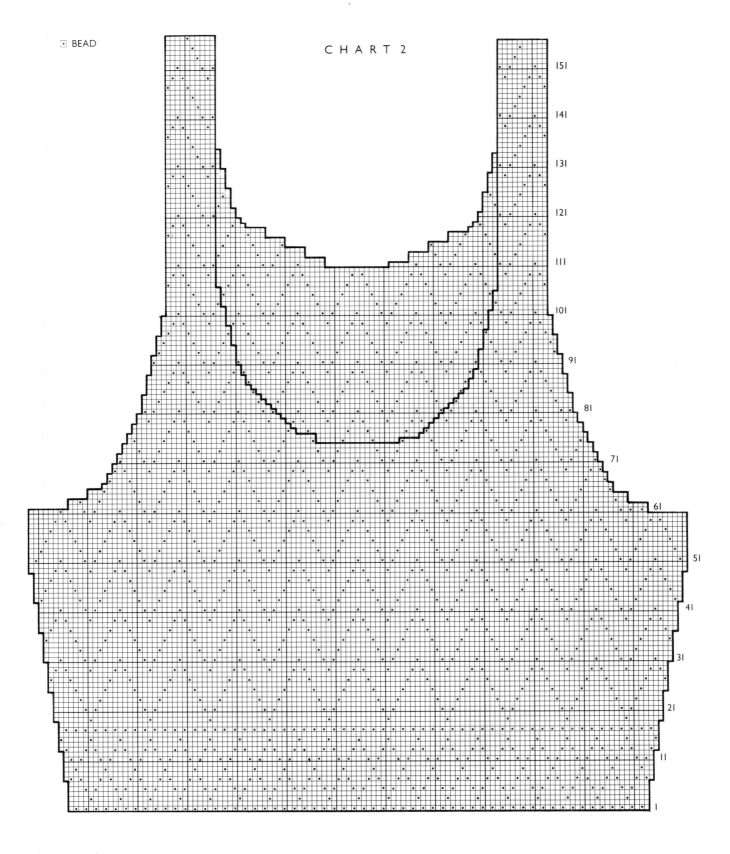

151

141

131

121

111

101

91

81

71

61

51

41

31

21

11

1

Work straight until row 110 has been completed.

Shape neck
Next row Patt 32, turn and leave rem sts on a spare needle.
Cont on these sts for first side of neck.
Cast off 4 sts at beg of next and foll 3 alt rows. 16 sts. Dec one st at neck edge on next 2 rows, then on foll alt row. Dec one st at same edge on every foll 4th row until 10 sts rem.
Work straight until row 156 has been completed. Cast off.
With RS of work facing, rejoin yarn to next st and cast off centre 13 sts, patt to end. 32 sts.
P 1 row. then complete to match first side of neck.

FRONT

Work has given for back (threading rem beads on yarn at beg of bead patt on bodice) up to beg of armhole shaping, ending with row 60.

Shape armholes
Cast off 8 sts at beg of next 2 rows, 4 sts at beg of foll 2 rows and 3 sts at beg of next 2 rows. Dec one st at each end of next and foll 3 alt rows. 95 sts.
P 1 row.

Shape neck
Next row K2tog, patt 37, turn and leave rem sts on a spare needle.
Cont on these sts for first side of neck.
Next row Cast off 4 sts, P to end.
Next row K2tog, patt to last 2 sts, K2tog.
Next row P2tog, P to end.
Rep these 2 rows twice more. 25 sts.
** Dec one st at armhole edge on 3rd and every foll 4th row and **at the same time** dec one st at neck edge on next 4 rows (5 rows for right side of neck), then on foll 2 alt rows.
Cont to dec at armhole edge as before, dec one st at neck edge on every foll 4th row until 12 sts rem. Keeping armhole edge straight, cont to dec one st at neck edge as before until 10 sts rem.
Work straight until row 156 has been completed. Cast off.
With RS of work facing, rejoin yarn to next st and cast off centre 17 sts, patt to last 2 sts, K2tog. 38 sts.
P 1 row.
Next row Cast off 4 sts, patt to last 2 sts, K2tog.

A sociable trio – Anna (left) is wearing 'Bronze Belle' with its jacket 'Windsor Glow', Nick (centre) is in 'Venetian Carnival' (page 131) and Elisabeth (right) wears 'Regency Stripes' (page 125).

Next row P to last 2 sts, P2tog.
Next row K2tog, patt to last 2 sts, K2tog.
Next row P to last 2 sts, P2tog.
Rep last 2 rows once more.
Complete as given for first side of neck from ** to end noting the bracketed exception.

TO MAKE UP
Omitting bead areas press lightly on WS using a warm iron over a damp cloth. Join shoulder seams, then join side seams.
Using the 3.00mm (US D/3) hook, work 2 rounds of dc (sc) evenly all round neck, lower edge and armhole edges.

WINDSOR GLOW

Designed in a carnival mood of bright spicy colours to be worn with 'Bronze Belle', this bolero jacket is knitted in Rowan Cabled Mercerised Cotton. In contrast to the soft pastels and tones that I prefer for day wear, here the Fair Isle patterns, intermingled with beaded stitches, glow with an unusual mixture of hot colours.

SIZES

To fit 81[86:91]cm (32[34:36]in) bust
Length to shoulder 37.5[40:42.5]cm (14¾[15¾:16¾]in)
Sleeve seam 49cm (19¼in)
Figures in square brackets [ ] refer to larger sizes; where there is only one set of figures, it applies to all sizes

MATERIALS

3[3:3]×50g balls of Rowan Cabled Mercerised Cotton in main shade A (Pippin 339)
2[2:2] balls in shade C (Speedwell 334)
3[3:4] balls in shade D (Aspen 335)
2[2:2] balls in shade E (Saffron 336)
2[2:2] balls in shade F (Geranium 338)
1[1:1] ball in shade G (Firethorn 337)
Approximately 2,750 beads (B on Chart)
Pair each of 2¼mm (US1) and 3mm (US3) knitting needles
A 2¼mm (US1) circular needle

TENSION

34 sts and 40 rows to 10cm (4in) over patt using 3mm (US3) needles

BACK

Using 3mm (US3) needles and A, cast on 129[137:145] sts.
Beg with a K row, cont in st st and work 6[10:10] rows in patt from Chart. Strand yarns loosely across WS of work to avoid drawing in the knitting.
Thread the required number of beads onto yarn before commencing bead patterns and work bead rows as folls:
On **knit** rows work to position of bead, bring yarn forward to RS of work, slide a bead down the yarn close to the last stitch worked, slip the next stitch purlwise from left-hand needle, pass bead in front of slipped stitch tightly, then take yarn to back of work and K next st.
On **purl** rows work to position of bead, take yarn back to RS of work, slip next stitch purlwise from left-hand needle to right-hand needle and slide a bead down the yarn as close to right-hand needle as possible. Bring yarn forward to front of work and P next stitch.
Cont to work the 82-row patt repeat from Chart, inc one st at each end of next and

11.5[12.5:14]cm/ 4½[5:5½]in   14[14.5:15]cm/ 5½[5¾:6]in

BACK

16[18.5:21]cm/ 6¼[7¼:8¼]in   20.5cm/ 8in

RIGHT FRONT   LEFT FRONT

45.5[48:50]cm/17¾[19:19½]in

42.5cm/16¾in

SLEEVE

49cm/19¼in

18cm/7in

every foll 4th[4th:5th] row until there are 155[163:171] sts.
Work straight until row 64[74:84] has been completed.

Shape armholes

Cast off 4 sts at beg of next 2 rows. Dec one st at each end of next 6 rows.
135[143:151] sts.
Work straight until row 146[156:166] has been completed.

Shape shoulders

Cast off 16[16:17] sts at beg of next 2 rows, 16[17:17] sts at beg of foll 2 rows and 16[17:18] sts at beg of next 2 rows. Cast off rem 39[43:47] sts.

LEFT FRONT

** Using 3mm (US3) needles and A, cast on 29[33:37] sts.
Beg with a K row, cont in st st and patt from Chart, work 3 rows (2 rows for right front). Thread the required number of beads onto yarn before commencing bead patterns.
Next row (front edge) Cast on 6 sts, patt to end.
Next row Patt to end.
Next row Cast on 6 sts, patt to end. **
1st size only
Next row Inc one st, patt to end.
2nd and 3rd sizes only
Work 1 row.
All sizes
Cast on 3 sts at front edge on next and foll alt row. 48[51:55] sts.
Inc one st at side edge on next and every foll 4th[4th:5th] row and **at the same time** inc one st at front edge on next 6 rows, then on foll 3 alt rows. Cont to shape side edge as before, inc one st at front edge on foll 4th row once, then on every foll 6th row until there are 67[70:73] sts.
*** Keeping front edge straight, cont to shape side edge until there are 72[76:80] sts.
Work straight until row 64[74:84] (row 65[75:85] for right front) has been completed. ***

Shape armhole and front edge

1st size only
Next row Cast off 4 sts, patt to end.
Next row Patt to end.
Dec one st at armhole edge on next 6 rows.
Work 6 rows straight.
2nd size only
Next row Cast off 4 sts, patt to end.
Next row Patt to end.
Dec one st at armhole edge on next 6 rows.
3rd size only
Next row Cast off 4 sts, patt to end.
Next row Patt to end.
Dec one st at armhole edge on next 6 rows and **at the same time** dec one st at front edge on next and foll 4th row.
Work 2 rows.

CHART I

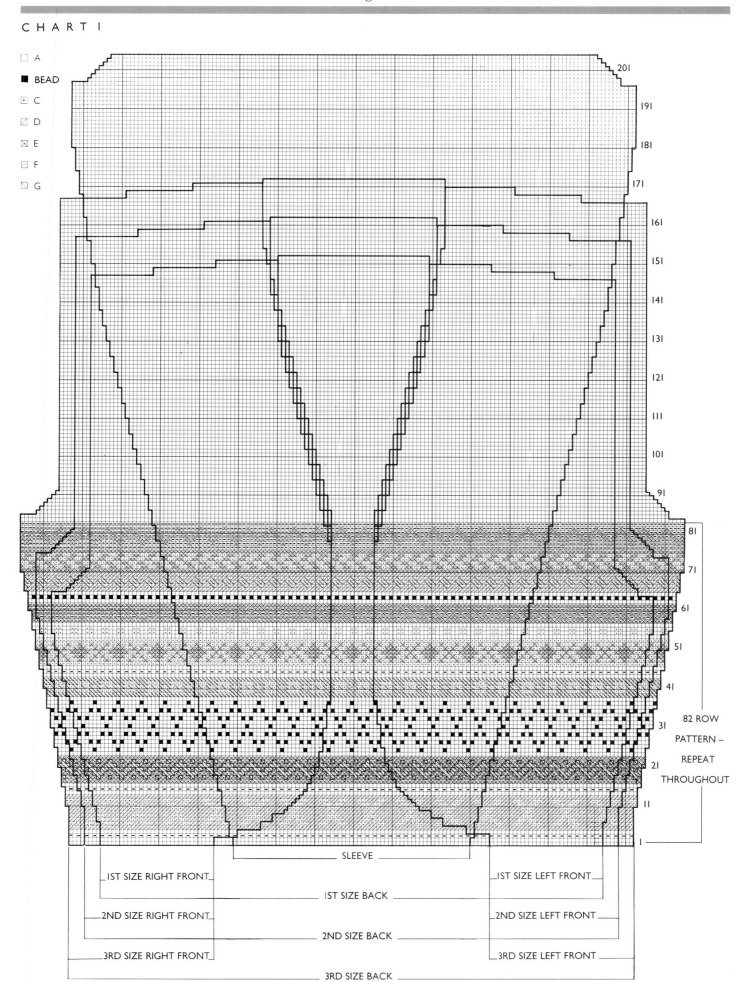

- □ A
- ■ BEAD
- ⊡ C
- ☑ D
- ☒ E
- ⊟ F
- ◩ G

201
191
181
171
161
151
141
131
121
111
101
91
81
71
61
51
41
31
21
11
1

82 ROW
PATTERN –
REPEAT
THROUGHOUT

SLEEVE

1ST SIZE RIGHT FRONT
1ST SIZE BACK
2ND SIZE RIGHT FRONT
2ND SIZE BACK
3RD SIZE RIGHT FRONT
3RD SIZE BACK

1ST SIZE LEFT FRONT
2ND SIZE LEFT FRONT
3RD SIZE LEFT FRONT

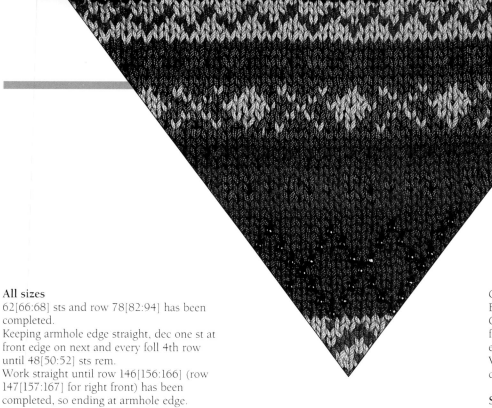

All sizes

62[66:68] sts and row 78[82:94] has been completed.

Keeping armhole edge straight, dec one st at front edge on next and every foll 4th row until 48[50:52] sts rem.

Work straight until row 146[156:166] (row 147[157:167] for right front) has been completed, so ending at armhole edge.

Shape shoulder

Cast off 16[16:17] sts at beg of next row and 16[17:17] sts at beg of foll alt row. Work 1 row. Cast off rem 16[17:18] sts.

RIGHT FRONT

Work as given for left front from ** to ** noting the bracketed exception.

Work 1 row.

1st size only

Next row Cast on 3 sts, patt to last st, inc in last st.

Next row Patt to end.

Next row Cast on 3 sts, patt to end.

2nd and 3rd sizes only

Cast on 3 sts at beg of next and foll alt row.

All sizes

Inc one st at front edge on next 6 rows, then on foll 3 alt rows and **at the same time** inc one st at side edge on 2nd row and every foll 4th[4th:5th] row. 60[63:67] sts.

Cont to shape side edge as before, inc one st at front edge on foll 4th row, then on every foll 6th row until there are 67[70:73] sts. Now work as given for left front from *** to *** noting the bracketed exception.

Shape armhole and front edge
1st and 2nd sizes only

Next row Cast off 4 sts, patt to end.

Dec one st at armhole edge on next 6 rows. 62[66] sts.

3rd size only

Next row Cast off 4 sts, patt to end.

Dec one st at armhole edge on next 6 rows

and **at the same time** dec one st at front edge on next and foll 4th row. 68 sts.

Work 2 rows.

All sizes

Now complete to match left front noting the bracketed exception.

SLEEVES

Thread the required number of beads onto yarn before commencing bead patterns.

Using 2¼mm (US1) needles and A, cast on 61 sts.

Beg with a K row, work 9 rows st st, so ending with a K row.

Next row K to end to mark hemline.

Change to 3mm (US3) needles.

Beg with a K row, cont in st st and patt from Chart, inc one st at each end of 3rd and every foll 4th row until there are 131 sts, then on every foll 6th row until there are 145 sts. Work straight until row 196 has been completed.

Shape top

Cast off 4 sts at beg of next 2 rows. Dec one st at each end of next 6 rows. Cast off rem 125 sts.

FACINGS AND EDGINGS

Join shoulder and side seams.

Left half

With RS of work facing, A and using the 2¼mm (US1) circular needle, beg at centre back neck, pick up and K19[21:23] sts across neck to shoulder seam, 134[144:154] sts along front edge to end of curve and 92[100:108] sts along lower edge of front and across to centre back. 245[265:285] sts.

P 1 row.

Next row K1A, *3G, 1A, rep from * to end.

Next row P2A, * 1G, 3A, rep from * to last 3 sts, 1G, 2A.

Cont with A only, K 1 row.

Next row K to end to mark foldline.

Beg with a K row, work 8 rows st st. Cast off.

Right half

Work as given for left half but beg at centre back of lower edge and end at centre back neck.

TO MAKE UP

Avoiding beaded areas, press lightly on WS using a warm iron over a damp cloth. Set in sleeves, matching centre to shoulder seam. Join sleeve seams. Fold facings to WS and slipstitch in position. Press seams.

REGENCY STRIPES

Stripes are a fascinating medium for design; they can be thick or thin, two-coloured or multi-coloured, repeated regularly or at random – the possibilities are endless. I love the warm spicy Oriental colours of antique textiles: I have used them in this scoop neck jacket knitted in a fine cotton yarn. The vertical striping is easily achieved by working horizontal stripes from side edge to side edge instead of the conventional hem to neck direction.

SIZES

To fit 86[91:97]cm (34[36:38]in) bust
Actual size 97[102:107]cm (38[40:42]in)
Length to shoulder 38[40:43]cm
(15[15¾:17]in)
Sleeve seam 44cm (17½in)
Figures in square brackets [ ] refer to larger sizes; where there is only one set of figures, i applies to all sizes

MATERIALS

2[2:2]×50g balls of Rowan Cabled Mercerised Cotton in shade A (Saffron 336), 2[2:2] balls in shade B (Pippin 339), 3[3:3] balls in shade C (Firethorn 337), 1[1:1] ball in shade D (Speedwell 334) and 2[2:2] balls in shade E (Aspen 335)
Pair each of 2¼mm (US1) and 3mm (US3) knitting needles
7[8:9] small buttons

TENSION

31 sts and 40 rows to 10cm (4in) over stripe patt using 3mm (US3) needles

SLEEVES

Using 3mm (US3) needles and E, cast on 158 sts loosely for underarm and work in a sideways direction.
P 1 row.
Beg with a K row, cont in st st and stripe sequence from Chart, shape underarm of sleeve as folls:
Rows 1 and 2 K34 sts, bring yarn to front of work, sl next st from left-hand needle onto right-hand needle, take yarn to back of work, sl the st back onto left-hand needle, turn and P to end.
Rows 3 and 4 K34 sts, K2tog the next st and loop wrapped around it, K5, bring yarn to

front of work, sl next st from left-hand needle onto right-hand needle, take yarn to back of work, sl the st back onto left-hand needle, turn and P to end – the movement on both rows will be referred to as 'wrap'.
Following the stripe sequence on chart, cont to take 6 extra sts on every K row, in this way until 2 rows have been worked thus: K142, K2tog next st and loop wrapped around it, K5, wrap next st, turn and P to end. 148 sts.
Next row K across all sts.
Beg with a P row, cont in stripe sequence, work 79 rows straight, so ending with a P row.
Shape side edge as folls:
Next 2 rows K148, wrap next st, turn and P to end.
Next 2 rows K142, wrap next st, turn and P to end.
Cont in this way, working 6 sts less on every K row until 2 rows have been worked thus: K34, wrap next st, turn and P to end.
Next row Using E, K34, K2tog next st and loop wrapped around it, then K across all sts. 158 sts.
P 1 row. Cast off loosely for underarm.

BACK

* Using 3mm (US3) needles and E, cast on 55[63:71] sts loosely for side edge.
P 1 row.
Beg with a K row, cont in st st and stripe sequence from Chart, shape side edge as folls:
Rows 1 and 2 K10[11:12], wrap next st, turn and P to end.
Rows 3 and 4 K10[11:12], K2tog next st and loop wrapped around it, K4[5:6], wrap next st, turn and P to end.
Cont to take 5[6:7] extra sts on every K row, work 8 more rows, so ending with a P row.

Shape armhole

With appropriate yarn and using a spare 3mm (US3) needle, cast on 62 sts.
Next row K across these 62 sts, then onto same needle K across main knitting, cont to take 5[6:7] extra sts as before until a row has been worked thus: K to last 10 sts. K2tog next st and loop wrapped around it, turn and P to end.
Next row K across all sts.
117[125:133] sts.

Shape shoulder

Beg with a P row, work 7[12:17] rows straight. *
Inc one st at shoulder edge on next and every foll 10th row until there are 122[130:138] sts.
Work 9 rows straight.

Shape first side of neck

Dec one st at shoulder edge on next and every foll 3rd row until 118[126:134] sts rem.
Work 27 rows straight.

Shape second side of neck

Inc one st at neck edge on next and every foll 3rd row until there are 122[130:138] sts.

Previous page *'Regency Stripes' is a
versatile design for evening wear. Elisabeth
wears it here with a velvet dress, but it
looks just as good with a skirt or trousers.
The clever combination of colours can be
dressed up with gold jewellery.*

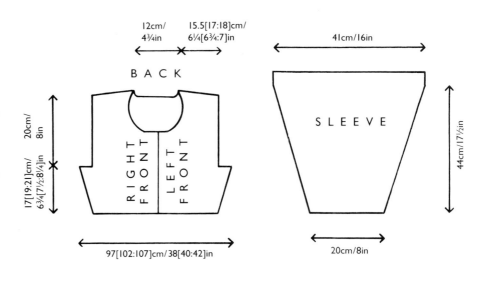

Shape shoulder

Work 9 rows straight.
Dec one st at shoulder edge on next and every
foll 10th row until 117[125:133] sts rem.
** Work 7[12:17] rows straight, so ending
with a P row. Shape for side edge as folls:
Next 2 rows K to last 10 sts, wrap next st,
turn and P to end.
Next 2 rows K to last 15[16:17] sts, wrap
next st, turn and P to end.

Shape armhole

Next 2 rows Cast off 62 sts, K to last
20[22:24] sts, wrap next st, turn and P to
end.
Cont to work 5[6:7] sts less on every K row
until a row has been worked thus: K10[11:12]
sts, wrap next st, turn and P to end.
Next row With E, K across all sts.
P 1 row. Cast off loosely. **

LEFT FRONT

Work as given for back from * to *.
Inc one st at shoulder edge on next and every
foll 10th row until there are 121[129:137] sts.
Work 9 rows straight.

1st and 3rd sizes only
Shape neck
Next row Inc in first st, K30, turn and leave
rem sts on a spare needle.
Cont on these sts for neck as folls:
Cast off 6 sts at beg of next and foll 3 alt
rows. Work 2 rows. Cast off rem 8 sts.
With RS of work facing, rejoin yarn to next st
and cast off next 12 sts, K to end. 78[94] sts.
Work 1 row.

2nd size only
Shape neck
Next row Patt 86 sts, turn and leave rem sts
on a spare needle.
Cont on these sts for first side of neck.
All sizes
Cast off 4 sts at beg of next row, then dec one
st at neck edge on next 3 rows, then on foll 4
alt rows. 67[75:83] sts.
Work 19 rows straight.
Using C only, beg with a P row, work 5 rows,
so ending with a P row.
Change to 2¼mm (US1) needles.
P 1 row to form foldline.
Beg with a P row, work 10 rows st st. Cast off.
2nd size only
With WS of work facing, rejoin yarn to next
st and cast off next 12 sts, P to last st, inc in
last st. 32 sts.
Work 1 row.

Cast off 6 sts at beg of next and 3 foll alt
rows.
Work 1 row. Cast off rem sts.

RIGHT FRONT

Using 2¼-mm (US1) needles and C, cast on
67[75:83] sts.
Beg with a K row, work 6 rows st st.
Buttonhole row (RS) K1, (yfwd, K2tog, K8)
6[7:8] times, yfwd, K2tog, then **for 1st and
2nd sizes only** K4[2].
Work 3 rows, so ending with a P row.
Next row P to end to form foldline.
Change to 3mm (US3) needles.
Beg with a P row, work 3 rows, then work the
buttonhole row again.
Work 6[7:6] rows straight.
Beg with a P[K:P] row, cont in st st and stripe
sequence from Chart, work 14[15:14] rows
straight.

Shape neck
Inc one st at end of next and foll 4 alt rows,
then on 2 foll rows, so ending at neck edge.
Next row Cast on 4 sts, work to end.
78[86:94] sts.
1st and 3rd sizes only
Next row P to end, turn and cast on 12 sts.
90[106] sts.
All sizes
Using a separate pair of needles and B, cast
on 8 sts.
Beg with a K[P:K] row, work 2[1:2] rows st st.
Next 2 rows K to end, turn and cast on 6 sts,
P across these sts, then P to end of row.
Cont in stripe sequence from Chart, rep last 2
rows 3 times more. 32 sts.
1st and 3rd sizes only
Next row K2tog, K to end, then onto same
needle K across the 90[106] sts of main
knitting. 121[137] sts.

2nd size only
Next row K to end, turn and cast on 12 sts.
44 sts.
Return to main knitting.
Next row P to end, then onto same needle P
across the 44 sts to last 2 sts, work 2tog.
129 sts.
All sizes
Dec one st at shoulder edge on every foll 10th
row until 117[125:133] sts rem.
Now work as given for back from ** to **

NECK FACING

Join shoulder seams. With RS of work facing,
C and using 2¼mm (US1) needles, beg at
start of stripe sequence, pick up and K67 sts
up right front neck to shoulder, 38 sts across
back neck and 67 sts down left front neck.
172 sts.
Next row K to end to mark foldline.
Beg with a K row, work 6 rows st st. Cast off.

LOWER FACING

Join side seams. With RS of work facing, C
and using 2¼mm (US1) needles, pick up and
K243[265:285] sts evenly along lower edge.
Next row K to end to mark hemline.
Beg with a K row, work 3 rows st st.
Next row Cast off 6 sts, P to end.
Work 6 more rows. Cast off.

TO MAKE UP

Press lightly on WS using a warm iron over a
damp cloth. Sew sleeve tops in position,
matching centre of sleeve to shoulder seam
and sewing final rows to groups at underarm.
Fold all facings to WS and slipstitch in
position. Fold 10 sts at lower edges of sleeves
to WS and slipstitch in position. Sew on
buttons. Press seams.

CHART I

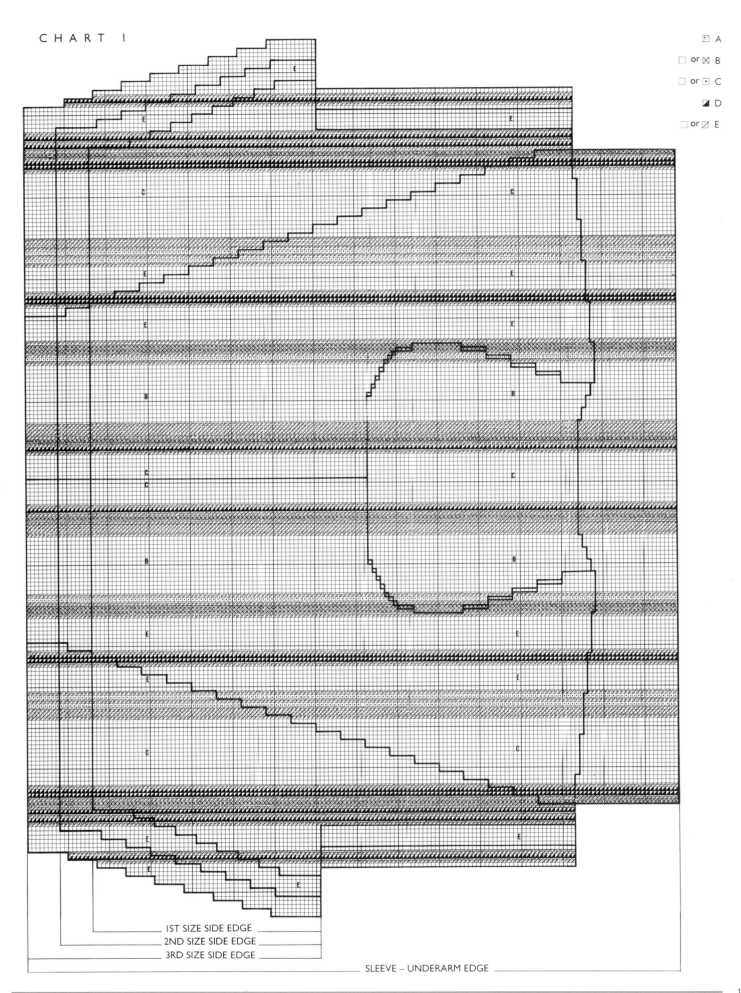

A
or B
or C
D
or E

1ST SIZE SIDE EDGE
2ND SIZE SIDE EDGE
3RD SIZE SIDE EDGE
SLEEVE – UNDERARM EDGE

VENETIAN CARNIVAL

The inspiration for this design came from a pair of porcelain Harlequin figures dating from the mid-eighteenth century. Although the idea may be hundreds of years old, this man's waistcoat knitted in 4 ply botany wool looks very contemporary. I chose muted masculine tones for the harlequin patterned fronts with vertical stripes of the same colours across the back.

SIZES

To fit 97[102:107]cm (38[40:42]in) chest
Actual size 105[109.5:114]cm
(41½[43¼:45]in)
Length to centre back neck 44[46:48]cm
(17½[18:19]in)
Figures in square brackets [ ] refer to larger sizes; where there is only one set of figures, it applies to all sizes.

MATERIALS

9[9:10]×20g balls of Rowan Edina Ronay Silk and Wool in shade A (Pine 860)
3×20g balls of Silk and Wool in shade B (Blueberry 859)
4×25g hanks of Rowan Botany in shade C (Peppercorn 603)
1×50g hank of Rowan Silkstones in shade D (Chilli 826)
Pair each of 2¼ (US1) and 3mm (US3) knitting needles
5 small buttons

TENSION

Front 27 sts and 40 rows to 10cm (4in) over patt using 3mm (US3) needles
Back 32 sts and 39 rows to 10cm (4in) over patt using 3mm (US3) needles

POCKET LININGS
(make 2)

Using 2¼mm (US1) needles and A, cast on 28[29:29] sts.
Beg with a K row, work 26[30:34] rows st st, ending with a P row.
Cut off yarn and leave these sts on a holder until required.

LEFT FRONT

Using 2¼mm (US1) needles and A, cast on 65[68:71] sts.

The four-colour knitted diamonds on the front of this waistcoat resemble a woven fabric. There are concealed pockets at the lower edge of the fronts.

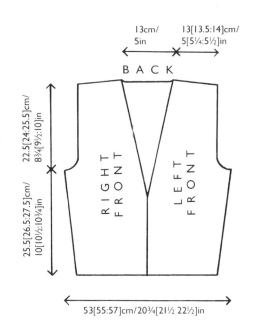

BACK

13cm/5in   13[13.5:14]cm/5[5¼:5½]in

22.5[24:25.5]cm/8¾[9½:10]in

RIGHT FRONT   LEFT FRONT

25.5[26.5:27.5]cm/10[10½:10¾]in

53[55:57]cm/20¾[21½ 22½]in

Beg with a K row, work 10 rows st st, so ending with a P row.
Next row P to end to form hemline.
P 1 row.
Change to 3mm (US3) needles.
Beg with a K row, cont in st st and foll shade sequence on Chart, work 36[40:44] rows shaping side edge on 17th and foll 14th[14th:16th] row. Use separate small balls of yarn for each diamond. Link one shade to the next by twisting them around each other on the WS to avoid making gaps.

Place pocket lining

Next row Patt 16[16:17], sl next 28[29:29] sts onto a holder, patt across 28[29:29] sts of pocket lining. patt to end.
Cont shaping side edge on every 14th[14th:16th] row until there are 71[74:77] sts.
Cont without shaping until row 92[96:100] has been completed.
Dec one st at end (for right front at beg) of next row and foll 6th row. 69[72:75] sts.
Work straight until row 102[106:110] (for right front row 103[107:111]) has been completed.

Shape armhole

Cont to shape front edge on every 6th row as before, cast off 4 sts at beg of next row. Dec one st at armhole edge on next 6[8:10] rows, then on every foll alt row until 47[48:48] sts rem. Keeping armhole edge straight, cont to dec at front edge as before until 36[37:38] sts rem. Work straight until row 192[202:212] (for right front row 193[203:213]) has been completed.

Shape shoulder

Cast off 12[13:12] sts at beg of next row and 12[12:13] sts at beg of foll alt row. Work 1 row. Cast off rem 12[12:13] sts.

CHART 1

⊟ A
⊠ B
☐ C
⊡ D

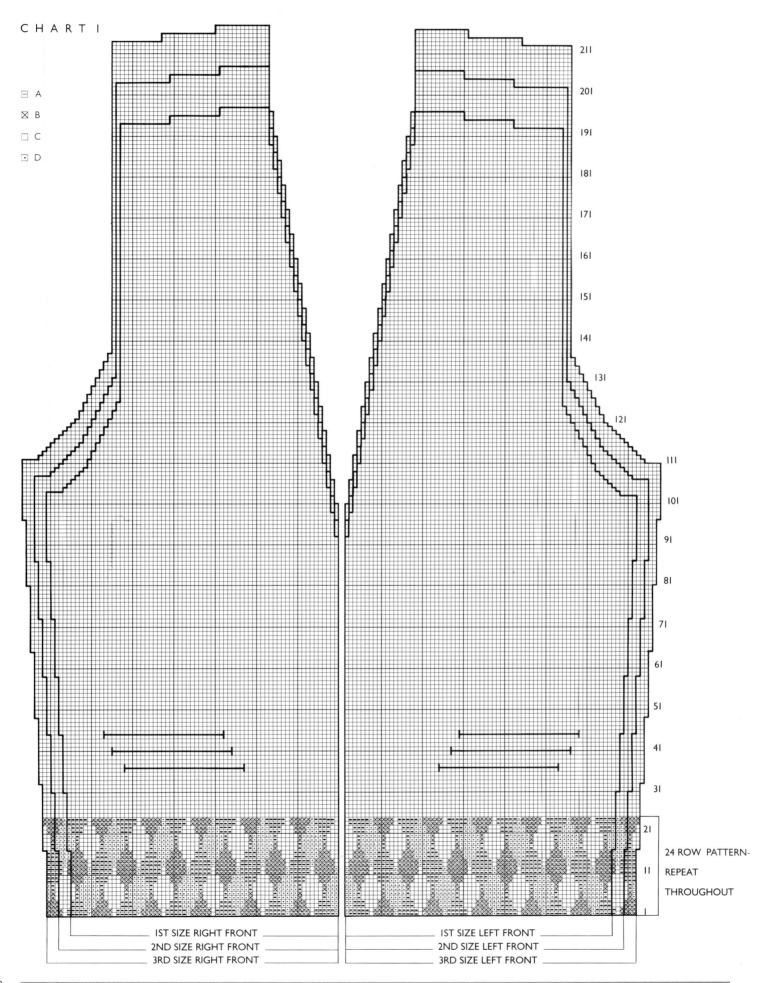

211
201
191
181
171
161
151
141
131
121
111
101
91
81
71
61
51
41
31
21
11
I

24 ROW PATTERN-
REPEAT
THROUGHOUT

1ST SIZE RIGHT FRONT
2ND SIZE RIGHT FRONT
3RD SIZE RIGHT FRONT

1ST SIZE LEFT FRONT
2ND SIZE LEFT FRONT
3RD SIZE LEFT FRONT

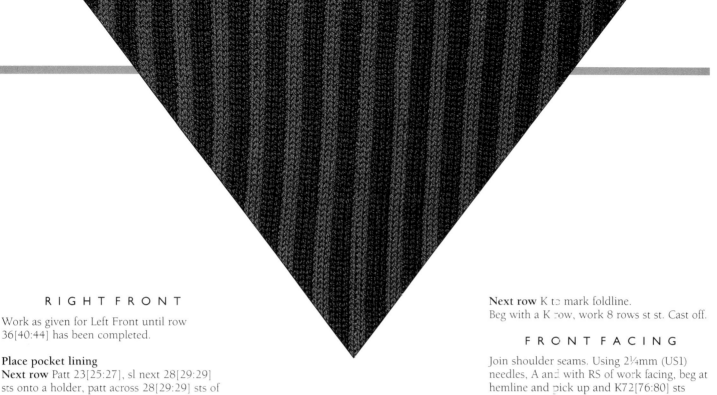

RIGHT FRONT

Work as given for Left Front until row 36[40:44] has been completed.

Place pocket lining
Next row Patt 23[25:27], sl next 28[29:29] sts onto a holder, patt across 28[29:29] sts of pocket lining, patt to end.
Now complete as given for Left Front noting the bracketed exceptions.

BACK

Using 2¼mm (US1) needles and A, cast on 153[161:169] sts.
Beg with a K row, work 10 rows st st, so ending with a P row.
Next row P to end to mark hemline.
P 1 row.
Change to 3mm (US3) needles.
Passing the yarn not in use loosely across the WS of the work to avoid drawing in the knitting, cont in st st stripes as folls:
Row 1 (RS) For 3rd size only K2C, then **for all sizes** 3[1:3]A, * 3C, 3A, rep from * to last 6[4:8] sts, 3C, 3[1:3]A, then **for 3rd size only** 2C.
Row 2 For 3rd size only P2C, then **for all sizes** 3[1:3]A, * 3C, 3A, rep from * to last 6[4:8] sts, 3C, 3[1:3]A, then **for 3rd size only** 2C.
Cont in stripe sequence, shaping sides on 13th and every foll 12th row until there are 167[175:183] sts.
Work straight until back measures same as fronts up to beg of armhole shaping, ending with a P row.

Shape armholes
Cast off 6 sts at beg of next 2 rows. Dec one st at each end of next 11[13:17] rows, then at each end of foll 3[4:3] alt rows.
127[129:131] sts.

Work straight until back is 3cm (1¼in) less than fronts up to beg of shoulder shaping, ending with a P row.

Shape shoulders and back neck
Cast off 14[14:15] sts at beg of next 2 rows.
Next row Cast off 14[15:15] sts. patt until there are 19 sts on right-hand needle, turn and complete this side first.
Next row Cast off 4 sts, patt to end.
Cast off rem 15 sts.
With RS of work facing, rejoin yarn and cast off centre 33 sts, patt to end. 33[34:34] sts.
Next row Cast off 14[15:15] sts, patt to end.
Next row Cast off 4 sts, patt to end.
Cast off rem 15 sts.

POCKET TOPS AND FACINGS
(make 2)

Using 3mm (US3) needles and with RS of work facing, rejoin yarn to 28[29:29] pocket sts on holder and patt 8 rows.
Change to 2¼mm (US1) needles and using A only, K 1 row.

Next row K to mark foldline.
Beg with a K row, work 8 rows st st. Cast off.

FRONT FACING

Join shoulder seams. Using 2¼mm (US1) needles, A and with RS of work facing, beg at hemline and pick up and K72[76:80] sts along right front edge to beg of shaping, 76[84:92] sts to shoulder seam, 40 sts from back neck, 76[84:92] sts down left front to end of shaping and 72[76:80] sts down to hemline. 336[360:384] sts.
Buttonhole row 1 P3, (cast off 2, P until there are 15 sts on right-hand needle after cast-off group) 4 times, cast off 2, P to end.
Buttonhole row 2 K to end, casting on 2 sts at each cast-off group.
Next row K to mark foldline
Buttonhole row 1 K263[287:311] sts, (cast off 2, K until there are 15 sts on right-hand needle after cast-off group) 4 times, cast off 2, K to end.
Buttonhole row 2 P to end, casting on 2 sts at each cast-off group.
Beg with a K row, work 8 rows st st. Cast off.

ARMHOLE FACINGS
(alike)

Using 2¼mm (US1) needles, A and with RS of work facing, pick up and K156[164:172] sts evenly all round armhole.
Next row K to mark foldline.
Beg with a K row, work 6 rows st st. Cast off.

TO MAKE UP

Press on WS using a warm iron over a damp cloth. Join side seams. Fold front, lower edge and armhole facings to wrong side and slipstitch in position. Sew down pocket linings on WS of work and pocket tops on RS of work, then turn facings to WS and slipstitch in position. Press seams. Sew on the buttons.

ROYAL PEACOCK

The idea for this sweater derived from a white muslin apron, made in England in about 1715, with peacock motifs worked in white linen thread. The absence of any colour meant that I could interpret the design as I imagined it. Choosing a chunky yarn for outdoor wear, I began with a rich chestnut background. I used gold for outlining the motifs and completed the rest of the pattern with my favourite autumnal shades.

SIZE

To fit up to 102cm (40in) bust
Actual size 134cm (52¾in)
Length to shoulder 67cm (26½in)
Sleeve seam 46cm (18in)

MATERIALS

29×25g hanks of Rowan Lightweight DK in main shade A (brown 71)
9×25g hanks of Rowan Botany in shade B (mustard 521) – use 3 strands together throughout
1×100g hank of Rowan Chunky Cotton Chenille in shade C (Wild Cherry 370) – used single throughout
1×100g hank of Chunky Cotton Chenille in shade D (Beech 374) – used single throughout
2×25g hanks of Lightweight DK in shade E (olive 407)
1×50g ball of Rowan Fine Cotton Chenille in shade F (Privet 394)
1×25g hank of Lightweight DK in shade G (deep blue 54)
Pair each of 4mm (US6) and 5mm (US8) knitting needles

NOTE

All yarns are used double throughout the design with the exception of Chunky Cotton Chenille, which is used as a single strand and Botany which is used as 3 strands together

TENSION

18 sts and 23 rows to 10cm (4in) over patt using 5mm (US8) needles

---

Diagram labels:

23cm/9in 22cm/8¾in

BACK AND FRONT

67cm/26½

67cm/26½in

51cm/20in

SLEEVE

46cm/18in

25cm/10in

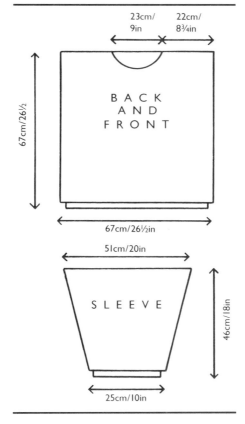

BACK

Using 4mm (US6) needles and B, cast on 120 sts.
Join in A and work 2-colour rib as folls:
Row 1 (RS) P1A, (K2B, P2A) to last 3 sts, K2B, P1A.
Row 2 K1A, (P2B, K2A) to last 3 sts, P2B, K1A.
Rep these 2 rows twice more but inc 1 st at end of last row. 121 sts.
Change to 5mm (US8) needles.
Beg with a K row, cont in st st and work 148 rows in patt from Chart 1. Strand yarns loosely across back of work where appropriate or use small, separate balls of yarn for individual motifs. Link one shade to the next by twisting them around each other where they meet on the WS to avoid making gaps.

Shape shoulders
Cast off 40 sts at beg of next 2 rows.
Cast off rem 41 sts.

FRONT

Work as given for back until row 132 of Chart 1 has been completed.

Shape neck
Next row Patt 55, turn and leave rem sts on a spare needle.
Cont on these sts for first side of neck.
Cast off 3 sts at beg of next and foll alt row.
Dec one st at neck edge on next 8 rows, then on foll alt row. 40 sts.
Work 2 rows straight, so ending at side edge.
Cast off rem 40 sts for shoulder.

Walking in the park Anna looks very regal in her 'Royal Peacock' sweater. The colours echo the rich woodland hues and a mixture of wool and chenille yarns gives a subtle variety of textures. Vertical striped ribbing in two colours at the lower edge, cuffs and neck adds decorative detail.

CHART I

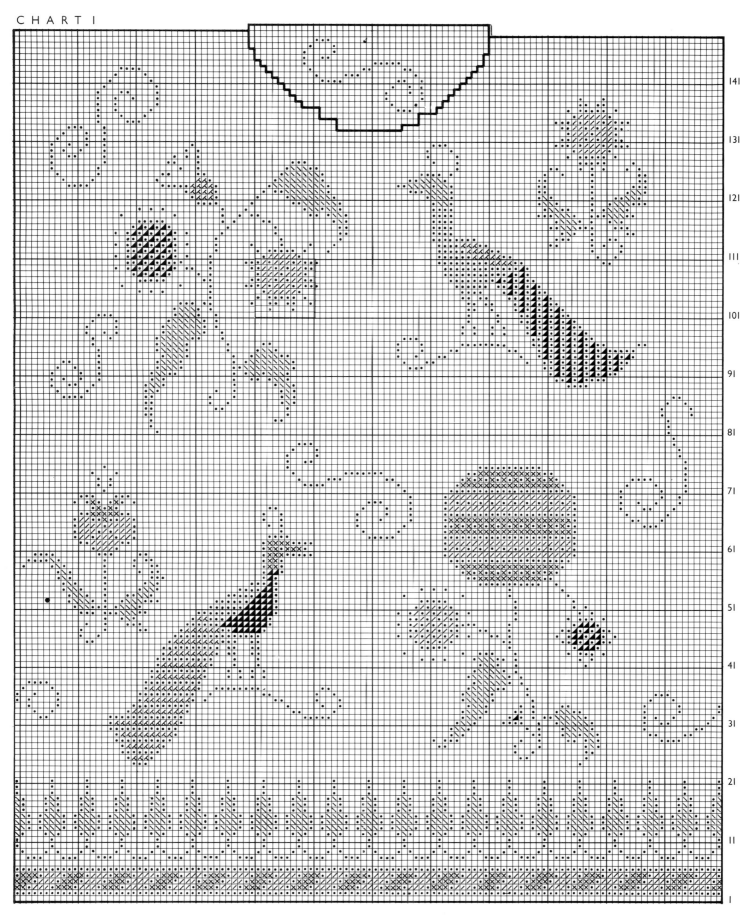

141

131

121

111

101

91

81

71

61

51

41

31

21

11

1

□ A ☑ D ◨ G
⊡ B ◩ E
⊠ C ▨ F

CHART 2

□ A
· B
⊠ C
◩ D
◰ E
◪ F
◢ G

SLEEVE

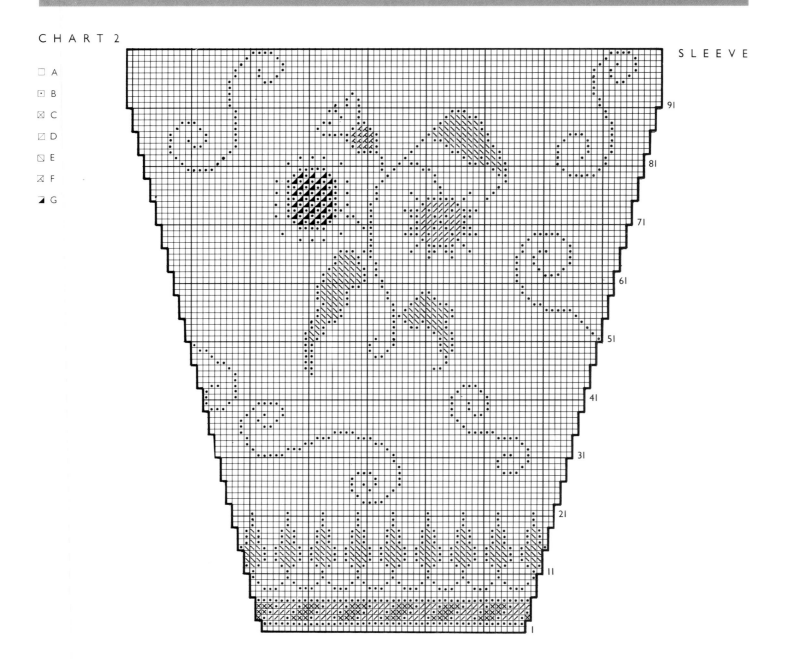

91
81
71
61
51
41
31
21
11
1

With RS facing, rejoin yarn and cast off centre 11 sts, patt to end. 55 sts.
Work 1 row, then complete to match first side.

SLEEVES

Using 4mm (US6) needles and B, cast on 44 sts.
Join in A and work 6 rows in 2-colour rib as given for back but inc 1 st at end of last row. 45 sts.
Change to 5mm (US8) needles.

Beg with a K row, cont in st st and patt from Chart 2, inc one st at each end of 3rd and every foll 4th row until there are 91 sts.
Work straight until 100 rows have been completed. Cast off loosely.

NECKBAND

Join right shoulder seam. Using 4mm (US6) needles, A and with RS of work facing, pick up and K22 sts down left front neck, 11 sts from front neck, 22 sts up right front neck and 41 sts from back neck. 96 sts.

Join in B and work 6 rows in 2-colour rib as given for back. Using B cast off evenly in rib.

TO MAKE UP

Press on WS using a warm iron over a damp cloth. Join left shoulder and neckband seam. Mark position of underarms 25.5cm (10in) down from shoulders on back and front. Sew in sleeves between markers, matching centre of sleeve top to shoulder seam. Join side and sleeve seams. Press seams.

KNITTING TECHNIQUES

All the patterns in this book contain general information (Sizes, Materials, Tension), written and/or charted instructions and details of how to assemble the garment. Everything is presented in a logical order; it is important that you read the pattern through before you start knitting so that you have a general understanding of the work.
The information here relates to reading the patterns section by section and describes the techniques that are used consistently.

SIZES

The patterns are usually written in a range of sizes; instructions for the first size are given outside a set of square brackets, [ ], with the larger sizes following on in order within the brackets.
Look at the *actual* measurement when choosing the size to make. Some garments have a generous amount of 'ease', so you may prefer to knit a smaller size than normal if the finished result is too large for your taste. Once you have decided on a size, mark the relevant figures throughout the pattern to avoid confusion.

MATERIALS

In this book the designs are all knitted in Rowan yarns – the names and shades of which are quoted with the individual instructions. To avoid the frustration of being unable to obtain specific yarns there is a table of generic equivalents (any standard 4 ply, double knitting, etc) on page 143. Only substitute a different yarn after first making a tension swatch and checking that the number of stitches and rows is the same as the original.
Changing yarns could mean that you will need more or less yarn than stated in the pattern, even though both yarns may be packaged in the same weight balls. Due to the composition of the fibres each type of yarn has a different metreage (yardage) – the actual length of yarn in each ball. Therefore the actual amounts quoted in the pattern can only be used as a guide.
Many of the designs in this book use a number of different colours, some in very small quantities. Yarns are frequently only available in 50g (2oz) balls which means that there is a lot left. Extra yarn may be welcome for future projects, but if you want to be more economical take advantage of the kits being offered for various garments (see page 143). The yarns included in a kit are wound off in more accurate quantities with little wastage.

TENSION

The tension quoted in a pattern has been achieved by the designer of the garment who uses it to make all the stitch and row

calculations. As the tension of your work is personal to you, and to ensure that your sweater finishes up the size that you intended, you *must* make a tension swatch before starting work.
Using the yarn and needles stated and working in the appropriate stitch or pattern, knit a swatch about 15cm (6in) square. Place the finished swatch on a padded surface, gently smooth it into shape, then secure the edges with pins placed at right angles to the fabric.

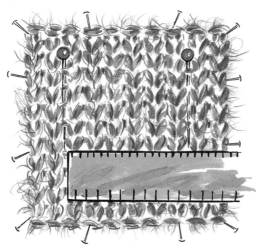

Measuring the stitch tension.

With pins as markers at each end, measure out 10cm (4in) horizontally across the centre of the swatch for the stitch tension; or vertically down the swatch for the row tension. Fewer stitches than stated means that your work is too loose and you need to try again with smaller needles; more stitches than stated indicates that you are knitting too tightly and should try again with larger

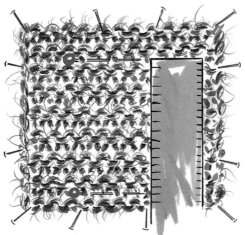

Measuring the row tension.

needles. Changing the needle size is not important as long as you obtain the correct number of stitches and rows to 10cm (4in).

CHARTS

Many designs in this book involve intarsia knitting which is a form of creating colour patterns usually against a background of stocking stitch. To see how the design evolves, sections of a garment are often shown as charts.
The charts are based on a grid of squares; reading horizontally across the grid each square represents a stitch, and vertically up the grid squares indicate the rows of knitting. Symbols represent the various colours: if you find it difficult to 'read' the symbols, photocopy the chart and shade the squares in the appropriate colours. It is also possible to enlarge a chart, if the grid is too small, by using the special facility on a photocopier. Solid lines show the markings for various sizes as well as indicating shaping such as armholes or neck. Only use the lines as a guide for placing the pattern; always follow the written detailed instructions for shaping.

MAKING AN OPEN INCREASE (Yo)

An open increase, known as 'yarn over' and abbreviated as 'yo', is made by putting the yarn over the needle between two stitches; this creates a hole (for buttonholes or decorative, lacy effects) when it is worked on the following row. Exactly how the yarn is placed over the needle depends on the stitches at either side.
Increasing between two knit stitches – at the appropriate position bring the yarn forward to the front of the work between two needles. Knit the next stitch in the usual way.
Increasing between a knit and a purl stitch – work to the position of the increase, then bring the yarn forward to the front between the two needles. Now take the yarn over the top of the right-hand needle point and round to the front again between the two needles. Purl the next stitch in the usual way.
Increasing between a purl and a knit stitch – when you reach the position of the increase, you will see that the yarn is already at the front of the work from purling the previous stitch. Instead of taking the yarn to the back, as you would normally do before knitting, simply proceed to knit the stitch. As you do this, you automatically bring the yarn over the needle so creating an extra loop.
Increasing between two purl stitches – take the yarn completely round the right-hand needle point and to the front again between the two needles. The yarn is now in position to purl the next stitch.

KNITTING WITH COLOUR

There are two main methods of working with colour – Fair Isle knitting and intarsia. Fair Isle work generally involves using two or

139

more colours, with no more than a few stitches between them, repeating across a row of knitting. Intarsia uses small or separate balls of yarn for isolated areas of colour or individual motifs.

Stranding yarns across a purl row.

Fair Isle In Fair Isle knitting, where two colours are used in one row, the yarn not in use is stranded across the back of the work as long as it passes no more than five stitches. On a knit row work the required number of stitches in one colour, then take up the second colour and work with that – and so on – stranding the yarns across the back of the work. Keep the strands fairly loose without them forming a loop; if you pull the yarns across too tightly the work will pucker and the knitting loses its elasticity.

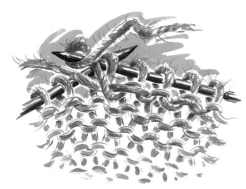

Stranding yarns across a knit row.

On a purl row, work in the same way, allowing the strands to form across the front of the work.
If the yarn must pass over more than five stitches avoid long, loose strands at the back

140   *Weaving yarns across the back.*

of the work by weaving it over and under the working yarn every three or four stitches.
Intarsia When working an isolated area of colour or a motif, use a separate length of yarn or wind off a small ball (depending on the size of the motif) for each area of colour. It is important to link each colour to the next by twisting the yarns together on the wrong side of the work when you change colour – otherwise the different areas of colour separate.

Linking yarns when changing colour.

MAKING UP

After the many hours that it takes to complete a knitted garment, do not spoil the finished effect by rushing the final stages. First make sure that all the loose ends of yarn are secured to prevent them unravelling later on. Always leave a long end of yarn for darning in when you start a new ball of yarn. Thread the end into a blunt-ended wool needle and neatly weave it into the back of the knitting behind the stitches of the same colour. Trim the loose end close the fabric.
For sewing up the garment use matching yarn in the main colour and a blunt-ended wool needle. If the original yarn is unsuitable for sewing up (ie. too thick or textured) choose a similar colour in a finer, smooth quality.

Blocking and Pressing
For a perfect fit the finished pieces of knitting should be blocked (ie. pinned out to the measurements indicated in the diagrams) and pressed according to the specific instructions given on the yarn label. Blocking requires a padded surface. Lay a folded blanket on a table and cover it with a sheet. Place the knitted pieces right side down on the sheet and smooth them out to the correct measurements. Check that the fabric is not distorted and that the lines of stitches and rows are straight, then secure to the pad using pins placed at right angles to the edge of the knitting. For most natural fibres cover the knitting with a damp cloth and, using a warm iron, place it gently on the fabric and lift it up again – without moving the iron in a continuous action. Allow the knitting to dry completely before removing the pins.
Do not press any areas of ribbing or stitch work patterns where the texture of the knitting can easily be damaged.

Backstitch Seam
The most popular seam in common use, the backstitch seam gives a strong firm finish to

most edges, but forms a ridge on the inside of the garment. To work the seam place the pieces to be joined with right sides together and matching any patterns row for row and stitch for stitch. Work in backstitch along the seam, close to the edge, sewing into the centre of each row or stitch to correspond with the row or stitch on the opposite edge.

Invisible Seam
This is a very useful seam when working with thick yarns where a backstitch seam would be too bulky. The seam is virtually undetectable from the right side of the work – the only sign is a slight ridge on the inside of the garment. Place the pieces to be joined edge to edge with the right sides facing upwards. By sewing under the horizontal strands (linking the edge stitch and the following stitch) of alternate edges the two pieces are gradually 'laced' together from the right side.

Overcast Seam
Although the seam is worked through two edges placed together, when it is opened out it lies completely flat. Use an overcast seam for areas of ribbing such as welts and cuffs, or for attaching front bands and collars. With the right sides of the two pieces to be joined together and matching stitches and rows, insert the needle behind the knot of the edge stitch on one side, then through the same part of the corresponding stitch on the second side. Draw the yarn through and repeat these actions to join each pair of row ends.

CARE OF HANDKNITTING

The majority of yarns used in this book are made up of natural fibres; all of them can be hand-washed or dry-cleaned in certain solvents, but only the cotton yarns are suitable for machine-washing. Follow the washing instructions printed on the ball band or label.

Hand-washing
Use hand-warm water in which a mild soap has been dissolved. Never allow the garment to soak, or rub it in the water, as the fabric will become felted. Instead gently squeeze the knitting, supporting it all the time so that the weight of the water does not pull the garment out of shape. Rinse in several changes of water until there is no trace of soap, then spin dry for a short time only.
Never tumble dry a knitted garment or hang it up to dry. Smooth the garment gently into shape and leave it to dry on a flat surface covered with a towel.

Machine-washing
It is possible to machine-wash some cotton yarns on a gentle cycle, but always refer to the instructions with the yarn.
Rowan-Den-m-nit Cotton is indigo dyed and possesses the same unique features as denim jeans. It will shrink with the first wash and continue to fade with subsequent washes. Where this yarn has been used, the making up instructions give details of washing the knitted pieces before they are assembled.

HINTS FOR AMERICAN KNITTERS

The patterns in this book should be easy for American knitters to follow. In case of difficulties the following tables and glossaries offer guidance.

TERMINOLOGY

UK	US
cast off	bind off
cont without shaping	work straight
colour	shade
ball band	yarn label
double crochet	single crochet
slip stitch in position	tack down
stocking stitch	stockinette stitch
tension	gauge
treble	double crochet
triple treble	double treble

The following table shows the approximate yarn equivalents in terms of thickness. Always check the tension of substitute yarns before buying sufficient to complete the garment.

UK	US
four-ply	sport
double knitting	knitting worsted
Aran-weight	fisherman
chunky	bulky

METRIC CONVERSION TABLES

Length (to the nearest ¼in)				Weight (rounded up to the nearest ¼oz)	
cm	in	cm	in	g	oz
1	½	55	21¾	25	1
2	¾	60	23½	50	2
3	1¼	65	25½	100	3¾
4	1½	70	27½	150	5½
5	2	75	29½	200	7¼
6	2½	80	31½	250	9
7	2¾	85	33½	300	10¾
8	3	90	35½	350	12½
9	3½	95	37½	400	14¼
10	4	100	39½	450	16
11	4¼	110	43½	500	17¾
12	4¾	120	47	550	19½
13	5	130	51¼	600	21¼
14	5½	140	55	650	23
15	6	150	59	700	24¾
16	6¼	160	63	750	26½
17	6¾	170	67	800	28¼
18	7	180	70¾	850	30
19	7½	190	74¾	900	31¾
20	8	200	78¾	950	33¾
25	9¾	210	82¾	1000	35½
30	11¾	220	86½	1200	42¼
35	13¾	230	90½	1400	49¼
40	15¾	240	94½	1600	56½
45	17¾	250	98½	1800	63½
50	19¾	300	118	2000	70½

NEEDLE SIZE CONVERSION TABLE

Use the needle sizes quoted in the patterns as recommended starting points for making a tension sample. The needle size actually used should be that on which you achieve the stated tension.

Metric	US	Old UK
2mm	0	14
2¼mm	1	13
2½mm		
2¾mm	2	12
3mm		
3¼mm	3	10
3½mm	4	
3¾mm	5	9
4mm	6	8
4½mm	7	7
5mm	8	6
5½mm	9	5
6mm	10	4
6½mm	10½	3
7mm		2
7½mm		1
8mm	11	0
9mm	13	00
10mm	15	000

ABBREVIATIONS

alt – alternate
beg – begin(ning)
ch – chain
cm – centimetres
cont – continue(ing)
dc (sc) – double crochet (single crochet)
dec – decrease(ing)
foll(s) – follows(ing)
g – grams
in – inch(es)
K – knit
K-wise – knitwise
lp(s) – loop(s)

Ml – make one stitch by picking up horizontal loop between stitches and knitting into the back of it
mm – millimetres
P – purl
patt – pattern
psso – pass slipped stitch over
P-wise – purlwise
rem – remain(ing)
rep – repeat
RS – right side
skpo – slip one, knit one, pass slipped stitch over

sl – slip
sp(s) – spaces(s)
sl st – slip stitch
st(s) – stitch(es)
st st – stocking (stockinette) stitch
tbl – through back of loop(s)
tog – together
tr (dc) – treble (double crochet)
tr tr (d tr) – triple treble (double treble)
WS – wrong side
yfwd – yarn forward
yo – yarn over (needle)

THE
ROWAN
STORY

We are proud to announce the publication of *The Original Annabel Fox* and *The Kim Hargreaves Collection*. The first two **Rowan Originals**, they combine outstanding knitting design with the range and quality of Rowan Yarns.

Rowan is a Yorkshire-based yarn marketing and design company whose name has become synonymous with the revolution that has swept the needlecraft and handkitting industry and changed its image and practice forever. Gone are the limited colours and synthetics offered by most other spinners; we have created a whole new generation of exciting natural-fibre yarns – from kid silk to chenille – in a myriad colours.

Working with the cream of contemporary designers, including Kaffe Fassett, Edina Ronay and Susan Duckworth, Rowan Yarns commissions special handknitting and needlepoint collections, taking what was once a hobby into the realms of high fashion. Rowan's design collections are now in fashion journals worldwide, while every glossy home supplement bears tasteful evidence of Rowan's artistic craftwork.

Home for Rowan is an old stone mill in a narrow green valley in the shadow of the Pennines overlooking Holmfirth. Rowan Yarns was set up just over thirteen years ago by myself and my colleague Simon Cockin. From the beginning our aims were different from our competitors. We took our palette of yarns to top designers; we worked with them to create yarns in colours to match their specific requirements. Some have proved so popular they have become a permanent part of the Rowan range.

Our yarns are now marketed worldwide and the sheer appeal of the variety and subtlety of colours and textures, combined with our willingness to experiment, ensure our continuing success.

Rowan Originals set new standards in quality from the very best contemporary designers. The books are produced with the same care and attention that is given to our yarns and the same eye for form and colour that has been our lifelong hallmark.

We hope that you will enjoy this new range of original designs using Rowan's yarns.

Stephen Sheard.

KITS & SUPPLIERS

The Rowan yarns used for designs throughout this book are named in each pattern and can be obtained from suppliers of good quality knitting yarns.

In case of difficulty, write to the addresses below for a list of suppliers in your area or consult the yarn list here before substituting a generic equivalent.

4-ply wool	–	Rowan Botany
Heavy 4-ply wool	–	Rowan Lightweight Double Knitting
Double knitting wool	–	Rowan Designer Double Knitting, Rowan Lambswool Tweed, Rowan Foxtweed Double Knitting
Aran-weight	–	Rowan Magpie
Chunky wool	–	Rowan Foxtweed Chunky
Heavy 4-ply yarn	–	Rowan Grainy Silk, Rowan Silkstones
4-ply yarn	–	Rowan Edina Ronay Silk and Wool, Rowan Mulberry Silk, Rowan Wool and Cotton
4-ply cotton	–	Rowan Sea Breeze, Rowan Cabled Mercerised Cotton
Heavy 4-ply cotton	–	Rowan Cotton Glacé
Double knitting cotton	–	Rowan Fine Cotton Chenille
Chunky cotton	–	Rowan Chunky Cotton Chenille

United Kingdom
Rowans Yarns, Green Lane Mill, Holmfirth, West Yorkshire HD7 1RW.
Tel 0484 681881
Fax 0484 687920

USA
Kenneth Bridgewater, Westminster Trading Corporation, 5 Northern Boulevard, Amherst, New Hampshire 03031.
Tel 603 886 5041
Fax 603 886 1056

Canada
Christopher Peacock, Estelle Designs and Sales Ltd, Units 65/67, 2220 Midland Avenue, Scarborough, Ontaria M1P 3ES.
Tel 416 298 9922
Fax 416 298 2429

Australia
Ron Mendelsohn, Sunspun Enterprises PTY Ltd, 191 Canterbury Road, Canterbury 3126, Victoria.
Tel 03 830 1609
Fax 03 816 9590

West Germany
Minke Heistra, Textilwerkstatt, Friedenstrasse 5, 3000 Hanover 1.
Tel 0511 818001
Fax 0511 813108

Germany
Naturwolle Fritzsch, Gewerbepark Dogelmuhle, 6367 Karben 1.
Tel 060 39 2071
Fax 060 39 2074

Denmark
Sonja Kristensen, Designer Garn, Aagade 3, Roerbaek, O Hobro.
Tel & Fax 9855 7811

Holland
Henk & Henrietta Beukers, Dorpsstraat 9, 5327 AR Hurwenen.
Tel 04182 1764
Fax 04182 2532

New Zealand
John Q Goldingham Ltd, PO Box 45083, Epuni Railway, Lower Hutt.
Tel 04 5674 085
Fax 04 5697 444

Norway
Jorun Sandin, Eureka, PO Box 357, 1401 Ski.
Tel 09 871 909

Japan
Mr Iwamoto, Diakeito Co Ltd,
1-5-23 Nakatsu Kita-Ku, Osaka 531.
Tel 06 371 5657

Sweden
Eva Wincent Gelinder, Wincent.
Luntmarkargaten 56, 113 58 Stockholm.
Tel 08 327 060
Fax 08 333 171

Italy
Daniella Basso, La Compagnia Del Cotone, Via Mazzini 44, 10123 Torino.
Tel 011 878 381
Fax 011 957 4096

Belgium
Studio Hedera, Diestsestraat 172,
B - 3030 Leuven.
Tel 016 232 189

Singapore
Francis Kiew, Classical Hobby House, 1 Jln Anak Bukit, No B2-15 Bukit Timah Plaza, Singapore 2158.
Tel 4662179
Fax 7762134

Mexico
Moses Semaria, Estembresy Tejidos Finos S.A.D. C.V., A.V Michoacan 30 – A, Local 3 Esq Av Mexico, Col Hipodromo Condesa 06170, Mexico 11.
Tel 2 64 84 74

Iceland
Malin Orlyggsdottir, Stockurinn, Orlygsdottir, Kjorgardi, Laugavegi 159, 101 Reykjavik.
Tel 010 354 1 18258

Finland
Helmi Vuorelma – Oy, Vesijarven Katu 13, SF – 15141 Lahti.
Tel 010 358 (918) 268 31
Fax 010 358 (918) 517 918

ROWAN KITS
Write to the Rowan distributors above for a list of suppliers of the following designs:

Sloane Square (page 25)
Kensington Gardens (page 47)

ACKNOWLEDGEMENTS

This is my chance to thank the many people – friends and colleagues – whose time and energy have turned my dream of a book into reality.

First I want to mention Stephen Sheard of Rowan Yarns who has taught me so much over the years and who I admire greatly, then Kaffe Fassett for his continual encouragement, Simon Cockin who keeps everything running smoothly at the mill and Kathleen Hargreaves who always gives two hundred percent of everything and who is a huge influence on me.

Next I want to thank the marvellous team that I worked with on the photographic shoot – photographer Tim Bret-Day who is responsible for the wonderful pictures in the book, Lizzi Zita who styled the clothes and was so supportive and Ken O'Rourke who created the beautiful hair and make-up. The models who showed the knitwear so professionally were Anna Drummond, Elisabeth, Nick, Warren and youngsters, Rahiama and Jennifer.

Many thanks also to the editorial team – Margaret Maino, my editor, for her hours of help and hard work, David Fordham for his brilliant book design and Mike Wicks of Rowan Publishing whose endless enthusiasm made this book possible.

Lastly, but not at all least, I want to thank Elizabeth Armitage whose time is dedicated to looking after the Rowan knitters. To all the loyal knitters who have been involved with the garments in this book – and you are too numerous to mention by name – I hope that you know how grateful I am for your marvellous work.

CREDITS

Clothes and accessories were lent by the following suppliers: *clothes* – Byblos, Hobbs, Browns, Whistles, Donna Karan, Ally Cappellino; *hats* – Andrew Wilkie; *shoes and handbags* – Hobbs; jewellery – Dinny Hall; *shawls/wraps* – Wright and Teague; *tights* – Wolford.

Photograph on page 142 by Andrew Sanderson.